Medieval Masculinities

Medieval Cultures

Series Editors

Rita Copeland
Barbara A. Hanawalt
David Wallace

Sponsored by the Center for Medieval Studies at the University of Minnesota

Volumes in the series study the diversity of medieval cultural histories and practices, including such interrelated issues as gender, class, and social hierarchies; race and ethnicity; geographical relations; definitions of political space; discourses of authority and dissent; educational institutions; canonical and noncanonical literatures; and technologies of textual and visual literacies.

Volume 7. Edited by Clare A. Lees
Medieval Masculinities: Regarding Men in the Middle Ages

Volume 6. Edited by Barbara A. Hanawalt and Kathryn L. Reyerson
City and Spectacle in Medieval Europe

Volume 5. Edited by Calvin B. Kendall and Peter S. Wells
Voyage to the Other World: The Legacy of Sutton Hoo

Volume 4. Edited by Barbara A. Hanawalt
Chaucer's England: Literature in Historical Context

Volume 3: Edited by Marilyn J. Chiat and Kathryn L. Reyerson
The Medieval Mediterranean: Cross-Cultural Contacts

Volume 2: Edited by Andrew MacLeish
The Medieval Monastery

Volume 1: Edited by Kathryn Reyerson and Faye Powe
The Medieval Castle

Medieval Masculinities

REGARDING MEN IN THE MIDDLE AGES

Clare A. Lees, editor
with the assistance of
Thelma Fenster and Jo Ann McNamara

Medieval Cultures, Volume 7

MIN NE SO TA

University of Minnesota Press
Minneapolis
London

Published by the University of Minnesota Press
2037 University Avenue Southeast, Minneapolis, MN 55455-3092
Printed in the United States of America on acid-free paper

Library of Congress Cataloging-in-Publication Data

Medieval masculinities : regarding men in the Middle Ages / Clare A. Lees, editor, with the assistance of Thelma Fenster and Jo Ann McNamara.
p. cm. —(Medieval cultures ; v. 7)
Includes bibliographical references and index.
ISBN 0-8166-2425-9 (hc : acid-free paper. — ISBN 0-8166-2426-7 (pb : acid-free paper)
1. Masculinity (Psychology)—History. 2. Civilization, Medieval. 3. Men in literature. 4. Feminist criticism. 5. Men's studies. I. Lees, Clare A. II. Fenster, Thelma S. III. McNamara, Jo Ann, 1931– . IV. Series: Medieval cultures ; 7
HQ1088.M45 1994
305.3—dc20 93-37311

Contents

Acknowledgments

I wish to thank Thelma Fenster and Jo Ann McNamara, who saw this project through its beginning stages and were most helpful with their suggestions and advice when I became editor. In addition, my thanks to Gillian R. Overing and her colleagues at Wake Forest University, whose enthusiastic response to my summary survey of this collection helped me refine my ideas about its significance. Pauline, Jack, and Julian all helped when Jacob came a little early: they know how much I owe them. Finally, I thank the anonymous readers of the University of Minnesota Press, who offered insightful and pertinent comments on all of the essays, and Lisa Freeman, my editor, whose assistance and support have been invaluable.

Clare A. Lees

Preface: Why Men?

Thelma Fenster

We should not be working [exclusively] on the subjected sex any more than a historian of class can focus exclusively on peasants.

Natalie Zemon Davis, 1975[1]

To the extent that feminist discourse defines its problematic as "woman," it, too, ironically privileges the man as unproblematic or exempted from determination by gender relations. . . . That men appear to be and (in many cases) are the wardens, or at least the trustees in a social whole, should not blind us to the extent to which they, too, are governed by the rules of gender.

Jane Flax, 1987[2]

As this volume goes to press, the discipline of men's studies, and gender studies along with it, has earned its place in scholarship; the date of Natalie Davis's prescient remark, quoted above, shows that the ground for men's studies was broken early in the feminist movement. There has nevertheless been a concomitant resistance to it within the movement, one that was still in evidence in 1990, when Fordham University hosted its conference on men in the Middle Ages, a meeting that inspired a number of the essays in the present collection. Titled "Gender and Medieval Society: Men," the conference was in fact a sequel to Fordham's 1988 congress, "Gender and the Moral Order in Medieval Society"; although the earlier meeting aspired to advance *gender* studies, the papers presented – though eminently worthy[3] – discussed gender primarily with *women* as their referents. As I later co-organized (with Jo Ann McNamara) the 1990 conference, I often heard this question: "*Men's* history? *Men's* culture? Isn't that what we've been studying for centuries, in the guise of *human* history?" History, some protested, was written "by men about men";[4] they could have added that it was written largely *for* men, too.

Those objections are addressed, I think, by certain of the assumptions underlying men's studies. Though they are no longer new, they may bear repetition, especially in a collection such as this, whose individual essays push the perimeters of men's and medieval studies beyond merely demonstrating how the assumptions work.

Although the subjects of traditional historical discourse were for the most part men, that discourse was still not precisely "about men." The conventions of modern historiography inscribed the stories of the few—the hegemonic males[5]—as generic, human history.[6] Readers often complied with that project, agreeing to read partial histories as comprehensive ones. As if clinging sometimes to a mythical idea of kingship, in which the fates of (Fisher?) king and country become inseparable, historiography offered the story of kings as that of nations and all their people; the pluralism of the societies they ruled was collapsed in the name of a simplicity that served a yearning for transcendence. While apotheosizing its perceivedly important men, historical discourse effaced the perceivedly unimportant ones—the millions of men who were only men.

As that reductive narrative obscured the many, flattening diversity and failing to record difference, obliterating *men as men*, it projected the local, the gendered, and the temporally bounded onto a universal, genderless, and atemporal screen, willingly ignoring the power imbalances thus served. In that way women were rendered invisible; but, ironically enough, so were gendered men. The terms *he*, *his*, and *man*, claimed as both grammatically masculine and neuter and allowing of no visible feminine, paradoxically also masked the particularity and materiality of their masculine referents.

The study of men's culture, through its challenge to an intellectual process that left men above examination, also corrects the peculiar "objectification" of women that feminist studies produced by studying women alone as gendered. The study of women's culture has almost always proceeded by asking how a woman's gender may shape what she does, and has even asked how the (woman) investigator's gender might bear on her study, but the relationship between a man's gender and his acts remains to be examined.[7] Women have been treated as material and local, whereas men have remained untouchable and unreachable, enjoying the privileges of the rarely present and rarely engageable Father. Feminism thus risked encouraging the sort of dichotomy that kept women in their (second) place.

Gender studies have underscored the "politics of representation" at work within traditional historical discourse, as some forms of feminism share with postmodernism the belief that history is not told, but re-presented:[8] not to have questioned that history, especially in its methodological assumptions, would have complied with its desire to be accepted as having unity, as rigorous, closed, and definitive—tautologously, the very qualities called upon to vouch for its correctness. If feminism had continued to perceive the revision of history as the adumbration of a separate history of women, to be inserted into the existing narrative, it could well have left intact a narrative that retained its edge of privilege.

It is true that men have not really clamored to have equal time (to leave linear time for cyclic time)[9]—in short, to be studied *as gendered*. Perhaps that is related to the privilege of genderlessness, as the gendered condition may be perceived as a second-class one: overwrought and overdetermined ideals of masculinity, those that emphasize great physical strength and emotional neutrality (such as the North American construction of the impenetrable macho man), suggest their promoters' unease with a simple, gendered masculinity. For some, being (simply) a man is, uncomfortably, being (like) a woman.

The idea that women might study men upsets established, gendered power relations. It makes women the readers, men the read, in a move that places women not at the margin but in the center. For some men (Freud, for example), studying women has seemed like a "normal" act of penetration; the reverse is "not normal." Then, too, transcendence offers a shelter from prying eyes, for it provides a place that is out of sight, beyond the gaze.

That the study of masculinities originates within feminism—and in my view feminism has done much clearing of the field—could leave some readers uncomfortable, as if men should study men and women should study women, yet another version of essentialism. But feminism, in its larger meaning as a system of thought and a practice, is far from being merely the study of women. In its best sense, feminism should be, as Myra Jehlen argued a long time ago, "the investigation . . . of everything."[10] Apprehended in that way, feminism is available to both female and male practitioners. To construe it any more narrowly by assuming that women alone may practice feminism or, alternatively, that women should be left to their feminism while men examine masculinities, would raise the specter of an unfortunately prefeminist worldview.

In the feminist movement itself the enterprise has opened a new door: if in the 1960s and early 1970s feminism analyzed what men had said and written in order to demystify the patriarchy, in the present stage, as we look once more at men, it is masculinities that provide the object of inquiry, not "the patriarchy," with all that the difference in terms implies.[11]

New sorts of inquiries, ones that were previously shunned, can be envisaged. Some issues, imputed to the man's arena, present a certain urgency for the lives of women—certain forms of violence, for example. Feminists have not generally addressed them, however, in part because these issues were consigned to a place ("men") for which feminism had no recognized discursive structure. The decision to exclude topics such as violence, on the grounds that they more properly belong within the man's purview, was probably an unwittingly essentialist choice. In my own field of French medieval literature, for instance, feminists have only sporadically examined the epic, and when we have, it was to look at the epic's sparse roles for women.[12] Yet the French epic of the Middle Ages is a repository for depictions of violence, presented as both gendered and institutionalized. Should we continue to ignore those representations, to treat them as if they had only an archaic literary relevance? Should we turn away in distaste from teaching all but the canonical epic(s), leaving it to other colleagues to sanction, however silently, the equation many French epics offer between masculinity and anger, physical action, and lack of reflection? Should we disdain the epic further because it "promotes the patriarchy"? Yet, a feminist examination might begin with the observation that the French epic speaks not to the father, but to the son—not to the relatively powerful, but to the relatively powerless—against a background of the culture's many myths containing fathers who would kill or sacrifice their sons: Abraham and Isaac, Laius and Oedipus, the Christian God the Father and Jesus.[13]

But after all, feminism *has* always studied men, for the study of women has necessarily—relationally—held implications for men's studies. Through both its philosophy and its praxis, feminism has equipped itself to approach the varieties of human experience. As explicit examples of types of men's studies, then, the essays in the present collection, written by both men and women, locate men as material, gendered entities. They assume that gender is constructed, that it depends on a network of oppositions and dependencies that are context bound. Seeing gender as relational, they ask how the categories of man and woman in the Middle Ages determined each other as exclusionary, and how fixed or fluid the categories were.[14] Clare A. Lees's introduction links each essay to other work in the medieval period and to the broader theoretical claims of gender and men's studies in the disciplines of history and literature.

Notes

1. Davis's comment was made in the keynote address to the 1975 Berkshire conference on women's history; cited in Elizabeth H. Pleck and Joseph H. Pleck, *The American Male* (Englewood Cliffs, N.J.: Prentice-Hall, 1980), 3-4.

2. Jane Flax, "Postmodernism and Gender Relations in Feminist Theory," *Signs* 12 (1987): 629. I thank Clare A. Lees for reading and commenting helpfully on this preface.

3. A selection of essays from the 1988 conference is published in *Thought* 64, no. 254 (1989).

4. A group of students from another university put it that way in a letter they wrote to me asking why we were having a conference about men.

5. Joseph H. Pleck, *The Myth of Masculinity* (Cambridge: MIT Press, 1981).

6. Harry Brod, "The Case for Men's Studies," in *The Making of Masculinities*, ed. Harry Brod (Winchester, Mass.: Allen & Unwin, 1987), 264; see also Brod's "A Case for Men's Studies," in *Changing Men: New Directions in Research on Men and Masculinity*, ed. Michael S. Kimmel (Newbury Park, Calif.: Sage, 1987).

7. A good example of such a study is Hanna Fenichel Pitkin's *Fortune Is a Woman: Gender and Politics in the Thought of Niccolo Machiavelli* (Berkeley: University of California Press, 1984).

8. See Linda Hutcheon, *The Politics of Postmodernism: New Accents* (London: Routledge, 1989).

9. Julia Kristeva's formulation in "Women's Time," *Signs* 7 (1981): 13-35; trans. of "Le Temps des femmes," in *34/44: Cahiers de recherche de science des textes et documents* 5 (1979): 5-19

10. Myra Jehlen, "Archimedes and the Paradox of Feminist Criticism," in *Feminisms: An Anthology of Literary Theory and Criticism*, ed. Robyn R. Warhol and Diane Price Herndl (New Brunswick, N.J.: Rutgers University Press, 1991), 76; reprinted from *Signs* 6 (1981): 575-601.

11. Arthur Brittan discusses the terms *masculinities, masculism*, and *patriarchy* in *Masculinity and Power* (Oxford: Basil Blackwell, 1989), 3-6.

12. For example, see Penny Schine Gold, *The Lady and the Virgin* (Chicago: University of Chicago Press, 1985); or Sarah Kay's synopsis of work by women on the French epic in E. Jane Burns, Sarah Kay, Roberta Krueger, and Helen Solterer, "Feminism and the Discipline of Old French Studies: *une bele disjointure*," in *The Discipline of the Discipline*, ed. R. Howard Bloch and Stephen G. Nichols, Jr. (Baltimore: Johns Hopkins University Press, forthcoming).

13. Harry Brod, "Scholarly Studies of Men: The New Field Is an Essential Complement to Women's Studies," *Chronicle of Higher Education*, 21 March 1990.

14. Flax treats approaches to gender in "Postmodernism and Gender Relations," 621-43.

Introduction

Clare A. Lees

Men's Studies, Women's Studies, Medieval Studies

Medieval Masculinities looks at men in the Middle Ages from the perspective of gender studies. In consequence, it is a project that appears to be simultaneously a timely and a risky business, and for similar reasons. It is timely because the groundwork for men's studies, laid out by social theorists, anthropologists, historians, and literary specialists in the last decade or so, offers medievalists theoretical insights and practical data with which to survey again the traditional study of men in the medieval period.[1] Building on such work, *Medieval Masculinities* helps to revise the emphasis on "hegemonic" males—the kings, princes, lawmakers, and so forth—that can obscure the rich and varied evidence for men's history in ways similar to the better-known silencing of women's history. Essays in this collection take a fresh look at, for example, the traditional male pursuits of warfare, territorial expansion, and aggression, and their literary representations, as well as focus on the less well studied areas of, for example, the concepts of the confessor, the bachelor, and the husband, and the literary construction of "manhood."

Medieval Masculinities is timely too because the important feminist contributions to medieval studies, which have necessarily concentrated on recovering and reconstructing women's history, now invite a complementary revision of what is often seen as the other side of this binary, asymmetric coin.[2] The question that runs throughout this collection in various formulations is, What does it mean to be a man in this historical period? Or, as Stanley Chojnacki asks in response to Joan Kelly's seminal question of whether women had a Renaissance: "whether, which, and how men had a Renaissance." As Chojnacki stresses, the latter questions do not cancel out the former: both, moreover, have ramifications not only for the study of the Renaissance but for the study of the Middle Ages. The focus on men in *Medieval Masculinities* is therefore not a return to traditional subjects that implies a neglect of feminist issues, but a calculated contribution to them, which can be formulated as a dialectic. The search for women in the cultural record, the breaking down of disciplinary barriers to that search, and the resultant new inquiries into cultural, social, and representational forms afford medievalists a glimpse of a very different history of men. That study, in turn, will modulate the premises, methods, and goals of a feminist inquiry. And, indeed, many of the essays in *Medieval Masculinities* address this dialectic. There are, of course, many ways of studying men and many different male experiences that still need to be recovered; this collection offers just one approach, one beginning, forged in part from the huge advances in women's history in medieval studies, and in part from the increasing body of contemporary gender theory.

The rise of men's studies in the late twentieth century, for example, can be studied in relation to the prior growth of the feminist movement. And, as is well known, the relationship between men's and women's studies can sometimes be troubled. What for some is a welcome repositioning of the older "men in feminism" debate in terms of a larger inquiry into gender is for others an indication of both male fears—a reassertion of "traditional" male values, practices, and behaviors threatened by feminism—and an erosion of the aims and goals of the feminist agenda. When placed within the larger context of postmodern theoretical critiques of subjectivity itself, the question of what it means to be a man or a woman (although initiating and motivating such discussions) appears to be old-fashioned, and increasingly irrelevant—at best, in other words, a risky business.

With the gendered study of men still in its infancy, critical anxiety about its relation to feminism has been swift to surface, as Thelma Fenster indicates in her preface to this collection. To take another, nonmedieval, example, Tania Modleski has recently demonstrated how feminist methods and goals can be appropriated for antifeminist, patriarchal ends.[3] Vital though it is to acknowledge the danger of appropriation, this is hardly a problem restricted to feminism. Modleski's solution in *Feminism without Women*, a book devoted to a feminist inquiry into men, is curiously lame. She advocates those studies of men "of the kind that analyzes male power, male hegemony, with a concern for the effects of this power *on the female subject* and with an awareness of how frequently male subjectivity works to appropriate 'femininity' while oppressing women."[4] What is lame is not her rationale, however—many of the essays in *Medieval Masculinities* demonstrate just this awareness—but her methodology. Men's studies is here incorporated into and embraced by women's studies, in a political move that places women's issues at the top of the agenda, with men's firmly subordinate to them. Seen as a political intervention, this approach certainly has its merits, but it remains problematically hierarchical, rather than dialectical. Aside from the issue of who is to police theory (an issue Modleski never addresses directly), this solution forecloses the kinds of investigations into men, masculinity, and patriarchy already under way in many disciplines and also at the heart of *Medieval Masculinities*, not the least by assuming that male power oppresses *only* women, equally. Any argument that runs this close to advocating ignorance is hardly promising.

In spite of Modleski's contempt for "gender studies," concepts of gender would seem to be a promising way to think through the dialectic of men's and women's studies.[5] But theories of gender too are currently subject to radical revision. Judith Butler's critique of identity, sex, and gender in *Gender Trouble* throws into relief the theoretical challenge of studying men or women in any period by appearing to offer a way out of the impasse of an emphasis on women (that may exclude men) or men (that may exclude women).[6] For Butler, who represents one logical endpoint of much postmodern thought, the terms *sex, gender*, and *subjectivity* are all discourse effects. Consonant with the postmodern premise that there is nothing outside the text, Butler combines a Foucauldian description of the genealogies of the discourses of "sex" and "gender" and a Lacanian/feminist psychoanalysis of subjectivity. Her thesis is familiar: the self, sexed or gendered, is knowable only through language into which it is subjected and that produces its agency. Butler's dilemma is also familiar. *Gender Trouble* wrestles with a laudable desire to get out of a fundamental binary impasse that bedevils gender studies, wherein to call oneself "woman" or "man" is to risk alignment with a patriarchal discourse that uses subject positions to enforce the "compulsory heterosexuality" that it requires for its reproduction.[7] To call oneself a man or a woman at the same time as urging a radical rethinking of gender politics risks inviting appropriation by the "other," as well as the silencing of "others." Most of us are fully aware of this vexing issue, for, although considerable gains for women and men have been achieved in the name of "woman," equally disquieting are our failures. Such is the way of coalition politics and, I would argue, gender theories have always found practical expression in broad-based, often conflicting, political movements. Butler suggests that the way out of the impasse is to subvert gender/sex distinctions from within (how else?), with a free play of gender roles that undermine and demystify the concept of fixed and stable categories of sexual or gender identity.[8] Although I appreciate the dilemma that Butler highlights, and the sophistication of her theoretical solution, I believe the greatest challenge of her work is to think through the relationship between theory and praxis—to imagine how the cause of women's and men's oppression is advanced by resisting the classifications of male and female.

Studies such as those by Modleski and Butler are representative of certain trends in the academy that make collections like *Medieval Masculinities* appear not only risky but, as I have already suggested, irrelevant and old-fashioned, if not downright impossible. In fact, although Butler appears to offer a way of thinking about gender that embraces many different genders, sexualities, and identities, the pluralism she advocates is severely strained by her theoretical analyses. Two interrelated areas in particular stand out: history and agency. Although Butler repeatedly gestures toward the importance of history, and historical methodologies, her emphasis on discourse in fact denies history any validity other than as text. Consequently, there is little historical study in *Gender Trouble*. This is perfectly consonant with a theory of language as the *only* human system of signification productive of meaning (upon which all others are modeled). But to say that social, historical reality is exhausted by, and can be reduced to, language is to stretch the specificity of language beyond meaningful bounds. For one thing, Butler's position may be read as implying that the history of male or female oppression is knowable *only* as a narrative of that discourse (despite her rhetorical assertions to the contrary). Such oppression is felt in the flesh and blood of bodies, however restricted to language our representation of it is.

The same is true of sexuality. Whether or not there is "a physical body prior to the perceptually perceived body" (a question that Butler sees as impossible to answer)[9] is set in relief by the issues raised in *Medieval Masculinities*. Consider, for example, Vern L. Bullough's account of the physical examinations necessary to the proof of impotence required for annulment of marriage, or the dead bodies (symbolic and/or real) that litter accounts of medieval aggression in the name of expansion or consolidation of political, social, or cultural power in the essays by Louise Mirrer and Christopher Baswell. As Kate Soper reminds us, "the body is neither simply the effect of discourse nor simply a point of 'brute' resistance to it, but a center of experience which is actively involved in the construction of discourse itself."[10]

Following Foucault and Lacan, Butler argues that subjectivity is produced by language, and therefore so too is agency.[11] The agents of oppression or change are thus the effects of the specific discourse that produces them. The problem is not one of the enormous power of language as a representation of reality, but one of the reductive notion of agency within history analyzed as discourse: "discourse" can no more deal with change than it can with oppression. Given the complex intersection of social, economic, and cultural factors that produce, for example, the phenomenon of the bachelor in fifteenth-century Venice studied by Chojnacki, the emergence of the institution of the husband outlined by Susan Mosher

Stuard, the twelfth-century shift in the sex/gender system documented by Jo Ann McNamara, or the role of the male mendicant orders in female mysticism indicated by John Coakley in *Medieval Masculinities*, I wonder just how adequate discourse can be as an explanatory tool. Even those studies into literary representation by, for example, Christopher Baswell, Clare Kinney, and Harriet Spiegel, which might fit conveniently into an analysis of literary discourse, engage much more with the complexity of lived experience as manifested in literary genres.

However uncomfortable the insights into male and female oppression afforded by its study in the medieval or other historical periods, only such studies will permit a fuller understanding of the cycles of crises and resolutions that underpin patriarchy, ensure its hegemony, and trace its varied manifestations in different sociocultural formations. In short, it does no harm to state the obvious: the relations between and within the sexes constitute a complex historical, hence sociocultural, phenomenon in which the language of sex and gender plays an important but not exhaustive role.

Indeed, *Medieval Masculinities* is timely above all precisely because it constitutes a challenge to those contemporary theories of sex, gender, and patriarchy that gesture toward but cannot adequately deal with the study of the past. All of the essays in the collection reveal the influence of contemporary thought and in various ways engage with it: I think, for example, of Christopher Baswell's work on the homosocial bonds in the *Roman d'Eneas*, informed by John Boswell's work on homosexuality and Eve Sedgwick Kosofsky's on homosociality; or McNamara's delineation of the *Herrenfrage*, which makes use of Thomas Laqueur's theory of the single-sexed body.[12] But the context of this book is also one of a discipline increasingly comfortable with examining its own presuppositions and increasingly uncomfortable with the frequent complacent ignorance of the period by postmedieval scholars and theorists. Lee Patterson, for example, has argued strenuously and correctly that the medieval period is often cast as the "other" of postmedieval disciplines, most significantly by those working in the Renaissance and early modern periods, who locate "modernity" and all that "modernity" implies—preeminently the "discovery" of the individual—in these later periods.[13] To take another example, the effects of a traditional literary history that arranges areas of investigation into closed series, enabling the casting of the medieval period as either "after" (the classical period) and "before" (the early modern), as Hans Robert Jauss elucidates, is being revised by historians, literary scholars, and archaeologists.[14] The history of the discipline itself is now a vital area of investigation that helps to restore and redefine the connections between past and present.[15] In opening up the study of a discipline already particularly well equipped for interdisciplinary and multicultural approaches, medievalists are exploring contemporary theories of, for example, historiography, textuality, and subjectivity and, at the same time, interrogating the assumptions of these theories against the "alterity" of the period.[16] In all of these avenues, medievalists seek dialogue with their more contemporary colleagues, and *Medieval Masculinities* is one such contribution, offering medievalists and nonmedievalists alike the opportunity to examine the historical and theoretical implications of the study of men, of women, and of gender, using the evidence of one particular period.

In consequence, this book builds upon those areas of study vital to redefining the subject that is the Middle Ages. Replacing the conventional emphasis on Anglo-French materials (doubtless the result of the prominence of these disciplines in the academy), *Medieval Masculinities* includes essays on Anglo-Saxon, Middle English, French, Italian, and Spanish subjects; covers a period from roughly the tenth to the fifteenth centuries; and offers insights into masculinity from political, legal, social, and religious history, as well as from literary texts (both canonical and noncanonical). This combination of different methodologies, periods, and theoretical emphases necessarily revises the object of analysis: as a result, no single and unified picture of masculinity in a seamless medieval world emerges. There is no "Man" in this collection, but there are studies of men, explored from a diversity of viewpoints, cultures, and representations. Such studies are vital in putting men back into the picture, as it were, in order to understand the multifaceted dynamic of male experience without succumbing to the temptation to see all men as the Same against which all women, as "Other," are defined.

McNamara, for example, charts the fluctuation of shifts in the sex/gender system that construct masculinity within patriarchy. She thus refines the concept of patriarchy in terms of specific sociocultural moments. By identifying moments where patriarchy consolidates its hegemony and others where both individuals and groups are able to resist this dominant ideology, McNamara demonstrates how medieval societies could imagine and even, however briefly and locally, realize different structurings of the gender system—different relationships between men and women. Bullough's analysis of medieval theories of the construction of masculinity contributes to our understanding of the history of sexuality with an exploration of the narrow definition of maleness as virility or potency in religious and medical discourse. His work on heterosexual anxieties, manifest both in isolated examples of cross-dressing and more prominently in "lovesickness," complements interestingly Clare Kinney's discussion of Gawain's erotic challenge to his manhood. Indeed,

Kinney's careful study of the construction and deconstruction of Gawain's body underlines just how flexible the cultural components of even a physical masculine identity are.

Encouraged by recent feminist and materialist work on the reproduction of patriarchy that focuses on the nature of work, the household, and the family, the essays by Chojnacki and Stuard offer important revisionary studies of the "institutions" of the husband and the bachelor, and Spiegel's examination of Marie de France's remodeling of the fable genre offers insights into the dynamic of male/female worlds in both public and private spheres. Moving from civil to spiritual institutions, Coakley's discussion of male-female and male-male relationships in accounts of medieval spirituality complements recent exploration of the distinctively female contributions to this medieval expression of belief. Finally, the ideology of masculinism and its relationship to male power and aggression is explored in analyses of literary representations of epic and empire by Baswell, Mirrer, and my own work. Indeed, Mirrer extends this emphasis by examining verbal aggression in the oppression of "other" men.

All of these essays, in other words, offer examples of the varied cultural manifestations of masculinity in the Middle Ages, drawing upon and contributing to key interdisciplinary areas of study that have relevance both within and without the period, for example: the idealized gender roles that men and women are encouraged to play in any given society and the strains of such roles, measured in both real lives and representation; the importance of economic and political factors in structuring the family and other social institutions; the dynamic of masculinist ideology in fostering and maintaining power through oppression of both men and women.

Medieval Masculinities

The emphasis of this collection is on masculinities as opposed to masculinity, as reflected by the grouping into three sections on constructing masculinities, men in institutions, and epic and empire. Nevertheless, the essays resist to some extent tidy classification by period or group. Recurrent themes surface throughout and bring to prominence factors that contribute to our understanding of the cultural construction of masculinity in the medieval period. Most notable is the complex interrelationship of the concepts of potency, power, patriarchy, and politics.

Analogous to Bullough's account of sexual potency in definitions of masculinity is my own study of the channeling of aggression into the reproduction of the elite warrior class in the Anglo-Saxon *Beowulf*. Christopher Baswell's revisionist reading of the Angevin *Roman d'Eneas* points to similar conclusions—dynastic expansion and consolidation is fueled by a fostering of patrilineal goals, quite literally harnessing an image of empire to the prerogatives of genealogy and legality through the trope of *translatio studii*. Equally notable is Louise Mirrer's study of Castilian frontier ballads and the epic *Cantar de Mío Cid*, which leaves us in no doubt that stereotypes of male aggression and sexual potency are used to celebrate the representation of the conquering Christian warrior. Stanley Chojnacki and Susan Mosher Stuard also remind us how masculine power can be directed into the production and maintenance of political and social formations—the patrician class in Venice whose fathers controlled the city, for example, or the consolidation of political, economic, and legal powers in the husband.

As we must expect in societies broadly conceived of as patriarchal, the success of such powerful interrelationships rests on the expulsion or redefinition of elements perceived as threatening to the hegemony. Or, to put it another way, the burden of masculine potency (symbolic or real), shadowed by impotence, exacts a heavy price. Bullough charts how psychosexual anxieties of impotence manifest themselves in lovesickness, the cures for which often only recommend further heterosexual intercourse, whereas Kinney examines how the spectacle of the male knight and courtly lover and his disappearing and reappearing "body" is a means by which social identity is gained and lost in *Sir Gawain and the Green Knight*. The successful negotiation of these conflicting roles for Gawain rests on a dynamic interplay of male and female subject-positions, as the famous seduction scenes suggest. Indeed, the "feminization" of Gawain in this section of the poem is perhaps paralleled by the peculiar position of the unmarried man in the patrician class that is the subject of Chojnacki's essay. While speculating that the bachelor can also be seen as "feminized," in the sense that the social position occupied by the bachelor is not dissimilar to that of his married sister, Chojnacki reminds us that the bachelor still enjoys political privileges from which the woman is barred. Chojnacki suggests that one reason for the number of bachelors in Venice may be the flourishing of a gay subculture, but warns us of the dangers of oversimplifying what is, in fact, complex historical evidence. Christopher Baswell too draws intriguing attention to the image of male bonding that is at the center (or heart?) of the *Roman d'Eneas*.

Nevertheless, as Stuard notes, most men in the Middle Ages were married, although the institution of husbanding has rarely received critical attention. Stuard's own analysis documents how men became subject to a new set of marriage values in the twelfth century that resulted in the legal definition of the husband. Although confirming the privileges of this status—the right to act as head of the household, for one—Stuard points out the cost, measured not only in legal responsibility but in an increasing economic burden, largely as the result of the management of dowry. Husbanding can be seen as a narrowing of the possibilities of male identity and roles; it carries with it an even greater narrowing of female roles. The wife, incapacitated before the law and dependent on her husband's definition in at least the public sphere, is thus subject to redefinition in order to maintain masculine prerogatives. Perhaps we should not be too surprised that Marie de France, as Spiegel notes, is, to say the least, ambivalent about masculine power and male inability to assume nurturing roles. Similar redefinitions are analyzed by Baswell, who stresses how the construction of empire in the *Roman d'Eneas* is built in part on the marginalization and containment of female erotic desire. A more radical example might be *Beowulf*, whose focus on the male warrior class is achieved by the containment or expulsion of women, including, most notably, mothers.

Jo Ann McNamara offers some explanations for these redefinitions and restructurings in her study of the *Herrenfrage* by pointing to the enforcement of clerical celibacy in the twelfth century as a driving force that motivated a crisis in the social system of gender relations in the medieval period. The *Herrenfrage* resulted in a reestablishment of social gender along circumscribed lines: as celibate men took over positions of power within the church, increasingly prescriptive models of behavior were offered to laymen. As a result, married men, subject to medicoreligious definitions of their sexuality, were relegated to a second-class secular world, and women removed from most spheres of ecclesiastical, social, and political influence. Licensing the oppression of women, the church also licensed the oppression of men, and an apposite example is Louise Mirrer's essay on the representation of "other" men in Castilian literature, which demonstrates how Muslim and Jewish men, like women in general, were accorded the sexuality and status of the powerless. Even within the church, however, men could be distanced from their own male role models, as is clear in John Coakley's analysis of the relationship between the mendicant friars and the male and female cults of saints they promoted. Specific gender differences in the hagiographic texts of these saints may be the result of a different and differently enriching mode of interaction between saint and venerator. The male venerator thus explores a different relationship with God through these saints: the increased intimacy and emotional charge in female sanctity offers the friars an indirect connection to an interiority often denied both friars and male saints.

In sum, many of these essays examine how ideologies of masculinity promote sameness and, at the same time, reject difference. It is therefore appropriate that the collection includes an essay speaking from that different perspective. Spiegel's essay on Marie de France considers the significance of her representations of men in the highly conventional genre of the fable. Spiegel examines how this genre becomes a vehicle for Marie de France's ambivalent look at the world of men and women from the outside, showing how this world constructs its own, frequently impoverished, definitions of manhood. *Medieval Masculinities* opens with a preface written by another woman, Thelma Fenster, who regards men from the perspective of late twentieth-century feminism. That the essays in this book should include two studies that use a female perspective to look at men is not representative of all the contributions, but neither is it exactly fortuitous. Together, they provide the two axes along which the other essays, written by both men and women, proceed. Some concentrate on the ways that contemporary twentieth-century theories of gender, and of men specifically, can be brought into a dialogue with medieval society and culture. Others concentrate on the reconstruction of assumptions about gender prevalent in the varied and dynamic social and cultural formations of this historical period. In sum, the collection looks at the past from the perspective of the present as well as at the present from the perspective of the past.

All the essays in *Medieval Masculinities*, including those by Fenster and Spiegel, share the same sense of the timely intervention in gender studies and medieval studies that a focus on men represents. This book is the first sustained attempt to explore the newly emerging field of men's studies in relation to medieval studies.[17] Its emphasis on difference and diversity provides a range of possibilities and approaches for future debate and analysis on a subject that, until recently, has attracted little interest; many more such avenues need to be explored. Nevertheless, as a result of this new focus, these essays will not only help us understand theories of men in their historical, social, and cultural dimensions, but equally—and equally important—they will help us understand theories of women.

Notes

1. See, for example, Joseph A. Boone and Michael Cadden, eds., *Engendering Men* (London: Routledge, 1990); John Boswell, *Christianity, Social Tolerance, and Homosexuality* (Chicago: University of Chicago Press, 1980); Stanley Brandes, *Metaphors of Masculinity: Sex and Status in Andalusian Folklore* (Philadelphia: University of Pennsylvania Press, 1980); Arthur Brittan, *Masculinity and Power* (Oxford: Basil Blackwell, 1989); Harry Brod, ed., *The Making of Masculinities* (Winchester, Mass.: Allen & Unwin, 1987); David D. Gilmore, *Manhood in the Making: Cultural Concepts of Masculinity* (New Haven, Conn.: Yale University Press, 1990); Joseph H. Pleck, *The Myth of Masculinity* (Cambridge: MIT Press, 1981); and Eve Kosofsky Sedgwick, *Between Men: English Literature and Male Homosocial Desire* (New York: Columbia University Press, 1985).

2. Providing a useful bibliography of work on women in medieval studies is beyond the scope of either this introduction or the book as a whole. I recommend the biannual bibliog-

raphies included in the *Medieval Feminist Newsletter* as a fruitful and increasingly valuable resource for those interested in feminist scholarship in this period.

3. Tania Modleski, *Feminism without Women: Culture and Criticism in a "Postfeminist" Age* (New York: Routledge, 1991), 3-22.

4. Ibid., 7.

5. Ibid., 5-6.

6. Judith Butler, *Gender Trouble: Feminism and the Subversion of Identity* (New York: Routledge, 1990).

7. Ibid., 5, 17-18.

8. Ibid., 142-49.

9. Ibid., 114.

10. Kate Soper, *Troubled Pleasures: Writings on Politics, Gender and Hedonism* (London: Verso, 1990), 11.

11. Butler, *Gender Trouble*, 24-26.

12. Thomas Laqueur, *Making Sex* (Cambridge, Mass.: Harvard University Press, 1991).

13. Lee Patterson, "On the Margin: Postmodernism, Ironic History, and Medieval Studies," *Speculum* 65 (1990): 87-108.

14. Hans Robert Jauss, "Literary History as a Challenge to Literary Theory," in *Toward an Aesthetic of Reception*, trans. Timothy Bahti (Brighton, Sussex: Harvester, 1982), 3-45.

15. See, for example, Allen J. Frantzen, *Desire for Origins: New Language, Old English, and Teaching the Tradition* (New Brunswick, N.J.: Rutgers University Press, 1990); and R. Howard Bloch and Stephen G. Nichols, Jr., eds., *The Discipline of the Discipline* (Baltimore: Johns Hopkins University Press, forthcoming).

16. See, for example, Kevin Brownlee and Stephen G. Nichols, eds., *Images of Power: Medieval History/Discourse/Literature*, Yale French Studies no. 70 (New Haven, Conn.: Yale University Press, 1986); Kevin Brownlee, Marina Scordilis Brownlee, and Stephen G. Nichols, eds. *The New Medievalism* (Baltimore: Johns Hopkins University Press, 1991); Laurie A. Finke and Martin B. Shichtman, eds., *Medieval Texts and Contemporary Readers* (Ithaca, N.Y.: Cornell University Press, 1987); and Allen J. Frantzen, ed., *Speaking Two Languages: Traditional Disciplines and Contemporary Theory in Medieval Studies* (Albany: State University of New York Press, 1991).

17. For examples of individual studies of masculinity and medieval texts, see David Aers, *Community, Gender, and Individual Identity: English Writing 1360-1430* (London: Routledge, 1988), 117-52; and H. Marshall Leicester, Jr., *The Disenchanted Self: Representing the Subject in the "Canterbury Tales"* (Berkeley: University of California Press, 1990).

PART I

Constructing Masculinities

CHAPTER 1

The *Herrenfrage*
The Restructuring of the Gender System, 1050-1150

Jo Ann McNamara

Experience indicates that the masculine gender is fragile and tentative, with weaker biological underpinnings than the feminine.[1] It requires strong social support to maintain fictions of superiority based solely on a measure of physical strength. The assignment of social roles and status on the basis of biological sex has customarily been justified as resting on the bedrock of natural law, decreed by God and nature and therefore beyond the reach of historical change. This has hitherto made the gender system almost impervious to challenge. In recent scholarship, however, the immutable laws of nature have been exposed as mere creatures of time and cultural change. Historians have come to see gender as an ephemeral, culture-bound style of self-presentation and biology itself as a largely constructed artifact. The gender system that defines male domination as an irreducible given has given way to a cultural fiction that relies on constant adaptation to new conditions. Thus, not only is gender a useful analytic tool for historians, but history is indispensable to understanding gender. After some decades of investigating the experience of women with astonishingly little impact on "mainstream" history, it is time at last to expose that traditional history as men's history.

Europe in the early twelfth century provides an exceptionally well documented restructuring of the gender system. Broad social changes, complicated by the ideological struggle between celibate and married men for leadership of the Christian world, precipitated a masculine identity crisis, which I have dubbed the *Herrenfrage*.[2] Its resolution dramatizes the dynamics that ensure that the more things change, the more they remain the same.

In the early eleventh century, the functional social order that divided men into those who pray, those who fight, and those who labor came under attack before the developing urban professions. Between 1110 and 1130, the conservative bishop of Limerick defended an equally threatened gender system: "I do not say that the function of woman is to pray or toil, let alone to fight, but they are married to those who pray, toil and fight and they serve them."[3] The prevailing biological definition of the female as a defective male subsumed women at the lower end of a single continuum. In that context, where dynastic needs occasionally decreed that princes should be women, family and class interests could supersede gender without threatening the right order of things. The noble blood of ladies triumphed over their female weakness in competition with men of inferior status. Family partnerships and supportive responsibilities extended through all three orders. When they were off to war, Carolingian emperors delegated the administration of their kingdoms to their wives.[4] Robert Guiscard's wife, Gaeta, rode into battle, harrying her husband's fleeing troops to make a stand and "fight like men."[5] The reforming papacy relied on Mathilda of Tuscany for military support against the emperor, though no one expected her or any other woman to "fight like a man" in physical combat. Similarly, the praying order could accommodate the occasional "manly" woman of exceptional spirituality.

By midcentury, this old social hierarchy was succumbing to the pressures of change.[6] Like the *Frauenfrage*, the *Herrenfrage* grew out of an expanding population that overburdened the agricultural economy. Primogeniture pushed the younger children of landowners, noble and serf alike, into pioneering new lands or into cities in search of new ways to earn their keep. New professions generated by the church, secular government, and towns themselves shaped new identities that had to be gendered as well as classed. Gradually a public sphere emerged that required a different division of labor from that characterizing the household/kinship society of the early Middle Ages. Status in urban institutions was less overtly pinned to masculine warrior qualities. That produced the *Herrenfrage*: How can men redefine manhood to prove women's incapacity to carry out public professional responsibilities? The displaced young men who were creating the learned professions reasserted the concept of woman as defective man from Galen and Aristotle.[7] This natural law theory privileged men in public life but did not guarantee that the new public sphere would be woman-free as long as dynastic interests were in play. Even a reordering of social priorities to give gender precedence over class would not automatically ensure male superiority in the new system without a violently exaggerated definition of masculinity.

Masculine claims to inherent superiority were already well grounded in theology. Woman's "natural" need to be ruled had been given divine sanction in the myth of the Fall. It was expressed socially in the rituals of marriage, which equated male adulthood with the assumption of responsibility for a family of dependents and relegated women to the status of perpetual children. The twelfth-century church promoted a model of marriage centered on the couple in preference to kindred. If men married the women who might have competed with them, they could subordinate them and secure the support of their talents at the same time. This worked fairly efficiently among the commercial and artisanal classes. The developing professions could have accommodated the exceptional manly woman as readily as had the warrior culture of the earlier period. As in that passing culture, however, this accommodation would have tended toward a hereditary professional caste.

The gender system destabilized because celibate men monopolized most of the new positions, excluding women rigorously during the sensitive period of social readjustment. The papal revolution of the 1070s presaged a new centricity of the sacraments that underscored the male monopoly of the Catholic priesthood. The imposition of clerical celibacy excluded women even from their nonsacramental functions. This woman-free space was inexorably expanded as clerical men monopolized new educational opportunities. The renaissance in classical learning reestablished the theoretical intellectual and moral inferiority of women and enabled men implicitly to absorb all the positive qualities of "mankind." The result was the ungendered public men who would henceforth be equated with "people," screened by such anthropomorphized institutions as "church" and "crown."[8] The process also protected the class system from the "new men" rising to bureaucratic prominence in courts and city governments. Priestly celibacy ensured that temporary lapses of the class system in favor of talented men over aristocratic women could be repaired in more stable times.

Women's absence from competitive space had the advantage of allowing for an ungendered definition of man. However, it deprived masculine individuals of objects for the sexual demonstrations that proved their right to call themselves men. An important class of men institutionally barred from marriage raised inherently frightening questions about masculinity. Can one be a man without deploying the most obvious biological attributes of manhood? If a person does not act like a man, is he a man? And what does it mean to "act like a man," except to dominate women? If men who repudiated connection with women not only remained men, but even claimed to be superior to other men, what did this mean to the self-image of men in the secular world?

Moreover, the whole male effort would collapse if women also became ungendered. Men's failure to marry meant that gender rules went unenforced over a growing surplus of women, unprotected, uncontrolled, undefined. The *Herrenfrage* precipitated the *Frauenfrage*: the problem of disposing of "excess" women. For many twelfth-century people, the logical answer to the *Frauenfrage* was syneisactic celibacy, a union of women and men free of sex and the gender roles that generally accompany sex. Monastic theory already defined celibate women as morally and intellectually equal to men. Thus, if they abandoned their family roles, nothing prevented them from following celibate men into the commodious spaces allotted to "mankind."

The entire gender system spun into a crisis. The polemics of clerical misogyny collided with the church's strengthened demand for lay monogamy and its accompanying sexual responsibilities. Secular men living ordinary procreative lives as prescribed by their religion heard women denounced as virulent agents of moral pollution, so contagious that prudent men must flee at their approach and shun all contact with them. Many reacted by seeking escape from the terrors of conjugal life, renouncing sex and the hierarchy that sex supported. The *Herrenfrage* forced men to take extreme measures against the encroachment of women in nearly every area of life. The resulting *Frauenfrage* threatened to undermine the whole ideological base of masculinism. By midcentury, the worst of the danger was over. Men who failed to cooperate in the enforcement of the gender system were bullied back into the ranks. Syneisactism became a clear indicator of heresy, and the penalties for heresy escalated as the century ended. Marriage regained its preferred status as the social norm and the celibate clergy reluctantly undertook the burden of controlling celibate women.

The Gender System under Threat

In the old tripartite order, as the bishop of Limerick envisioned it, the celibate were structurally nonexistent. A peculiarly Christian value primarily associated with women, celibacy by its very nature threatened any established gender system.[9] Women who abstained from sex were freed from the responsibilities and some of the constraints generally imposed upon them. In early Christian times, the anomaly had been solved by classifying such women as "manly."[10] In the monastic order, they performed many of the same tasks as men, sometimes in the same physical environment. Nuns shared the educational opportunities available to monks. Indeed, the devotion of monks to sedentary intellectual tasks tended to give them a somewhat "womanish" image. In the early twelfth century, convents still produced women of impressive learning, such as Hildegard of Bingen and Herrad of Hohenburg. Some monastic women ruled in princely fashion and even claimed episcopal privileges. Secular canonesses attached to cathedral chapters shared many of the liturgical and administrative roles of secular canons in the clerical hierarchy, though female exclusion from sacramental activity maintained a firm gender barrier between them. In effect, freedom from sexuality enabled women to develop the intellectual and spiritual gifts they shared with men. The insult to the gender system had been absolved in early medieval society by the legal fiction that monastic men and women were dead to the world and therefore excluded from the social structure.

In the tenth century, however, monastic men returned to the world with a vengeance and challenged episcopal leadership of the church, claiming a moral superiority based on renunciation of sex over the married secular clergy. The moral equality of women with men in the ascetic community threatened these ambitions. Around 995, Abbo of Fleury described three orders of Christian men—monks, clerks, and laymen—suggesting that the highest order of men were those furthest from women.[11] Their female partners in religion, traditionally ranked in a descending hierarchy of virgins, continent widows, and matrons, were relegated to a hidden "private" sphere within monasticism as within the laity. The monks of Cluny, who spearheaded monastic leadership, refused adamantly to admit female communities to their network of reformed monasteries, implying that women were incapable of sufficient spiritual merit. While claiming moral superiority over the secular clergy because of their sexual purity, the Cluniacs refused women's claim to share their social leadership by virtue of equal purity. As monks rose in the ecclesiastical hierarchy, they monasticized the secular clergy by imposing celibacy upon them, sometimes violently.

The Gregorian revolution aimed at a church virtually free of women at every level but the lowest stratum of the married laity. Once the secular clergy had been subjected to celibacy, the monastic orders were largely clericized. The co-optation of monks into the ordained priesthood doubly hedged religious women. Once priesthood became a prerequisite of higher education, nuns were institutionally disqualified from following monks into new areas of learning and administration, regardless of their natural endowments. Canonesses were attacked in the first great wave of reform legislation in 1059 and, from the 1120s on, many chapters were dissolved.[12]

Clerical celibacy was not easily imposed. As late as 1119, more than half a century after the original decrees, the laws were still being renewed with ever stronger sanctions.[13] Theological and social defenses of clerical marriage were reinforced by medical beliefs, as taught by Constantine Africanus (d. 1095), that men required regular sexual activity to ensure against an unhealthy buildup of effluvia.[14] Priests resisted giving up comfort, affection, and good health to satisfy the radical ideas of a few extremist monks. Ultimately, a theoretical separation of the priest's two bodies was achieved. Though the polemics against priestly marriage had come dangerously close to weakening the ancient protection of the priest from the moral failings of his humanity, donatism was soon restored to heretical status and defended him against critics of clerical immorality.

Psychologically, manhood itself was at stake. Men without women, if deprived of sexuality, came dangerously close to traditional visions of femininity. Celibacy deprived its practitioners of the necessary "other" upon which to construct a gender persona. Engaging in sex, if only in the sense of boasting to other men and joining with them in a common celebration of the physical subordination of women, was necessary to the construction of masculinity. In the 1120s, the clergy finally became celibate in the narrow sense that clerical orders were declared to be an immovable impediment to marriage. But for centuries to come, people took it for granted that most priests would enjoy the unsanctified companionship of concubines, and episcopal records suggest that others regarded the *cura monialium* as a grant of sexual privilege with nuns.[15] In effect, clerical men could affirm their masculinity only by committing sin.

Although hardly a morally impeccable solution, pragmatic tolerance achieved the institutional goal of excluding women from the unfamiliar territory that men were beginning to occupy. Separation from women reinforced the dislike and fear fostered by monastic polemic. We are so accustomed to thinking of the medieval clergy as violently abusive toward women that we have missed a chronological subtlety. Clerical misogyny reached a crescendo between the mid-eleventh and the mid-twelfth centuries. The struggle to separate men from women caused reformers to rave against married priests and, by implication, the whole sexual act. Sermons, pastoral letters, public statements of all sorts depicted women as dangerous and aggressive, poisonous and polluting. Yet the logic of clerical celibacy required a complementary lay society whose members were paired in heterosexual unions.

A psychological crisis developed, I think, around the whole question of sexuality. Among the clergy, obviously, misogyny had its uses. But the uncoupling of women and men posed a structural challenge to the secular orders. Laymen were increasingly pressed to marry. The spread of primogeniture created a surplus of younger sons, not all of whom could be absorbed into the clergy. Continual warfare and the normal accidents of procreation resulted in a proliferation of heiresses. The sinking of the white ship in 1120, for example, leaving only a female successor to William the Conqueror's crown, was but the most dramatic instance of a broad social phenomenon. Ambition urged fortune hunters toward marriage. The growing class of disinherited "youth" were obliged to make themselves pleasing to women if they were to compete successfully in securing their lost place in the social order.[16] In life as in literature, the harsh reality was that many men had to put women's tastes ahead of their own masculine image. Moralists, who were strangely silent about female vanity in the first half of the twelfth century, complained of men's effeminate fashions.[17] Men who shaved their beards, curled their hair, and cultivated other courtly vanities were blamed for causing soldiers to be confused with priests or women.[18] Canon lawyers insisted that the consent of the partners was the only requirement for marriage, opening up the possibility that young men might make desirable matches despite the disapproval of prudent parents. The ephemeral advantages of women in courtship dictated the "unnatural" subordination of men.[19] They were expected to profess a love that was defined as a disease whose only cure was marriage.

The laity were defined as the sexually active part of the population. Around 1140, canon lawyers who wanted to strengthen indissolubility were arguing that consummation was necessary to legitimate marriage.[20] Adalbero of Laon praised Robert thc Pious for discouraging laymen from inappropriate displays of religious enthusiasm in favor of procreation. The fighting class, locked into indissoluble unions, were expected to exercise their manly attributes of rationality and potency to control their wives, as they were expected to control the toiling classes.[21] Ironically, this involved temporary sacrifices of rationality and even potency to the passions of love and rage. The aristocratic model of marriage, though opposed to the Church ideal in some respects, agreed that men must control women. In society as in the bedroom, women's inherent incapacity to function without male guidance and protection had to be affirmed. Instead, scandals involving both male and female adultery, incest, and violence left the ruling class in disorder.[22] The pope excommunicated the king of France for his marital misdeeds.[23] Dynastic strategy alone cannot account for the number of husbands who repudiated their wives even as the clergy separated from theirs.

Lay people, reflecting upon diatribes by local preachers enforcing the celibacy decrees, must have wondered about the safety of their sexual lives.[24] Although there were many biological theories to choose from, and we cannot know how many people were aware of the debates of professors, the ideas of William of Conches, who studied in Paris until 1120, seem to reflect a growing anxiety about female potency and male impotence. He advocated the idea that female sperm is an active component of procreation, in opposition to the Aristotelian theory assigning all formative capacity to male sperm.[25] Female sperm added to female menses, from which the sperm was thought to take its fetal shape, almost rendered men unnecessary to procreation.[26]

Popular literature commonly showed women as more lustful than men, insatiably seeking satisfaction. Women themselves exhibited a strong sense of their conjugal claims, as, for example, that group of Norman women who demanded successfully that William the Conqueror send their husbands home from England to satisfy their sexual needs.[27] Polite literature exhibited a new focus on women's control over the act of love as well as her control over her courting lover.[28] Woman's right to sex was implicit in the church's emphasis on consent and marital affection as the foundation of marriage. Indissolubility increased the pressures that produced men's fear of marriage. Medical texts began anxiously to argue for the restriction of copulation to the "natural position," threatening that when women are on top, the effort of expelling the seed might cause lesions in the penis.[29]

A surprising number of men are known to have shrunk from the intimate responsibilities that marriage demanded. Sainthood through sexual abstinence was a virtue often associated with women in the early Middle Ages.[30] In the eleventh century, it became an attribute of kings. Henry II of Germany's biographer maintained that he would have avoided marriage but for the pressure of his nobles. He found a wife, Cunegund, with whom he conspired to renounce sex. The couple were not canonized until the later twelfth century, first Henry and then Cunegund. The hagiographic tradition exalting their chaste marriage grew with time and distance. Edward the Confessor's childless marriage was likewise ascribed to his purity.[31] In contrast to early hagiographic clichés that cast women as the leaders in embracing chastity, both queens were suspected of adultery. Thus, new concepts of women's sexual insatiability balanced a symbolic autocastration that protected some men from the burdens and dangers of marriage.[32]

The gender system required enforcers, but enforcement exposed men to the mysterious threat of female sexuality. Where did that leave the natural law of male dominance, upon which all masculinist theory rests? Male sexuality is constructed on the phallus as a symbol of power, a myth that grossly overburdens physical reality. In contrast to the phallic imagery of masculinism, the penis is rarely erect. Thus, the necessary myth of constant, uncontrollable potency has to be ritually strengthened in male gatherings through boasts and dirty jokes and occasional group aggression against women.[33] In reaction to the implied threat of virile women, masculine behavior was defined and promoted as rough and domineering. Several biographers made special efforts to depict their male subjects as brutal toward women, as though to reinforce a common stereotype. The story circulated that William the Conqueror dragged his future queen Mathilda around her father's house by her hair until she agreed to their marriage. Gilbert Crispin describes the parents of Herluin of Bec as a well-matched couple, the husband being barbaric and rough and the wife meek and gentle. Anselm of Bec recorded that he was brutalized by a male relative and healed by his mother.[34] The masculine identity crisis produced a complicated dialectic. Women, depicted as fearsome, required men to be brutal; men, depicted as brutal, required women to be gentle.

The need for unrelenting potency produced a fear of impotence that shadows a surprising number of early twelfth-century accounts. Guibert of Nogent claims, for example, that his father was prevented from consummating his marriage for seven long years by the witchcraft of enemies who opposed his choice of a wife. To prove his potency, he was driven to a prostitute.[35] Bertold, the husband of Saint Godeleva, attributed his inexplicable revulsion toward the woman he had married for love to witchcraft and felt justified in killing her when he could not overcome his sexual distress.[36] Christina of Markyate, who was forced into marriage, persuaded her young husband to respect her virginity and engage in a chaste marriage. His relatives and friends shamed him into attempting to rape her, promising to help him out if necessary.[37] Louis VI, the king of France, was subjected to intimidating mockery because of his reluctance to marry.[38] Yves of Chartres admonished him to take a wife because failure to take his place in the married order would exclude him from his place in Heaven as well.

In effect, the newly celibate clerical hierarchy reshaped the gender system to assure male domination of every aspect of the new public sphere. The imposition of celibacy on the clergy and clerical monopoly of the universities set up to produce a new professional class enforced masculinist claims for the incapacities of women. The myth of women's uncontrollable sexuality and its disorderly effects justified the segregation of the clergy, but it sent deeply troubling messages to the laymen upon whom the responsibility for governing women fell doubly hard.

Not all men accepted their roles as enforcers of the system. Many men and even more women saw celibacy as an opportunity to escape the burdens and the constraints of male dominance. Even among the champions of clerical celibacy at the Gregorian curia, chaste rhetorical romances seem to have flourished, as evidenced by the letters between the hysterical misogynist Peter Damien and the Empress Agnes.[39] Gregory VII himself was emotionally close to the widowed Beatrice of Tuscany and her daughter, Mathilda, whose marriages were commonly believed to have been unconsummated. In one moment of discouragement, he even proposed to take Mathilda on Crusade.[40] A well-publicized group of people saw renunciation of sexual relations as a means to free men as well as women from traditional gender roles. There was a moment in the early twelfth century when they might have led the way to a new and more equitable partnership that narrowed the social effects of biological differences and favored a wider development of the ungendered aspects of the individual personality. Alert to the danger, the defenders of the system struck back forcefully.

Innovation

The triumph of monasticism over the clergy threatened to introduce a sort of gender minimalism. The ideology that had long been associated with the renunciation of sexual activity pointed strongly toward the inclusion of women among the "people" rising to the top of the medieval hierarchy.[41] The famous surplus of women emerged in northwestern Europe, where, at the turn of the century, Urban II was preaching the crusade, renewing the battle against clerical marriage, and taking control of the Peace of God movement. For a brief period around the time of the first Crusade, it appeared that in the renunciation of sex, many women and men might find the key to a new gender system in which domination was not a central issue. Observers in the late eleventh century chronicled the multiplication of women who became hermits or anchoresses or who joined the following of itinerant preachers. These included fabled throngs of repentant prostitutes, who, I venture to suggest, may often have been the abandoned wives of priests who had formally been branded as concubines by the reformers. Women repudiated by their husbands mixed with women who took the initiative in rejecting not only husbands but the sexual life itself.

Many men saw abstinence as a means to drop out of the whole power system. Instead of using celibacy to control society, they renounced the burdens and corruptions of governance. These latter-day apostles began to experiment with a syneisactic life.[42] Robert d'Arbrissel, for example, turned from a preacher of clerical celibacy to an apostolate to abandoned women.[43] Like several of his contemporaries in the effort, he argued that Christ traveled with women and lived with them. His followers practiced the *imitatio Christi* by living in small huts with minimal sex segregation on uncleared land at Fontevraud.[44] More aggressively, Robert led the women in his company into the church of Ménat, where once the local saint had cursed all women. He defied the ban forbidding their entrance on pain of death, proclaiming that it was madness to exclude women from a building when Christ deemed them worthy to house his body and blood.[45] The same argument was advanced by Anselm of Bec, who maintained that the imitation of Christ was open to women as well as men.[46]

Abelard began his brief history of nuns with a discussion of the women around Jesus.[47] He stressed the equality of both sexes in the apostolic life.[48] The burgeoning cults of the Virgin Mary, Saint John, and Mary Magdalene reflected the growing enthusiasm for this mixed, chaste lifestyle of the apostolic past.

The renunciation of sex without separating women from men narrowed the definitional grounds between the genders. Proponents of the apostolic movement boasted that women proved themselves fit for the hardest ascetic practices and manual labor.[49] Norbert of Xanten settled some of his female followers in a community under Ricwere de Clastres in 1120. Within twenty years, thousands of women under the protection of Prémontré were serving the sick of urban communities.[50] In 1131, seven young women gathered around Gilbert of Sempringham, who had tried and failed to find men who would submit to his rigorous standards.[51] They took up a barren piece of land that monks had abandoned as too difficult to cultivate. Groups of women, relatives, or simply pensioners formed an aureole of recluseries and women's communities around many, perhaps most, male monasteries. The women attached to monasteries, often relatives of the monks, called themselves handmaids of the monks and performed services for them well within the boundaries of the conventional sexual division of labor. Bec, for example, was founded in partnership between Herluin and his mother, who acted as a handmaid, doing laundry and baking bread for her son and his companions. From 1080 to 1099, a community of women became an integral part of the Bec confraternity, almost a monastic family. Even a single Cluniac house, Marcigny, was founded in 1080. In England, where few convents survived the Conquest, scholars have uncovered more than forty monasteries housing both men and women between 1130 and 1165. In Germany, there was hardly a great house of monks without a nearby female house under its protection. In many cases, the women's community was made up largely of female relatives and separated wives of the monks (as at Vannes and Tart), opened to relieve the pressures of unplaced women.

The power relations of recluses were less clear, but we have numerous examples of men who subjected themselves to the tutelage of women.[52] Hermits living in rural solitude or even in urban areas looked to holy women as their mentors. Abbots of male communities drew spiritual sustenance from recluses clustered around their monasteries.[53] Eva, who lived with a preacher from the monastery of Trinité-la-Vendôme, had a wide circle of male admirers.[54] Roger the hermit left his cell to his pupil, Christina of Markyate, where she drew a community of women.[55] The abbot of Saint Albans assumed the care of her group and relied on her visions to guide him in making crucial decisions.[56] Hildegard of Bingen lent great prestige to the monastery that protected her community of recluses. It required several miracles to enable her to sever the relationship. From Aelred of Rievaulx, we know that recluses were known widely for educating young people from their retreats and, though we may assume that most of their clients were female, males were not excluded.

A syneisactic society, where women and men mingle and relate to one another without reference to accepted sex roles, is deeply threatening to the conventional order. The socialization of gender identity, a person's own view of maleness or femaleness, assumes heterosexuality and indeed leaves no room for deviation of any sort from the polarized sex roles into which each individual can be fitted or forced during the vulnerable period of early childhood.[57] A fluid relationship between women and men enabled women to take the lead when the normal variables of talent, age, experience, and social status made it appropriate. As a widow, Ida of Boulogne retired in 1099 to St. Vaast, which she restored and shared with Cluniac monks under her care; she was recognized as de facto abbot there.[58] Saint-Sulpice (ca. 1120) had one male and one female house, both under an abbess.[59] At Fontevraud, women ruled men as established by Robert before his death in 1117. These women gave vivid new meaning to the ancient formulas praising virgin saints as "virile" women, whose renunciation of sexual activity liberated their native manliness. They were seemingly the harbingers of a world in which the gender system might be utterly demolished. Men and women worked alike and dressed alike. They might become indistinguishable if they really escaped sexuality and its procreative results.[60] Indeed, if gender differences were reduced to the level of biology, sex itself might be changed.

It is worth pondering what the future may have looked like for a few people in 1120. The mingling of men and women was not necessarily confined to the marginal world of the extreme ascetic. Many women accompanied the first Crusade, some of them disguised as men.[61] Educated women shared, though marginally, the intellectual awakening and discovery of the age. Some of them are still remembered as the authors of letters, religious works, and fiction. Hildegard of Bingen, Herrad of Hohenberg, and others had an extensive classical education, as did their male contemporaries. A woman, whether or not named Trotula, was probably teaching medicine in an Italian university. The book attributed to her placed woman with man "above the other creatures by means of extraordinary dignity" with "freedom of reason and of intellect."[62] In some respect the developing science of sex was an effort by men to take control of the secrets of women.

Around 1120, Heloise, who may have been the child of a clerical couple, was living with her uncle in the cathedral close in Paris.[63] We shall never know what Fulbert had in mind when he procured the city's most famous scholar, Abelard, to tutor his niece. He may have been hoping for a marriage, but that does not seem reason enough for Heloise's elaborate education. Heloise herself never intended to be a nun, and she refused to marry her lover. Despite Abelard's careful masculinist depiction of himself as a cold-blooded seducer, his own testimony and that of Heloise's letters affirm that she entered into their affair with a strong sense of herself as a sexual, but not conjugal, person.[64] What could anyone have expected for a young woman famed for her intellect while still in her teens? Abelard was well known for his impetuous desertion of the cathedral school to embrace a career as an independent scholar. There was, at that time, no university and no formal system that excluded women or demanded clerical orders from its participants. Did Fulbert hope that an unusual woman such as Heloise might find some career in the learned sciences? Did she hope for it, or at least for some sort of career as Abelard's amanuensis, partner, or muse? Perhaps they had convinced each other that together they could restore the conditions of Paradise. Abelard once suggested that Adam and Eve might actually have enjoyed intercourse before their fall instituted the hierarchical gender system.[65] Did they envisage a life beyond the syneisactic experiment? The tone of Heloise's arguments against marriage suggests that she may have dreamed of an unconstrained sexual relationship in which she could somehow function independently of Abelard's legal and economic support.

That, perhaps, is too daring a speculation. But meanwhile, the followers of the apostolic life were living and working together, pursuing a common spiritual vision. Their occasional mischances were few compared with the chronic state of fornication in which many of the newly celibate clergy lived. Yet whoring priests were little criticized, and the prostitutes whose numbers were growing as a result of the husband shortage received a surprising degree of sympathy from moralists and canon lawyers alike.[66] Itinerant preachers, such as Henri of Lausanne, Fulk of Neuilly, and Vital of Mortain, were particularly concerned with this emerging evil and sought to solve it by urging single men to marry prostitutes as a charitable act. The people who came in for incessant, hysterical criticism were the syneisactics.

Reconstruction

I believe that it was fear of their success and not concrete evidence of wrongdoing that caused influential contemporaries from Odo of Cluny through Paschal II to criticize violently preachers who committed themselves to the ministry of women.[67] To restore the threatened boundaries between male and female, they had to restore the idea of man's raging, uncontrollable lust. Robert d'Arbrissel's bishop, Marbod of Rennes, repeated rumors circulating against the women serving the poor and sick in his hospices. He admitted that he had no serious doubts about Robert's purity, but went on to warn him of the dangers of poisonous, flaming, venomous women.[68] Naturally, there were occasional sexual lapses. The misdeeds of the nun of Watton who became pregnant by a monk of the community are well known.[69] In one of her hermitages, a young priest stripped off his clothing in hopes of seducing Christina of Markyate.[70] The same saint endured constant criticism for her close communion with the abbot of Saint Albans, though most of their relationship was conducted in dreams and visions.[71] Guibert of Nogent tied syneisactism to other "unnatural" behavior with an exemplary tale of a hermit who loved a nun and made a bargain with the devil through the mediation of a Jew.[72] The underlying argument of all the critics was that men could not consort innocently with women. This was most succinctly stated by Bernard of Clairvaux, who said that it was easier to raise the dead than to resist women.[73]

In 1123, while the ill-fated union of Heloise and Abelard was moving to its violent conclusion, the First Lateran Council issued a new bull against clerical marriage that firmly invalidated the marriages of priests. Thereafter, the barriers between the genders were gradually rebuilt. Abelard's account of his Calamities, written about 1132, illustrates the ambiguities of the age. By the time he wrote about it, Abelard seems singularly sanguine about his castration. After an even more dangerous sojourn in the segregated world of monks, he returned not only to Heloise but to a fuller syneisactic life at the Paraclete. He answered his critics that, like Origen, he had earned the right to teach women with impunity.[74] He was earnest and persistent in his efforts to persuade Heloise to abandon her memories of their sexual encounters and join him in chaste service to God. From the passionate tone of her letters, as contrasted to his chilliness, I am tempted to speculate that Abelard may have nursed a small secret sense of relief to have been excused from coping with her blazing passions any longer.

But his well-publicized castration was surely an object lesson to all those men who risked themselves in partnership with women. Outsiders who heard their story must have shuddered at the evidence of the real-life dangerous liaison so similar to the destructive unions being celebrated in romance and courtly love poetry.[75] The nuns at Watton who made their errant sister castrate her lover may have been motivated by a need to avenge their lost honor, and Aelred himself endorsed this interpretation.[76]

Nevertheless, the vision of a horde of ravening maenads must have confirmed his monastic readers in their fear of syneisactism. The chill distances between lovers prescribed in Andreas Capellanus's handbook on seduction take on new meaning in this light. His apparently anomalous third book, warning at great length that love (and women) are the root of all evil, becomes a fitting culmination to the entire opus.[77] The growing popularity of *The Song of Roland* brought a monasticized form of knighthood into fashion. Later twelfth- and thirteenth-century Arthurian tales also warned of the terrible dangers of male-female propinquity, whose cure could be found only in the heroic purity of knights such as Percival and Galahad.

Freedom from women became the test of a true fighting man. Around 1125, Robert the Monk published a new version of Urban II's speech launching the Crusade, adding an explicit warning that women should not go without male guardians because they would be more hindrance than help.[78] Guibert of Nogent argued that women had corrupted the Crusaders and praised King Baldwin for putting his wife in a convent to free himself from the struggle with the flesh.[79] In 1128, the Crusade produced that new militia who would be so enthusiastically praised by Bernard of Clairvaux as a manly brotherhood, spurning the effeminate trappings of worldly knights and, of course, sworn as monks to forgo the company of women.[80] The effeminate worldly knight in silks and curls was utterly disgraced by comparison with the Templars, who were celibate and bearded.

From the 1020s forward, people were intermittently condemned as heretics for their hatred of the flesh, the fighting, and the sexuality that defined the secular man.[81] Guibert of Nogent in 1124 and Peter the Venerable in the 1130s warned their readers against false monks practicing the *vita apostolica.*[82] Around 1136, Bernard of Clairvaux equated heresy with syneisactism.[83] He admitted that "there is nothing more blameless than the behavior" of certain sexually mixed religious groups who shared a common table and sleeping quarters. They attended church regularly, and participated in the sacraments. They honored the clergy and performed meritorious acts of self-mortification without stinting on useful labor.[84] But he argued casuistically that, because syneisactism scandalized him, men and women consorting together sinned against the Gospel that prohibited the spreading of scandal. Bernard dismissed the objection that women lived with Jesus and the apostles. His conclusion was simple: men and women who lived and worked together, however chaste and blameless they might appear, were in truth heretics subverting the church through scandal. The devastating effect of Bernard's successful condemnation may be seen in a tale of the late twelfth century. Gervase of Tilbury described the fate of an apparently blameless young woman burned at the stake as a member of the "Publican" sect. Her straitlaced disdain for a noble seducer had alerted her accusers to her heresy.[85]

Bernard was not a lone voice.[86] Prudent men began to flee the company of women. Stephen of Grandmont deserted Gaucher of Aureil because of the hermit's willingness to undertake the care of women. He went on to found a monastic order from which women were strictly excluded.[87] A hermit named Ailbert who had established a syneisactic community at Rolduc near Liège circa 1102 left the establishment when the women refused to live apart in a nearby cemetery.[88] For forty years, his successors tried to get rid of the women, whose defenders argued that there were women among the apostles.[89] But gradually the women, who were the original core of the community, were reduced from sisters to *conversae* and driven to its margins.

Marcigny, the first abbey for women admitted to the Cluniac network, pioneered the fanatic claustration that characterized twelfth-century monastic rules.[90] Fontevraud abandoned the active life of social service before the first generation died out and retained a mere shadow of its original syneisactic character. The monks took an oath to provide for the needs of the women, but they were protected from temptation by the strict enclosure of the nuns.[91] Even the offices for the dead were carefully designed to preserve the segregation of nuns and monks.[92] At the Paraclete, segregation was as complete as it was at Fontevraud. Abelard's rule, written at Heloise's request about fifteen years after the death of Robert d'Arbrissel, criticized the latter's insistence on the superiority of the abbess.[93] In 1147 the Cistercians flatly refused to take on the growing Gilbertine community,[94] but the ubiquitous Bernard of Clairvaux helped write a rule designed to segregate them at every point.[95] The Premonstratensian chapter general ended its nursing mission and cloistered the sisters within their monasteries. Then, for fear of scandal, they separated them from the male monasteries and finally, in 1137, suspended their recruitment altogether.[96] One of the abbots, Conrad of Marchtal, explained:

> We and our whole community of canons, recognizing that the wickedness of women is greater than all the other wickedness of the world, and that there is no anger like that of women, and that the poison of asps and dragons is more curable and less dangerous to men than the familiarity of women, have unanimously decreed for the safety of our souls, no less than for that of our bodies and goods, that we will on no account receive any more sisters to the increase of our perdition, but will avoid them like poisonous animals.[97]

While men were being taught to quarantine women through fear of pollution and chaos, they were being urged to establish their own dominance at whatever cost. Women were being retrained to fear the dangers of provoking the ungovernable male sex drive. The literature that emerged after 1130 or 1140 seems designed to reconstitute the separation of the sexes.[98] In 1164, just after his investigation of the notorious affair at Watton, Aelred of Rievaulx wrote a rule for recluses that was typical of the proliferating regulations that were hemming them in.[99] Aelred, like his contemporary hermit Godric of Finchale, consciously invoked his sister's virginity as a compensation for his own loss of purity. To safeguard it, he warned her against active relationships with men. Even confession, the delight of the meditative soul, was dangerous because women's "candid" confessions might stir the irresistible lusts of men. Aelred conceded only that a recluse could speak to a confessor for limited spiritual direction. She could also speak occasionally in the presence of a third person to an abbot or prior or other estimable person, but not frequently, for fear of temptation.[100] Networks with women in the community and the common practice of educating children from the cell window were also condemned as dangerous temptations that might bring seduction and even assault. A combined fear/threat of rape began to run through the prescriptive literature designed to keep unprotected women silent and immobile.

These strenuous efforts presumably saved the monks. The wider ecclesiastical order soon followed. Women were denied entry into the developing spaces where men received formal intellectual training. In the latter part of the twelfth century, the outlines of the future university, firmly monopolized by the celibate clergy, emerged. The monasteries, where women might still aspire to an education, fell behind in the new intellectual hierarchy. Why? Perhaps the creation of a woman-free environment was a necessity before the schoolmen could construct a cosmos and a terrestrial order that firmly supported the natural law of masculine superiority. Men fearful of women frightened women away from them, and where the *Herrenfrage* was solved by the exclusion or claustration of women, the balance seemed lost forever. Even womanly functions were claimed by men. The affectionate clerical rhetoric that has been identified as a "gay subculture" may easily have reflected the insecurity of men separated from women in expressing the affectionate relationships of "people" outside the old gender system.[101] Anselm of Bec saw both Jesus and himself as mothers. Having driven women out of his vision of communal life, Bernard advised abbots to treat their monks with a mother's nourishing love rather than fear.[102] Bernard's own vision of himself as a woman was equated with his humility and weakness. He said that he was not equal to the tasks imposed on man in the world.[103] Among monks, safely segregated from women, perhaps the safest way to restore the gender system was to play both roles and, by implication, deny the need for women in any capacity.

As a result, the *Frauenfrage* emerged. The surplus of women and their tendency to act for themselves urgently required a new, or at least reinforced, definition of woman and her proper relationship to man. A debate over whether women were made in God's image focused the argument.[104] In general, scholars agreed that the spiritual likeness of both women and men to God was not reflected in the biological differences of women. This anchored women to the animal functions of sex and reproduction, which proved that they could never hope to achieve the spiritual level that qualified men for the clergy and for fully human status. The clerical monopoly on learning, which was taken to rest on female incapacity to reason, opened the way to a polemic against the governing authority of women typified by Idung of Prüfenung: "It is not expedient for that sex to enjoy the freedom of having its own governance because of its natural fickleness and also because of outside temptations which womanly weakness is not strong enough to resist."[105] The body politic was increasingly womanless as university-trained administrators began to develop outside the kindred-based feudal system. Even the dynastic rights of women were severely undermined by the resistance of the English barons to the succession of Henry I's daughter.

Women were securely tied to a nature defined by sexual and reproductive functions and thus disqualified for participation in the new public spheres. Masculinist ideology revived and reinforced the dualism inherent in scholastic thinking. The Aristotelian theory that denied female sperm and thus also an active role for female pleasure and orgasm regained preeminence in the later twelfth century.[106] Even Trotula elucidated the Aristotelian dichotomies in her gynecological work. She contrasted the inwardness of women's generative organs to the outwardness of men, seeing the creation of women as bound to God's procreative plans.[107] Other women whose voices we can hear collaborated in constructing this better-calibrated gender system, though it is not clear if they understood its larger implications. Hildegard of Bingen, who began to reveal her visions around 1140, saw the disobedience of the first couple as a cosmic disaster transforming and distorting both genders by subjecting them to the passions of lust and the domination that transformed male sexuality as the tempests of menstruation and the pain of childbirth transformed female sexuality.[108]

By midcentury, the marital crisis was winding down.[109] The decrees on clerical celibacy were definitively reinforced in 1148. Gratian divided the social world into celibate clergy and married laymen, thus securely defining manhood in conjunction with activity in the public world. Bernard of Clairvaux, among others, re-visioned the social order as a new binarity, with the celibate clergy placed over the married laity.[110] As the twelfth century grew older, the presence of unattached and independent religious women, whether they were unimpeachably orthodox or dedicated heretics, provoked repeated papal and episcopal efforts to force monks back to the *cura mulierum*.[111] Heloise clung fiercely to her insistence on being Abelard's wife, not God's. But, as Abelard saw, the ranking of nuns as divine consorts flattered them with the intimacy of their bridegroom but also effectively pushed them out of the administrative hierarchy, as queens were being pushed aside by male ministers in terrestrial governments.[112] The imagery associated with celibate women as brides of Christ was revived in male rhetoric, where it firmly placed even the most resolute virgin in the gender system as a structural wife.[113]

Thus subordinated to the celibate, all-male clergy, the secular gender balance could be restored through the enhancement of the attractions of marriage and child rearing. Marriage had been reconstructed as an indissoluble union based on conjugal love, soon to be given sacramental status. Consummation was formally accepted as a central element in the legitimation of marriage by Alexander III. Hugh of Saint Victor and the canonists writing around 1140 praise the restrained and sober character of marital love in contrast to thc raging lust of romantic love.[114] Ida of Boulogne's biography, written around 1130, praises the saint as a mother and eulogizes marriage.[115] The romance of *Erec and Enid* recapitulated the whole process. The hero was placed in jeopardy of losing his manhood by long dalliance with his bride. By treating her roughly and passing a series of dangerous tests, he regained his masculinity. The heroine learned to subordinate herself and her superior intelligence to his manly pride. At last, the proper balance was restored and a happy marriage was made possible.

Once this relationship was confirmed, the motherhood of Mary received new respect, as did the humanity Jesus received from her. The motherhood of the church and of its clergy reflected its dignity in a revived respect for the motherhood of women.[116] Even in the scholastic view of the cosmos, man's reconciliation with nature provided women's procreative role a less blameworthy place in the divine scheme.

Conclusion

The late eleventh- and early twelfth-centuries experienced profound disturbances in the gender system. Celibacy freed men from women. It enabled the clergy to use elements from both genders to construct a new model of humanity in which men could play all the roles. But it also freed women from the immediate governance of men and from the biological constraints that defined them as women. If celibacy redefined masculinity, it also redefined femininity. Clerical celibacy and indissoluble secular marriage drove many men and women into syneisactic refuges. This precipitated the *Herrenfrage*, a crisis of masculine identity. It was resolved by biology's reaffirmation of the fearfulness of women. The debate on the creation of Eve reestablished correct gender relationships. The newly constructed system was enforced by stimulating women's fear of rape to counter male fear of castration. Men were urged to cease being "effeminate" even as they appropriated a claim to "femininity." Safe sex within marriage was reaffirmed by moralists, canon lawyers, and literature. The dialogue that redefined the natures of men and women and the construction of a public sphere that belonged to men alone had many repercussions. On one level, it defined men as people and blotted out the humanity of women. But the price was the loss of male humanity itself at the institutional level and the transformation of masculinity into a brutal caricature at the level where men intersected with women.

Men doomed themselves to support a construct of masculinity that defined them as those who fight, who dominate. The proponents of a less rigid, syneisactic system were silenced as heretics. Men burdened themselves with the task of imposing a masculinist perception of the universe and enforcing political, religious, and social orthodoxy on everyone. Increasingly constrained by these definitions, men lost the chance to share the burden of running the world with women or even with other men with different viewpoints. The more they succeeded, the more threatened they felt—indeed, the more threatened they were. They had deprived themselves of personality in the public world of the passive voice and the anthropomorphized institution. But they had also fused personhood with manhood, and to defend their manhood they had to become ever more manly. They had to persecute with ever-increasing severity anyone who threatened the uncertain inner core of that image. Women were victimized by their exclusion and male victims—heretics, homosexuals, Jews, any rebels who didn't fit the mold—were turned into women. The image of domination forced men into an endless competition to prove their manhood to one another. This was a tragedy for women and for the not-men, half-men, effeminate men who were the objects of this relentless persecution. In a subtler way, it was also a tragedy for the psychologically maimed creatures the system produced. This leaves us, I think, with a final formulation of the *Herrenfrage*, as puzzling and vital today as it was a millenium ago: Why do men feel the need to be "MEN"?

Notes

1. Arthur Brittan, *Masculinity and Power* (Oxford: Basil Blackwell, 1989), 46.

2. The effects of clerical celibacy affected every corner of Catholic Europe (though enforcement was long delayed in many areas). Concentration of sources in the northwest and other factors have constrained the universality of my own observations. It is my hope, however, that other researchers can make use of my relatively limited illustrations to expand the area of investigation. The term *Herrenfrage* has not gone uncriticized by readers sensitive to German nuances. I hope that someone may be moved to write an essay on the difficulties of balancing the *Frauenfrage* with *Herren, Männer*, or *Menschen*. In the end, I elected the term that elicited the most immediate recognition of its feminine counterpart and the one that pleased me most aesthetically, with its overtones of lordship so complementary to my thesis.

3. Georges Duby, *The Three Orders* (Chicago: University of Chicago Press, 1978), 287.

4. *Capitulare de villis*, 16, *Monumenta Germaniae Historica. Capitularia regum francorum* 1: 84. This was confirmed in the following century by Hincmar of Reims, *De ordine palatii*, 22, *MGH Capitularia* 2: 525.

5. Anna Comnena, *Alexiad*, trans. E. R. A. Şewter (Baltimore: Penguin, 1969), 147.

6. Suzanne F. Wemple and I examined the shift from family power to public power in "The Power of Women through the Family in Medieval Europe, 500-1100," in *Women and Power in the Middle Ages*, ed. Maryanne Kowaleski and Mary Erler (Athens: University of Georgia Press, 1988), 83-101.

7. Thomas Laqueur, *Making Sex* (Cambridge, Mass.: Harvard University Press, 1991), calls this the one-sex body and claims that the two-sex system, reinforcing women's incapacities with a fundamentally different biology incompatible with the tasks allotted to men, developed only in the eighteenth century.

8. This process ought to inspire a new reading of Ernst Kantorowicz's classic in medieval political theory, *The King's Two Bodies* (Princeton, N.J.: Princeton University Press, 1957).

9. I attempted to trace as much of this process as I could in *A New Song: Celibate Women in the First Three Christian Centuries* (New York: Haworth, 1983), chapter 3.

10. A long tradition, reaching back at least to Clement of Alexandria, situates gender solely in biology. Clement of Alexandria, *Paedagogus*, 5:4, *Sources Chrétiennes* 70, 108, 158 (Paris: Editions du Cerf, 1960-70); *Stromata*, 4:8, *Sources Chrétiennes* 30 and 38 (Paris: Editions du Cerf, 1951-54). "Souls have no sex" was the classic formulation of Jerome, *Epistola 122, Ad Rusticum*, 4, *Patrologia Latina* 22, 1045, which generally guided monastic thinking on the subject until the advent of Cluny.

11. Duby, *The Three Orders*, 87-90, links this to the rise of Cluniac leadership, peaking between 1020 and 1030, without systematic regard to gender.

12. J. Siegwart, *Die Chorherren und Chorfrauen-Gemeinschaften in der deutschsprachigen Schweiz vom 6 Jahrhundert bis 1160; mit einem Überblich über die deutsche Kanonikerreform des 10 und 11 Jh.* (Fribourg: Studia Friburgensia, 1962). C. J. Hefele, and H. Leclercq, *Histoire des Conciles* (Paris, 1910), 4, 1177, show that the cloistering of canonesses was given the same priority as the attack on simony, clerical marriage, and lay control of papal elections.

13. Riots in favor of priests' marriages took place in 1074. Urban II renewed the struggle in 1095. At the First Lateran Council of 1123, Calixtus voided priestly marriages and the bull was reissued in 1148. These dates are markers in the restructuring of the gender system. The chronology outlined by Henry C. Lea in *History of Sacerdotal Celibacy* (n.p.: University Books, 1966) has recently been fitted into a study of the polemics defending the married

clergy by Ann L. Barstow, *Married Priests and the Reforming Papacy: The Eleventh-Century Debate* (New York: Edwin Mellen, 1982), 159.

14. James A. Brundage, *Law, Sex, and Christian Society in Medieval Europe* (Chicago: University of Chicago Press, 1987), 187.

15. This is abundantly expressed not only in polemical literature condemning the intimacy of penitents and their confessors but in the visitation records of bishops. See particularly the analysis given by Penelope Johnson, *Equal in Monastic Profession* (Chicago: University of Chicago Press, 1991), 124-25.

16. Georges Duby, "In Northwestern France: The Youth in Twelfth Century Aristocratic Society," in *Lordship and Community in Medieval Europe*, ed. Frederic Cheyette (New York: Holt, Rinehart & Winston, 1968), 198-209.

17. My thanks to Diane Owen Hughes, who has shared with me this unexpected result of some of her extensive research into the history of medieval fashion.

18. Adalbero of Laon, from Duby, *The Three Orders*, 54-55; H. Platelle, "Le problème du scandale: les nouvelles modes masculines aux XIe et XIIe siècles," *Revue belge de Philologie et d'Histoire* 53 (1975): 1971-96.

19. Andreas Capellanus, *The Art of Courtly Love*, vol. 1, trans. John J. Parry (New York: Columbia University Press, 1941), 1.

20. Brundage, *Law, Sex, and Christian Society*, 188-89, places the circulation of the coital theory of marriage between 1123 and 1130. Around 1140 the discussion was dominated by Gratian, who made consummation necessary to complete marriage. *Decretum*, ed. Emil Friedberg, *Corpus Iuris canonici* (Leipzig: B. Tauchnitz, 1879), c. 27 q. 2 d.p.c.

21. Brundage, *Law, Sex, and Christian Society*, 183, describes the complete program and the resistance to its acceptance.

22. Georges Duby, *The Knight, the Lady and the Priest* (New York: Pantheon, 1985), 148-59, cites many instances of disastrous marital clashes that were well known to men at the time.

23. Duby, ibid., 5-8, sees the culmination of the marriage upheaval in the reign of Philip I ending in 1108.

24. See Brundage, *Law, Sex, and Christian Society*, 185, for instances of the widespread preaching that sowed fear of sexuality and of women throughout the West in these years.

25. William's object was to explain the resemblance of children to their mothers, which was an impossibility in the Aristotelian system. Danielle Jacquart and Claude Thomasset, *Sexuality and Medicine in the Middle Ages*, trans. Matthew Adamson (Princeton, N.J.: Princeton University Press, 1988), 53.

26. Ibid., 52. See also Laqueur, *Making Sex*, 58, for a reconciliation of Aristotle and Galen/Conches under the "one-sex" model and 122ff. for a discussion of the consequent unease about gender stability.

27. Brundage, *Law, Sex, and Christian Society*, 198, citing a case from Orderic Vitalis.

28. Jacquart and Thomasset, *Sexuality and Medicine*, 95. The countess of Die (born 1140) would allow the lover embraces and kisses that must stop short of the consummation that is the husband's prerogative.

29. Ibid., 92.

30. Duby, *The Three Orders*, 51. For a survey, see my "*Imitatio Helenae:* Sainthood as an Attribute of Queenship in the Early Middle Ages," in *Sanctus, Sancta*, ed. Mario A. Di Cesare (Binghamton: Medieval and Renaissance Texts and Studies, 1993).

31. Jo Ann McNamara, "Chaste Marriage and Clerical Celibacy," in *Sexual Practices and the Medieval Church*, ed. Vern L. Bullough and James A. Brundage (Buffalo, N.Y.: Prometheus, 1982), 22-33.

32. Some theologians extended the idea into speculation on the prelapsarian condition. Rupert of Deutz, who was in the Paris schools at about the same time as Abelard and William of Conches, pondered that sinless parents might have engendered sinless children in Paradise. *In Genesim* 2:9, *Corpus Christianorum: continuatio medievalis* 21 (Turnhout), 193-94.

33. The erection thus constitutes an embodiment of the discourse of masculinity in sport and combat, according to Brittan, *Masculinity and Power*, 74-75. A similar transformation of male-female relationships paralleling women's loss of power through kinship has been demonstrated for the Huron Indians in French Canada by Karen Anderson, *Chain Her by One Foot* (New York: Routledge, 1991).

34. Sally N. Vaughn, "St. Anselm and Women: Tradition and Novelty in Anglo-Norman Monasticism," paper presented at the meeting of the American Historical Association, 1989.

35. Guibert de Nogent, *Autobiography: Self and Society in Medieval Europe*, ed. and trans. John Benton (New York: Harper & Row, 1970), 64.

36. *Vita sanctae Godelevae* (died c. 1070), *Acta Sanctorum* 6 July, 405-11.

37. C. H. Talbot, ed., *The Life of Christine of Markyate: A Twelfth-Century Recluse* (New York: Clarendon, 1987), chapter 10.

38. Duby, *The Knight, the Lady and the Priest*, 167, suggests that his failure to marry might have exposed him to implications of homosexuality.

39. Reto R. Bezzola, *Les origines et la formation de la littérature courtoise en occident (500-1200). I: La tradition impériale de la fin de l'Antiquité au XIe siècle* (Paris: Bibliothèque de l'école des Hautes Etudes, Lib. Honoré Champion, 1944), 286. Bezzola sees in this correspondence early evidence of the literary conventions of courtly love.

40. *The Correspondence of Pope Gregory VII: Selected Letters from the Registrum*, trans. E. Emerton (New York: Columbia University Press, 1932), 60-61.

41. For the development of this ideology in ancient Christianity, see Jo Ann McNamara, "Sexual Equality and the Cult of Virginity in Early Christian Thought," *Feminist Studies* 3 (1976): 145-58.

42. Marie-Dominique Chenu, "The Evangelical Awakening," in *Nature, Man and Society in the Twelfth Century* (Chicago: University of Chicago Press, 1968), 239-69. Chenu, who discusses the changing definitions of the *vita apostolica* among various twelfth-century groups of reformers, is entirely silent on this attempt to incorporate women.

43. Jean-Marc Bienvenu, *L'étonnant fondateur de Fontevraud, Robert d'Arbrissel* (Paris: Nouvelle Editions Latines, 1981); and Jacques Dalarun, *L'impossible sainteté: La vie retrouvée de Robert d'Arbrissel (v. 1045-1116) fondateur de Fontevraud* (Paris: Editions du Cerf, 1985).

44. Peter of Sully, *Concordia inter monasterium S. Sepulchri Sulliensis et Coenobium Fontis Ebraldi*, *PL* 162, 1090.

45. Dalarun, *L'impossible sainteté*, 287-89.

46. Vaughn, "St. Anselm and Women."

47. Letter 6, written at Heloise's request, in *The Letters of Abelard and Heloise*, trans. Betty Radice (Baltimore: Penguin, 1974). As befit the humanism of the age, which looked back to the textual tradition of late antiquity as well as to the Gospels, he drew support from Augustine and Leo IX.

48. Epistola 7. Mary M. McLaughlin, "Peter Abelard and the Dignity of Women: Twelfth-Century 'Feminism' in Theory and Practice," in *Pierre Abelard, Pierre le Vénérable: Les courants philosophiques, littéraires et artistiques en occident au milieux du XIIe Siècle, Colloques National internationaux du Centre de la Recherche Scientifiques* (Paris: CNRS, 1975), 287-334, places him in a larger syneisactic movement with Norbert and Arbrissel, calling him a "practical feminist" who emphasized equality in the Christian army and the special dignity of women conferred by Mary's role in the incarnation, an idea more extensively formulated by Hildegard of Bingen.

49. Particularly, Hermann de Tournai, *De miraculis S. Mariae Laudunensis, Patrologia Latina* 156, 1001-2, on women adopting the Cistercian rule.

50. See C. Dereine, "Le premier ordo de Prémontré," *Revue Bénédictine* 58 (1948): 84-92.

51. Sharon K. Elkins, "The Emergence of a Gilbertine Identity," in *Distant Echoes*, ed. John A. Nichols and Lilian Thomas Shank (Kalamazoo, Mich.: Cistercian Publications, 1984), 169-82. Before dying in 1189, he wrote an account of the founding of the order as a

preface to the institutes printed in William Dugdale, *Monasticon Anglicanum*, ed. John Caley (1846).

52. Hubert Dauphin, "L'érémitisme en Angleterre aux XIe et XIIe siècles," in *L'Eremitismo in Occidente nei secoli XI e XII* (Milan: Vita e Pensiero, 1965), 271-310.

53. Women far outnumbered men in the reclusive life in Lorraine, according to J. Leclerc, "Reclus et recluses," *Revue de l'église de Metz* (1952): 315-62; (1953): 21-24; in England, according to Ann K. Warren, *Anchorites and Their Patrons in Medieval England* (Berkeley: University of California Press, 1986); and in Perugia, according to Carla Casagrande, ed., *Prediche alle donne del secolo XIII. Test'i di Umberto da Romans, Gilberto da Tournai, Stefano di Borbone* (Milan: Bompiani, Nuova Corona, 9, 1978). Otmar Doerr, *Das Institut der Inklusen in Suddeutschland. Beitrage zur Geschichte des alten Mönchtums und des Benediktiner Ordens* (Münster: Ildesons Herwegen, 1934), makes the same claims for Bavaria.

54. A. Wilmart, "Eve and Goscelin," *Revue Bénédictine* 50 (1938): 42-83.

55. Talbot, *The Life of Christine of Markyate*, 20-21.

56. Ibid., 49.

57. Brittan, *Masculinity and Power*, 14-15.

58. Sally Vaughn's emphasis based on Ida of Boulogne's correspondence with Anselm contrasts interestingly with Duby's interpretation, based on her biography of about 1130, which emphasizes her dependence on male advisers. See Vaughn, "St. Anselm and Women"; Duby, *The Knight, the Lady and the Priest*, 137.

59. J. von Walter, *Die ersten Wanderprediger Frankreichs: Robert von Arbrissel* (Leipsig: Studien zur geschichtes der theologie und kirche 9, 1903), 104.

60. This may explain the inordinate attention that even friendly syneisactics such as Robert d'Arbrissel and Abelard gave to the habits of their nuns.

61. Norman Cohn, *The Pursuit of the Millennium: Revolutionary Messianism in Medieval and Reformation Europe and Its Bearing on Modern Totalitarian Movements* (New York: Harper & Row, 1961), 43.

62. Trotula, "Introduction," in *Diseases of Women*, cited in Jacquart and Thomasset, *Sexuality and Medicine*, 116, n. 77. Jacquart and Thomasset believe Trotula may be a male production, late twelfth or early thirteenth century, though they agree with Benton that there was a woman practicing at Salerno in the twelfth century, "Trotula, Women's Problems and the Professionalization of Medicine in the Middle Ages," *Bulletin of the History of Medicine* 59 (1985): 30-53.

63. C. N. L. Brooke, "Gregorian Reform in Action: Clerical Marriage in England, 1050-1200," in *Change in Medieval Society*, ed. Sylvia Thrupp (New York: Appleton-Century-Crofts, 1964), 49-71.

64. Newman's recent argument in the long debate over the authorship of the letters of Heloise and Abelard strongly confirms that both partners spoke for themselves. Barbara Newman, "Authority, Authenticity and the Repression of Heloise," *Journal of Medieval and Renaissance Studies* 22 (1992): 121-57.

65. *Expositio in Hexaemeron*, PL 178, 781 cd.

66. See Brundage, *Law, Sex, and Christian Society*, 248-49.

67. Odo of Cluny complained of clergy attracted to the society of women, especially nuns; *Collationes* 2, 8-9, PL 133, 555, with other citations in G. G. Coulton, *Five Centuries of Religion*, vol. 1 (New York: Cambridge University Press: 1923), 175. Paschal II, 1101, complained to Bishop Didacus of Compostella that monks and nuns were said to be living together throughout his province and ordered them to be separated; PL 163, 80.

68. Letter, c. 33, in von Walter, *Die ersten Wanderprediger Frankreichs*,182. Geoffrey of Vendôme, published in the same appendix, said that Robert was accused of talking privately with women and even having them into his chamber at night, as though this must mean that they were having sexual intercourse.

69. Aelred of Rievaulx, *De sanctimoniali de Wattun*, *PL* 195, 789-96.

70. Talbot, *The Life of Christine of Markyate*, c. 44.

71. Ibid., c. 70. Envious people, even some religious, gossiped about her close relationship with the abbot of Saint Albans. "Like another Jerome and Paula, though each had been praised separately for chastity, together they incurred slander."

72. When his companion was absent he and a visiting nun made love, and then he changed her into a dog to get her past his returning fellow hermit; Guibert de Nogent, *Autobiography*, c. 26, p. 115.

73. Sermo 65, *Sermones in Cantica Canticarum, PL*, 1088-93. According to the *Golden Legend*, Saint Bernard froze himself in a pond to cure lust and entered the Cistercian order after two women tried to seduce him because it was not safe to dwell with the serpent (of lust, presumably).

74. *Historia Calamitatum* (Radice), 99.

75. Jacquart and Thomasset, *Sexuality and Medicine*, 96. This original notion of woman's control over pleasure pointed in the direction of severe gynephobia "of which the fabliaux are the most brutal but perhaps the least harmful expression."

76. Giles Constable, "Aelred of Rievaulx and the Nun of Watton: An Episode in the Early History of the Gilbertine Order," in *Medieval Women*, ed. Derek Baker (Oxford: Basil Blackwell, 1978).

77. Capellanus, *The Art of Courtly Love*.

78. Edward Peters, *The First Crusade: The Chronicle of Fulcher of Chartres and Other Source Materials* (Philadelphia: University of Pennsylvania Press, 1971). This work includes various versions of Urban's speech, 1-16. This is not reflected in the Gesta, 1100-1101, nor in Baldric of Dole, early twelfth century, nor Guibert of Nogent, who was there.

79. Duby, *The Knight, the Lady and the Priest*, 220.

80. Bernard's *Praise of the New Militia*, PL 182.

81. "Aspiring to reproduce chastely like bees, reviling marriage, preaching continence, dreaming of castration," they sought a desexualized order. Duby, *The Three Orders*, 131, claims that the attack on the "primordial social barrier" was the principal cause of their failure.

82. Giles Constable, "Renewal and Reform in Religious Life: Concepts and Realities," in *Renaissance and Renewal in the Twelfth Century*, ed. Robert L. Benson and Giles Constable (Cambridge, Mass.: Harvard University Press, 1982), 55.

83. Bernard of Clairvaux, *Sermones in Cantica Canticarum, PL*, 1088-93, Sermo 65, on clandestine heretics, whose preposterous religion and care for hiding its secrets are revealed by their scandalous companionship with women, 4.

84. Ibid., c. 5.

85. Ralph of Coggeshall, *Chronicle*, in G. G. Coulton, *Life in the Middle Ages*, vol. 1 (New York: Cambridge University Press, 1967), 29. Bernard: "He who does not listen to the church, shall be to you as an ethnicus and a publican" (Matthew 18:6-9; 17).

86. Alain de Lille complained that Waldensians excused themselves for entering women's communities on the grounds that the apostles did it. *Contra haereticos libri quattuor*, 1, 2, *PL* 210, 379. Stefanus de Bourbon criticized women who preached in their homes, in the streets, and even in the church and accused men of heresy for saying that a preacher's sex is irrelevant to good preaching. *Anecdotes*, 292, in Johann J. Döllinger, *Beiträge zür Sektengeschichte des Mittelalters* (New York: Burt Franklin, 1960), 2, 6, 300.

87. The rule of Grandmont specifically states that they are not to undertake the guidance of women. Like similar prohibitions of the period, it was soon ignored.

88. Dereine, "Le premier ordo," 204.

89. *Annales Rodensis*, 203. Michel Parisse, *Les Nonnes au Moyan Age* (Le Puy: Christine Bonneton, 1983), 54-55, finds this pattern of gradual separation elsewhere.

90. A priory of monks shared the church at Marcigny, separated by a wooden screen from the nuns. The prior was responsible for the temporals of the nuns and the claustral prior for their spiritual needs.

91. *Regulae Sanctimonialium Fontis Ebraldi*, 25, *PL* 162, 1080. The sisters were never given the kiss of peace, but kissed a stone passed through the window. Silence was particularly

stressed for female religious. William of Malmesbury, *Gesta Regum Anglorum* 5, 440 (London: Camden Society, 1846), v. 34, says whenever silence is relaxed women become frivolous. Cloistered women were forbidden to work outside or even to attend services with the brothers without a grill or wall separating them. The abbess of Fontevraud screened all visitors, both lay and monastic, and she had to take precautions to get the residents out of the way when tourists wished to see the cloister. *Regulae*, c. 27-28.

92. Ibid., 41, p. 1081. They shall perform offices for the dead with the priest saying the collect at the altar. Then the sisters will go out to the cloister and the cellaress with a senior will be prepared to open the gate to the priests and brothers. Then the priests and brothers will bear the body to the tomb, the rest remaining in the cloister and never going out to the grave of the dead.

93. Priests from the nearby male monastery came through a hidden entrance to say mass for the sisters when they were not busy with their own offices. Only an elderly priest was left to administer communion after the deacon and subdeacon had withdrawn. The infirmary was arranged so that priests could give the sacraments unseen behind a screen even when the whole convent was attending their dying sister. As at Fontevraud, even death did not give license for women and men to come together. Letter 7, in *The Letters of Abelard and Heloise*, 216, states that the nuns would wash the body and bring it into the church, and then retire to pray in the oratory while the monks gave the dead proper burial.

94. Rose Graham, *Saint Gilbert of Sempringham and the Gilbertines* (London: 1901), 32. Around 1140, Gilbert was given Havenholme for his nuns after a colony of monks from Fountains had found it too hard a place.

95. The Gilbertine canons were closed off from the women even at mass. On Good Friday, two canons entered the nuns' church and placed the cross on the ground. After they had gone, the nuns and sisters entered to venerate the cross. The portress guarded the turntable receiving the holy water and the "stone of peace" that six brothers carried to the sisters for the kiss of peace. The Gilbertine canons could see the women only to give them last rites.

96. Jacques de Vitry, *Historia Occidentalis*, 15, ed. John F. Hinnebusch, *Spicilegium Friburgense* 17 (Fribourg: University Press, 1972).

97. R. W. Southern, *Western Society and the Church in the Middle Ages* (Baltimore: Penguin, 1972), 314. The note states, "Quoted by A. Erens, 'Les soeurs dans l'ordre de Prémontré,' *Analecta Praemonstratensis* (1929) 6-26, from E. L. Hugo, *Annales Praemonstratenses*, 2, 147." No date is given.

98. Christina of Markyates's parents and friends considered rape an acceptable method of persuading a reluctant bride. She once had a vision of herself in a field full of bulls who threatened her with their horns, but she was given to understand that if she stood perfectly still they could not touch her. Talbot, *The Life of Christine of Markyate*, c. 33. Even Hildegard of Bingen, who had grown up in Jutta's recluserie, saw the church as a bride threatened with the corrupting and seductive powers of greedy prelates. Barbara Newman, *Sister of Wisdom: St. Hildegard's Theology of the Feminine* (Berkeley: University of California Press, 1987). Elizabeth of Schönau (*Vita*, 7. 97 PL 195, 171 A) and Hildegard of Bingen (Epist. 48, PL 197) condemned marriage in almost Manichaean terms. Legitimate fear of rape and violence was reinforced by the models of Agnes, Catherine of Alexandria, and Ursula, ersatz saints constructed or reconstructed in the twelfth century. Models of female sainthood offered to religious women associated a terrible death with too public a display of feminine beauty, intelligence, and independence. In this context, even the sincerest male advisers could warn women of the threats awaiting if they exposed themselves in the world, participating in the rape continuum so lucidly described by Susan Brownmiller in the conclusion to *Against Our Will: Men, Women and Rape* (New York: Simon & Schuster, 1975).

99. Aelred of Rievaulx, *Rule of Life for a Recluse*, in *Works*, vol. 1 (Spencer, Mass.: Cistercian Publications, 1971), 43-102.

100. See Jean Delumeau, *La peur en occident* (Paris: Fayard, 1978), 304-45, for the growth of fear of women.

101. I am not as ready as John E. Boswell, *Christianity, Social Tolerance and Homosexuality: Gay People in Western Europe from the Beginnings of the Christian Era to the Fourteenth Century* (Chicago: University of Chicago Press, 1980), to plunge these men, continent by law, into a fully active homosexual life, but their modes of address are undeniably provocative.

102. Caroline W. Bynum, "Jesus as Mother, Abbot as Mother: Some Themes in Early Cistercian Writing," in *Jesus as Mother* (Berkeley: University of California Press, 1982), 110-68.

103. David Damrosch, "Non alia sed aliter: The Hermaneutics of Sainthood in Bernard of Clairvaux," in *Images of Sainthood in Medieval Europe*, ed. Timea Szell and Renata Blumenfeld-Kosinsky (Ithaca, N.Y.: Cornell University Press, 1991), 181-95, points out that he uses the same techniques of appropriation with Jews and heretics.

104. Newman, *Sister of Wisdom*, 131. Abelard, Yvo of Chartres, and Ernaldus of Bonneval say that she is in the likeness of man, who is in the likeness of God. Rupert of Deutz, Gilbert de la Porée, and the majority of theologians say she is fully in the likeness of God.

105. Idung of Prüfenung, "An Argument Concerning Four Questions by Idung of Prüfenung," in *Cistercians and Cluniacs: The Case for Citeaux*, ed. and trans. J. Leahey and G. Perigo (Kalamazoo, Mich.: Cistercian Publications, 1977), 143-92.

106. Jacquart and Thomasset, *Sexuality and Medicine*, 65. It makes women totally irresponsible for the fertility of their bodies.

107. Trotula, "Introduction," in *Diseases of Women*, cited in ibid.

108. Newman, *Sister of Wisdom*, 131.

109. Where Duby situates the resolution as early as 1108, Brundage places it even beyond the time of Gratian, between 1159 and 1181, when the doctrine of consent decisively took precedence over the need for consummation. See Duby, *The Three Orders*, 5-8; Brundage, *Law, Sex, and Christian Society*.

110. Duby, *The Three Orders*, 223.

111. The process is traced painstakingly, order by order, by Micheline de Fontette, *Les religieuses a l'âge classique du droit canonique* (Paris: J. Vrin, 1967).

112. For the position of queens, see Marion F. Facinger, "A Study of Medieval Queenship: Capetian France 987-1237," *Nebraska Studies in Medieval and Renaissance History* 5 (1968): 1-48. Abelard, letter 4, in *The Letters of Abelard and Heloise*, 137. It also reflects the "feminizing" of virginity, which peaked in the thirteenth century, according to John Bugge, *Virginitas: An Essay in the History of a Medieval Idea* (The Hague: Martinus Nijhoff, 1975).

113. Bynum points out that this imagery comes most frequently from Cistercian men basing themselves on the Bernardine image of the soul as bride. She feels that there is no reason to believe that this feminine imagery was particularly attractive to women, though they shared the same mystical tradition as men. Bynum, "Jesus as Mother."

114. Brundage, *Law, Sex, and Christian Society*, 198, 333-35.

115. Duby, *The Knight, the Lady, and the Priest*, 135.

116. John F. Benton, "Consciousness of Self and Perceptions of Individuality," in *Renaissance and Renewal in the Twelfth Century*, ed. R. L. Benson and G. Constable (Cambridge, Mass.: Harvard University Press, 1982), 263-95.

CHAPTER 2

On Being a Male in the Middle Ages

Vern L. Bullough

Medieval anatomical and physiological ideas of what constituted maleness were for the most part inherited from the classical period. Though medieval writers were willing to criticize classical authorities on specific points, many of the basic physiological concepts had a continuous life extending from the Greeks to modern times. In the medieval period, most of the anatomical and physiological theories were incorporated into Christian doctrine, where they had even greater influence on the medieval belief system than they would have if they simply had been confined to medicine. One of the basic assumptions of the classical writings on anatomy and physiology was that the male was not only different from the female, but superior to her.

Aristotle, for example, had held that men were not only intellectually superior to women but morally superior as well. As proof, he pointed to nature, where he said the male of each species demonstratively was more advanced than the female – larger, stronger, and more agile. This led him to conclude that male domination was the will of nature and that to try to challenge nature in the name of an imagined principle of equality was quite contrary to the interests of both the individual and the community.[1] Other evidence of the superiority of the male was the overwhelming importance of the male principle in reproduction. Aristotle held that the key to life was the male semen, which was the effective and active component of conception. The female semen was only a passive contributor, simply giving the material upon which the semen could work.[2] Man was more perfect than woman because the active force in the seed tended to the production of a perfect likeness in the masculine sex, whereas the production of the female came from a defect in the active force or from some material indisposition.[3]

Medieval physicians following Avicenna modified Aristotle somewhat and compared the process of generation to the manufacture of cheese. The male agent was equivalent to the clotting agent of milk and the female "sperm" to the coagulum. Just as the starting point of clotting was in the rennet, so the starting point of the clot that was to become a "person" was in the male semen.[4] St. Albertus Magnus made one further qualification to Avicenna's argument, namely, that the female semen could be called semen only in an equivocal sense, because it was the male who contributed the essential material for generation.[5] St. Thomas Aquinas, his pupil, also agreed that the female generative power was imperfect compared with the male because "in the arts the inferior art gives a disposition to the matter to which the higher art gives the form . . . so also the generative power of the female prepares the matter which is then fashioned by the active power of the male."[6] Aquinas, however, modified Aristotle's belief that the female came from a defect in the active force, as, he said, woman could not be misbegotten because she was part of God's intentions. This, however, did not mean that women were equal to men, for it was in the nature of the universe for men to govern and women to be subject to men because the discretion of reason was so predominant in man.[7]

Of equal importance to the beliefs about the anatomy and physiology of men and women was the medieval conception of their intellectual capacities. Particularly influential in formulating what came to be Christian ideas was the Alexandrian Jewish philosopher Philo. Philo taught that the male was superior to the female because the male represented the more rational parts of the body—that is, the soul—whereas the female represented the less rational. Thus a woman in order to progress had to give up most aspects of the female gender, the material, the passive world of mind and thought, and the easiest way for her to progress was to deny her sexuality, to remain celibate.[8] Conversely, males who demonstrated any feminine qualities could only be looked down upon. These views were more or less officially incorporated into Christianity. One of the major figures in establishing such beliefs was St. Jerome, who wrote that as "long as woman is for birth and children, she is different from men as body is from the soul. But when she wishes to serve Christ more than the world, then she will cease to be a woman and will be called a man."[9]

Further reinforcing the biological superiority of the male were the ideas about body temperature emphasized by Galen. He held that the male was superior to the female because he was warmer and it was this greater body warmth that allowed his sex organs to grow outside of the body and fully develop, whereas the woman's organs, like the eyes of the mole, could never fully develop and only remained embryonic.[10] Medieval etymology only emphasized this. Man was the complete being who drew his name (*vir*) from his force (*vis*), whereas woman (*mulier*) drew hers from her softness. Woman had to be physically weaker than man in order for her to be subject to him and so that she could not repel his desire, for, once rejected, he might then turn to other objects.[11] Isidore added that the word *femina*

> is derived from those parts of the thighs by which this sex is distinguised from men. Others think that *femina* is derived by a Greek etymology from "fiery force," because she lusts so strongly for the female is much more sensual than the male, among women just as among animals. Hence, love beyond measure among the ancients was called "womanly love," *femineus amor*.[12]

Isidore's etymologies continued to influence thought during the Middle Ages and are quoted again in the encyclopedias of the thirteenth century such as the *Speculum Naturale* of Vincent of Beauvais or *De Proprietatibus Rerum* of Bartholomew the Englishman.[13]

Finally, the proof of the superiority of the male came from the Bible itself; man, after all, had been created from clay and then changed to flesh by God, whereas woman had always been flesh. This was interpreted to mean that the female was an airy creature with a thin skin and thin skull who could not feel lust as the male did, but only a warm tenderness. In fact, if a woman felt a hot lust like a man she would not be able to bear children because she would become sterile, just as the earth becomes sterile from too much sun.[14]

Problems for the Male with Such Definitions

What these anatomical and physiological assumptions did was establish strict roles for each sex. In recent years, we have tended to look at the restrictions put upon the woman by such assumptions.[15] What is sometimes overlooked is that they also put limitations on male development. Medieval writers paid little attention to this, but modern writers have.

Some of these problems, which can apply to medieval males as well as modern, were summarized by the late Robert Stoller:

> While it is true the boy's first love object is heterosexual [the mother], he must perform a great deed to make this so; he must first separate his identity from hers. Thus the whole process of becoming masculine is at risk in the little boy from the day of birth on; his still-to-be-created masculinity is endangered by the primary, profound, primeval oneness with mother, blissful experience that serves, buried but active in the core of one's identity, as a focus which, throughout life, can attract one to regress back to the primitive oneness. That is the threat latent in masculinity.[16]

Though what constitutes manhood has varying definitions according to a society or culture or time period, the most simplistic way of defining it is as a triad: impregnating women, protecting dependents, and serving as provider to one's family.[17] Failing at these tasks leads not only to challenges to one's masculinity, but also to fear of being labeled as showing feminine weakness, however a society defines that. This puts restrictions upon the man that, though quite different from those on the woman, are nonetheless burdensome. A woman in a sense can be encouraged to adopt "masculine" ways of thinking, even "masculine" ways of action, but any male who demonstrates any inclination toward showing a more feminine side is deprecated, as this is a sign of weakness, not strength. A woman can raise her status and role in society by acting as a man (providing she does not show a woman's sexuality) without any threat to society. Males who fail to perform as males have their manhood questioned. It is almost as if the "superiority of the male" has to be demonstrated continually or else it will be lost.

To illustrate and support these arguments, I would like to look first at acceptable gender behavior, then at love, and finally at the sexual act itself. One way to look at acceptable gender behavior is to look at examples of those who crossed gender, performing in the role of the opposite sex. There are many examples of cross-gender behavior among medieval women, but almost none among medieval men. Technically, the Bible prohibits any cross-gender behavior that involves impersonation of the opposite sex. The statement in Deuteronomy (22:5) is often cited in support: "The woman shall not wear that which pertainent unto a man neither shall a man put on a woman's garment; for all that do so are an abomination unto the Lord thy God." Generally, however, in the medieval period, this statement was applied only to men, and not to women. A good illustration of this is the number of female transvestite saints, in fact at least forty of them, most of whom lived all their adult lives as males and were discovered to be females only when they died.[18] It is not only in the early medieval period that such male impersonators are found, but throughout the Middle Ages, both in reality and in fiction. A good fictional example is the the knight Silence, who appears in *Le Roman de Silence*, which was written in the third quarter of the thirteenth century by Heldris de Cournuälle and discovered only in the 1960s.[19] Though this tale only recently came to light, there are any number of other cases in medieval and early Renaissance literature, including the case of Bradamante in Ariosto's *Orlando Furioso*.

There are few similar stories or incidents about men, and when men do somehow seem to have worn women's gowns, they have been frowned upon. St. Jerome's enemies, for example, are alleged to have laid a trap for him (*insidias paraverunt*) that would lead him to disgrace. They placed a woman's garment near his bed while he was sleeping, and the saint, getting up in the dark to go to matins, reached out and put it on, mistaking it for his own. Thus "scandalously" dressed, he made his way to church. As the commentator said, his "enemies played this trick on him so that the people would think he had spent the night with a woman."[20]

The association of sexuality with cross-dressing as alleged in the case of St. Jerome also appears in a case reported by Gregory of Tours in the sixth century. Gregory reported that during a revolt of some nuns in the convent of Radegunde, the rebellious faction charged the abbess with keeping a man clothed in female garb and pretending that he was a woman. Everyone knew, they claimed, that he "was most plainly of the male sex" and that this person regularly served the abbess. The charges resulted in an investigation that did in fact find there was a male nun. He had donned female garb because as a little boy he had had "a disease of the groin" that was regarded as incurable. A physician, Reovalis, explained:

> His mother went to the holy Radegund and begged her to have the case examined. The saint summoned me, and bade me give all the help in my power. I then cut out his testicles, an operation which in former days I had seen performed by surgeons at Constantinople, and so restored the boy in good health to his anxious mother. I never heard that the abbess knew aught of the matter.[21]

As a result of this testimony, the charges against the abbess were dropped. In spite of the evidence in this case, the implication is strong that the only reason a man might don female garb and live in a convent was because it gave him freer access to potential sex partners. Later in the medieval period, about 1250, an inquisitor in southern France reported that a number of men disguised as women entered the home of a rich farmer, dancing and singing, "We take one and give back a hundred," a possible reference to a popular belief of the powers of the "good" to reward any house in which they had been given gifts. The suspicious wife of the farmer, however, did not accept them as powers of the good (*bonae*), especially given that they had carried out all the goods from her house. She reported the results to the bishop, who sent the agents of the inquisition to investigate.[22]

One fictional example occurs in the tale *Aucassin and Nicolete*, where Aucassin finds the king of Torelore in childbed. Aucassin asks him why he did this foolish thing:

"I'm a mother," quoth the King:
"When my month is gone at length,
And I came to health and strength,
Then shall I hear Mass once more
As my father did before,
Arm me lightly, take my lance,
Set my foe a right fair dance,
Where horses prance."[23]

Aucassin proceeds to beat the king until he is near to death; this leads the king to promise that "man shall never lie in child-bed" in his realm again. Aucassin then sets off to find the queen. When he locates her, she is with her troops, fighting a war with mushrooms, baked apples, and arrows pelted with good fresh cheese. Aucassin, who can hardly believe such a scene, takes over and routes the enemy.

Obviously, males who cross-dressed, even in fiction, were regarded with hostility, whereas a woman, such as the queen, could be forgiven her incompetence on the assumption that she was only a woman and thus did not know about such things. Again, this emphasizes the hostility to men acting in any way that could be interpreted as feminine. Men, however, were allowed to impersonate women, even to assume the manners and actions of the female, but only in carefully designated situations where the presence of women was considered unacceptable. One such place was on the stage, where for the most part proper women did not appear. Usually, the women's roles were acted by adolescent boys, and not by men, perhaps emphasizing that the boys were not yet men. Occasionally in the medieval period we get glimpses of some of the actors. This is the case with a young barber's apprentice at Metz, who is said to have performed the role of Saint Barbara so

> thoughtfully and reverently that several persons wept for pity: for he showed such fluency of elocution and such polite manners, and his countenance and gestures were so expressive when among his maidens, that there was not a nobleman or priest or layman who did not wish to receive this youth into his house to feed and educate him; among whom there was a rich widow . . . who wanted to adopt him as her heir.[24]

The youth's reputation as a female impersonator, however, was shortlived; the next year, when he acted the part of another woman saint, his voice had changed and the audience was not so impressed. He soon abandoned his acting career and went off to Paris to study for the priesthood.

The one major exception to these limitations on female impersonation that I have been able to document is the case of Ulrich von Lichtenstein, a thirteenth-century knight from Styria (now part of Austria). He is best remembered today for his narrative poem *Frauendienst*, or *Autobiography in Service of Ladies*.[25] Though when originally published at the beginning of the nineteenth century it was believed to be a highly reliable autobiography, modern scholars are not so sure. Some regard it as a fictional comedy work, a predecessor to Cervantes's *Don Quixote*, and certainly those scholars who have attempted to authenticate some of the events depicted in it have had difficulty in documenting them. One of the most remarkable of Ulrich's adventures took place in 1227, when, in order to honor his lady and all women, he disguised himself as the goddess Venus and as such engaged in a number of jousts on a trip he took from Venice to Styria, Austria.

Though he wore women's clothes all the way, and on first impression appeared as a woman, under his veil he apparently retained his beard. One countess who went up to kiss him remarked when Ulrich removed his veil:

> Why you're a man!
> I caught a glimpse of you just now.
> What then? I'll kiss you anyhow.
> From all good women everywhere
> I'll give a kiss. Because you wear
> a woman's dress and honor thus
> us all, I'll kiss for all of us.[26]

Apparently most of the people on his tour got into the act, and it seemed to be great fun. There is no question that Ulrich enjoyed his adventure. Even if the events did not actually take place, the account emphasizes that impersonation at the comedy level was certainly allowed as long as it was evident, as in Ulrich's ability to win at the jousting matches, that the impersonator was a real man.

Probably the only places where adult men could in any way regularly drop their masculine stance and experiment more freely with cross-gender attitudes were festivals or carnivals, where the usual standards of behavior were laid aside. Although few of these medieval carnivals have been studied in detail, we know that in some of them women were allowed to act the male role, and men, to impersonate women. In the Nuremberg festivals of the late medieval period, for example, a number of male dancers wore feminine masks and probably dressed as women. In fact, it seems to be such a common phenomenon that one authority has said that disguising as the opposite sex was a custom that was "peculiar to all carnivals."[27] The tradition continues today in the Mardi Gras festival in New Orleans and elsewhere, and in the Mummer's parade in Philadelphia.

Lovesickness

In some instances, the assumption of the male of behaviors regarded as feminine could be regarded as an illness. This appears in the medieval discussion of lovesickness. Generally the Greeks classified lovesickness as a form of madness, although the medical authorities who dealt with it were much less certain.[28] It entered the medical literature through Galen, who regarded it simply as one of a number of physiological diseases that can affect the body. Galen believed that both men and women could suffer from the condition. Caelius Aurelianus (fifth century of the modern era), who translated Soranus's lost treatise *On Acute and Chronic Diseases* (second century), regarded love as a form of mania and also implied that both men and women were affected by it. He debated whether sexual intercourse was a cure, and decided against it.[29]

As the ideas of love entered into the medieval period, however, a change took place, as can be seen in the work of Isidore. In his definition of *femina*, mentioned above, he said that love beyond measure was called "womanly love." This could be and was interpreted as meaning that a man in love acted as a woman and thereby lost status as a man. But how could he retain his status? What could he do to emphasize that he was a man? Here the medieval physicians turned to Ovid's *Art of Love*, which, among other things, recommended intercourse to demonstrate maleness.[30] This concept passed into medieval medical literature as well, primarily through the translations of Constantine the African (eleventh century). Constantine had crossed over from Africa with a large number of Arabic medical and scientific works, which he spent the rest of his life translating into Latin. His discussion of love appears in his *Viaticum*, an adaption of popular Arab handbooks for travelers. Passionate love is the subject of the twentieth chapter of the first book. Most important in terms of gender roles, Constantine located the sensations of love in the brain rather than in the heart. This meant that it was primarily a disease of men, rather than women, and that men who fell in love were, in a sense, getting a "feminine disease."[31] Moreover, it was likely to afflict noblemen more than commoners because they had more leisure and a much softer life; that is, they were already somewhat on the way to becoming effeminate. Here again, the cure for the disease according to Constantine and many of his medieval commentators was simply to have intercourse.[32] Though these ideas of the necessity of intercourse were eventually challenged by religious authorities, they continued to have great influence. Ideally, intercourse should be with the loved person, but given that it was often the inaccessibility of the loved one that caused the sickness, it was recommended that the act be performed with a different partner, or even a variety of partners, to avoid another fixation.

The emphasis on intercourse as a cure would seem contrary to regarding lovesickness as an illness of the soul or mind, but obviously such an illness, and threat to masculinity, called for drastic action. Late in the medieval period the disease came to be regarded as one of the genitals rather than of the mind or soul, and women once again were regarded as also being susceptible to the disease. Still, the treatment emphasis was on the male's removing the "feminine" feelings of helpless and inadequacy engendered by love by asserting his maleness – which seems to imply having intercourse.

Often this emphasis on male performance was put more subtly, not as a way to solve his problem but as a way to keep the woman in good health. Women had thin skins and thin skulls, and thus had to be kept moist in order to remain fertile; the most effective way for a woman to remain moist was through sexual intercourse. In fact, some authorities argued that unless women engaged regularly in sexual intercourse the uterus would dry up and lose weight, and in its search for moisture it would rise toward the hypochondrium, impeding the flow of breath. If the organ came to rest in this position, it would cause convulsions similar to those of epilepsy. If it mounted higher and attached itself to the heart, the patient would feel anxiety and oppression and begin to vomit. If it fastened to her liver, the woman would lose her voice and grit her teeth and her complexion would turn ashen. If it lodged in the loins, she would feel a hard ball or lump in her side. If it mounted as high as her head, it would bring pain around her eyes and nose, make the head feel heavy, and cause drowsiness and lethargy to set in.[33] Though such an assumption could allow the male to feel that by engaging in sex, he was doing so with the health of his partner in mind, it also put an added performance burden upon him. He could even feel he had to engage in sex in order to keep a woman healthy.

Moreover, it was not enough to have intercourse with a woman, but it was important she have an orgasm. There were two reasons for this. First, orgasm was necessary for the women to expel her seed, which, if stored up and unused, might cause hysteria; second, it was essential for procreation, something that the church regarded as the only justifiable reason for intercourse. This is the Galenic view:

> The mixing of the two sperms is necessary for two useful purposes. The first is that the woman's sperm is a suitable source of sustenance for the sperm of the man, because the sperm is thick and of a hot constitution, whereas the sperm of the woman is thin and of a cold constitution. Because of its thickness, the sperm of the man cannot spread sufficiently and through its heat it would spoil the substance of which the foetus is made, the sperm of the woman is thus necessary to moderate its thickness and heat. Its second use is the formation of the second membrane surrounding the foetus. For the man's sperm, moving forwards in a straight line, does not reach the horn-like extension and does not spread out over the whole internal surface of the womb. So the sperm of the woman is necessary to reach the places where the sperm of the man has not reached.[34]

Though some medieval writers were skeptical about the absolute necessity of the female orgasm to achieve pregnancy (they had interviewed women who claimed to have become pregnant without orgasm), there was still a widespread belief that this was a necessity and that it involved special efforts by the male. This was because in order for a woman to enjoy intercourse and have an orgasm, the male had to engage in what we would now call foreplay. Arnold of Villanova wrote that it was easy to recognize when a woman's heat level had been raised enough, because she would then give signs that she was ready for entry.[35]

It was not enough, however, for a man to get a woman either pregnant or contented simply by bringing her to orgasm. A man's maleness was also demonstrated by the sex of his child. Though there were various reasons, including astrological ones, believed responsible for whether a fetus developed as male or female, it was also considered to be influenced greatly by the sperm. Strong male sperm tended to reproduce in another being the sex and characteristics of the individual from whom it had come. In essence, if the child was female and resembled the mother in her individual characteristics, the female sperm was considered to have vanquished the male sperm. If, however, the child was a son bearing the characteristics of his father, then the male sperm had proved dominant in all respects. If it was a daughter resembling the father, the female sperm had been dominant in terms of sexual characteristics, but the male in terms of individual characteristics. There were various other alternatives, but clearly the dominant male would have sons who resembled him; if a man had a daughter who did not resemble him in any way, then quite clearly the wife's seed was dominant and all the world could see his weakness. This belief in the dominant seed influencing sex and other characteristics was first stated by Aristotle and was carried over into medieval thought by Albertus Magnus.[36]

Impotence

Quite clearly, male sexual performance was a major key to being male. It was a man's sexual organs that made him different and superior to the woman. But maleness was somewhat fragile, and it was important for a man to keep demonstrating his maleness by action and thought, especially by sexual action. It was part of his duty to keep his female partners happy and satisfied, and unless he did so, he had failed as a man. Inevitably, there was also concern with his ability to perform and to beget children. While there was a recognition that males as well as females could be sterile, sterility did not hinder the carrying out of the sexual act, and, lacking proof, the blame for sterility could often be assigned to the woman. Failure to perform, however, was a threat not only to a man's maleness but to society. Potency came to be not only the way in which a male defined himself, but how he was defined by society, and impotence was grounds for marital annulment or divorce.[37] Medieval medical authorities quite clearly recognized that there were differences in sexual temperament because different humours might be dominant. One English copyist at Heresford in the thirteenth century summarized the four types of males:

> The sanguine (hot and moist) "desire much and are capable of much."
> The choleric (hot and dry) "desire much and are capable of little."
> The phlegmatic (cold and moist) "desire little and are capable of much."
> The melancholic (cold and dry) "desire little and are capable of little."[38]

Still, even a melancholic man should be capable of achieving an erection, although he might be more difficult to arouse.

Because medieval legal authorities recognized that even impotence might be faked in order to have a marriage annulled, it was not enough for a man to declare himself impotent, or to have his wife do so; he had go through the humiliation of being proven impotent. This necessitated the intervention of medical authorities who sought signs and symptoms of impotence. John of Gaddesden, recognizing that there were many causes of impotence, attempted to differentiate male sterility and impotence by cause. One cause would have been accidental, such as a wound in the genitals or a hernia, and this could be revealed through questioning and examining the patient. Internal problems could also cause impotence, including infection within the genital organs. Some signs of impotence were relative lack of pubic hair, tight veins and coldness of the skin, and cold testicles. Possible causes of impotence included a complexion that was too hot or a temperament overabundant in dryness or moistness.[39]

It was also believed that impotence could be caused by witchcraft. Increasingly, in fact, when any discernible cause was lacking, supernatural intervention came to be accepted as proven. One of the supposed powers of a witch was the ability to make the penis disappear by casting a "glamour" over it. Once this happened, only the witch herself could restore normal sexual activity by making it reappear. Eventually, witchcraft came to be regarded as the main cause of male failure to achieve an erection; witchcraft was also believed to prevent women from conceiving or to cause them to miscarry. Witches supposedly caused impotence by tying knots in threads or laces of leather, thus creating ligatures or knots in the seminal vessels; impotence so caused would remain until the hidden knots were discovered or untied or until the witch lifted her spell.[40]

Regardless of the cause, it was still necessary to demonstrate that impotence was real. Guy de Chauliac described the procedure as it had evolved in the fourteenth century:

> Since justice has adopted the habit of asking the physician for an examination, the form the examination takes must be described. Once he has obtained permission from [the] justice, the [physician] must first of all examine the complexion and structure of the reproductive organs; then he must go to a matron used to such [procedures] and he must tell [the husband and the wife] to lie together on several successive days in the presence of the said matron. She must administer spices and aromatics to them, she must warm them and anoint them with warm oils, she must massage them near the fire, she must order them to talk to each other and to embrace. Then she must report what she has seen to the physician. When the physician has been informed, he must bear testimony in all truth before justice. He must, however, beware of being deceived, because numerous frauds are habitually committed in such cases, and there is a great peril in separating those whom God has joined together, if it is not for a very just cause.[41]

Summary and Conclusion

Medieval society had drawn up distinct gender behavior for men and women, but because women were such low-status creatures, their attempts to gain status by becoming more masculine were condoned and encouraged. Although men certainly had more status, in terms of gender behavior they had ever to be on the lookout for threats to their masculinity. Femininity in males was regarded as an illness, and many of the qualities associated with femininity were frowned upon if they appeared in the male. Ultimately, however, the male was defined in terms of sexual performance, measured rather simply as his ability to get an erection. This was essential for the functioning of society. It kept women from becoming hysterical, it led to pregnancy and childbirth, and, in brief, it was how a male was defined, both by himself and by society.

Medieval man's masculinity differed in a sense from the modern American definition of machismo as symbolized by what is sometimes called the John Wayne syndrome ("wham, bam, thank you ma'am") in one important particular, namely, the need to perform the sex act to the satisfaction of the female partner. Still the key to the male definition was in his virility. Ultimately, if he failed, he had an easy explanation at hand, or at least had one by the end of the Middle Ages, namely, the witch. This leads me to wonder if a previously overlooked explanation for the seeming rise of witchcraft at the end of the medieval period was a growing concern over male potency and performance. The only evidence is an increasing reference to witchcraft in the medical literature, but this might be a result of the fact that physicians were also increasingly called in to determine whether males were really impotent. Still, it makes for interesting speculation. Certainly, when masculinity is equated with potency and any sign of lack of virility is a threat to one's definition as a man, it becomes easy to accept the existence of malevolent feminine forces. In short, the medieval male was plagued by many of the same fears and anxieties as his modern counterpart, and being masculine was all-important.

Notes

1. Aristotle, *Historia animalium*, 608 B, trans. D'Arcy W. Thompson, in *The Work of Aristotle*, vol. 4 (Oxford: Clarendon, 1910). See also Aristotle, *Politics* 1.2 (1252 B), ed. and trans. H. Rackham (London: Heinemann, 1944).

2. Aristotle, *Generation of Animals*, 729 A, 25-34, trans. A. L. Peck (London: Heinemann, 1953).

3. Ibid., 728 A, 17ff.; 766 A, 19-35.

4. Avicenna, *Canon of Medicine*, 1, 196, trans. O. Cameron Gruner (London: Luzak, 1930), 23.

5. Albertus Magnus, *De animalibus libri XXVI*, lib. 9, tract 2, cap. 3, and lib. 15, tract 2, caps. 4-11, ed. Hermann Studler (Munster: *Beiträge zur Geschichte des Mittelalters*, vols. 15-16, 1916-20), 714ff., 1026ff.

6. St. Thomas Aquinas, *Summa Theologica* (New York: Berringer Brothers, 1947), pt. 3, q. 32, "Die conceptione Christia quod activum principium," iv. My translation.

7. Ibid., pt. 1, q. 92.

8. Philo, *On the Creation*, ed. and trans. F. H. Colson and G. H. Whitaker (London: William Heinemann, 1963), 69-70, 151, 162; Philo, *Questions and Answers on Genesis*, ed. and trans. Ralph Marcus (London: William Heinemann, 1961), 1, 40; Richard A. Baer, Jr., *Philo's Use of the Categories Male and Female* (Leiden: E. J. Brill, 1970), 46-51.

9. St. Jerome, *Commentarius in Epistolam ad Ephasios*, bk. 16, col. 56, in *Patrologiae Latina*, vol. 26, ed. J. P. Migne (Paris: Garnier Frâtres, 1884). My translation.

10. Galen, *On the Usefulness of the Parts of the Body (De usus partium)*, trans. Margaret Tallmade May (Ithaca, N.Y.: Cornell University Press, 1968), 14.6, 2:628-30.

11. Isidore of Seville, *Isidori Hispalensis Episcopi Etymologiarum sive Originum Libri XX*,. ed. W. M. Lindsay (Oxford: Oxford University Press, 1911), 11, 2:17-19. For an English translation, see *Isidore of Seville: The Medical Writings: An English Translation with an Introduction and Commentary*, ed. and trans. William D. Sharpe, *Transactions of the American Philosophical Society*, n.s. 54, pt. 2 (1964), 50.

12. Ibid., 2:24. The translation is by Sharpe.

13. Though the work of Vincent of Beauvais was extremely popular in the late medieval period, there is no recently edited text available of his work. See Vincent of Beauvais, *Speculum Naturale* (D. Nicolini, Venice, 1591). The same difficulties occur with Bartholomew Anglicus, *De Proprietatibus Rerum*. An English translation by John of Trevisa, *De Proprietatibus Rerum* (Westminster: Wynkyn de Worde, 1495), was made and from this a gleaning was prepared by Robert Steele, *Medieval Lore: An Epitome of the Science, Geography, Animal and Plant, Folk-Lore and Myth of the Middle Ages, Being Classified Gleanings from the Encylopaedia of Bartholomaeus Anglicus on Properties of Things* (reprint) (London: King's Classics, 1907). An early edition in the original Latin, edited by Georgio Bartholdo, was also reprinted (Frankfurt, 1964). See also J. J. Walsh, "Medicine in a Popular Medical Encyclopaedia," *Annals of Medical History*, n.s. 4, (1932): 273-82.

14. Paul Diepgen, *Frau und Frauenheilkunder in der Kultur des Mittelalters* (Munich: Bregman, 1937), 137ff.

15. See, for example, Vern L. Bullough, Brenda Shelton, and Sarah Slavin, *The Subordinated Sex* (Athens: University of Georgia Press, 1988).

16. Robert Stoller, "Facts and Fancies: An Examination of Freud's Concept of Bisexuality," in *Women and Analysis*, ed. Jean Strouse (New York: Dell, 1974), 358.

17. For a more complete discussion of this, see David D. Gilmore, *Manhood in the Making: Cultural Concepts of Masculinity* (New Haven, Conn.: Yale University Press, 1990), 223.

18. See Vern L. Bullough, "Transvestites in the Middle Ages," *American Journal of Sociology*, 79 (1974): 1381-94; John Anson, "The Female Transvestite in Early Monasticism: The Origin and Development of a Motif," *Viator* 5 (1974): 1-32. The most complete study of this is found in Valerie R. Hotchkiss, "Clothes Make the Man: Female Transvestism in the Middle Ages," Ph.D. diss., Yale University, 1990.

19. The romance exists only in one manuscript, Mi.LM.6, deposited on loan in the Muniments Room of the University of Nottingham. *Le Roman de Silence* comprises folios 181 to 223. It was first publicized in a a series of articles by Lewis Thorpe in *Nottingham Medieval Studies*, 5 (1961), 33-74; 6 (1962), 18-69; 7 (1963), 34-52; 8 (1964), 33-61; 10 (1966), 25-69; 11 (1967), 19-56. These articles were then brought together in book form and amplified; Lewis Thorpe, *Le Roman de Silence: A Thirteenth-Century Arthurian Verse-Romance by Heldris de Cournuälle* (Cambridge: W. Heffer, 1972). For a version in modern English, see Heldris de Cornuälle, *Le Roman de Silence*, trans. Regina Psaki (New York: Garland, 1991).

20. See Eugene F. Rice, Jr., *Saint Jerome in the Renaissance* (Baltimore: Johns Hopkins University Press, 1985), 28-29.

21. Gregory of Tours, *History of the Franks*, 2 vols., ed. and trans. O. M. Dalton (Oxford: Clarendon, 1927), 2:449.

22. Jeffrey Burton Russell, *Witchcraft in the Middle Ages* (Ithaca, N.Y.: Cornell University Press, 1972), 157, 292, 315.

23. *Aucassin and Nicolette*, trans. Eugene Mason (New York: E. P. Dutton, 1958), 32.

24. Quoted by Karl Mantzius, *A History of Theatrical Art*, vol. 2, *The Middle Ages*, trans. Lousie van Cossel (New York: Peter Smith, 1937), 89.

25. The narrative first appeared in print in 1812. Ulrich von Lichtenstein, *Frauendienst, oder: Geschichte une Liebe des Ritters un Sängers*, trans. Ludwig Tieck (Stuttgart, 1812). It

was translated in condensed form into English verse by J. W. Thomas, *Ulrich von Lichtenstein's Service of Ladies* (Chapel Hill: University of North Carolina Press, 1969).

26. Ibid., 110, quatrain 538.

27. Samuel L. Sumberg, *The Nuremberg Schembart Carnival* (New York: AMS, 1966).

28. For a more complete discussion of lovesickness, see Mary Frances Wack, *Lovesickness in the Middle Ages: The* Viaticum *and Its Commentaries* (Philadelphia: University of Pennsylvania Press, 1990), 1-24.

29. Caelius Aurelianus, *On Acute Diseases and on Chronic Diseases*, ed. and trans. I. E. Drabkin (Chicago: University of Chicago Press, 1950), 1, 5, 176-78, 556-59.

30. Ovid, *Art of Love*, ed. and trans. J. H. Mogley (London: William Heinemann, 1962).

31. The key sections of Constantine's treatment of love have been translated by Wack, *Lovesickness*, 186-93.

32. See, for example, the commentary of Gerard of Berry as edited by Wack in *Lovesickness*, 199-205.

33. Hippocrates, *Des maladies des femmes*, 1.7.32 and 2.123-127, in *Oeuvres complètes d'Hippocrates*, trans. E. Littré (Paris, 1851).

34. *Trois traités d'anatomie arab*, trans. P. D. Koning (Leyden: E. J. Brill, 1903), 397.

35. Arnoldus de Villanova, *De regimine sanitatis*, in *Opera* (Lyons: 1509), 213. See also Helen Rodnite Lemay, "Human Sexuality in Twelfth- Through Fifteenth-Century Scientific Writings," in Vern L. Bullough and James A. Brundage, *Sexual Practices in the Medieval Church* (Buffalo, N.Y.: Prometheus, 1992), 187-205.

36. Albertus Magnus, *Questiones super De Animalibus*, 18, q. 3; cited in Danielle Jacquart and Claude Thomasset, *Sexuality and Medicine in the Middle Ages*, trans. Matthew Adamson (Princeton, N.J.: Princeton University Press, 1988), 140.

37. See James A. Brundage, *Law, Sex, and Christian Society in Medieval Europe* (Chicago: University of Chicago Press, 1987), passim, especially 456-58. See also Pierre Darmon, *Trial by Impotence*, trans. Paul Keegan (London: Chatto & Windus, 1985).

38. Brian Lawn, *The Prose Salernitan Questions* (Oxford: Oxford University Press, 1979), B8, 6.

39. See H. P. Cholmeley, *John of Gaddesden and the Rosa Medicinae* (Oxford: Clarendon, 1912). See also Jacquart and Thomasset, *Sexuality and Medicine*, 170.

40. H. C. Lea, *History of the Inquisition of the Middle Ages*, 3 vols. (reprint) (New York: S. A. Russell, 1955), 1: 162-70.

41. For the Latin text, see G. Hoffman, "Beiträge zur Lehre von der durch Zauber verusachten Krankheit und ihrer Behandlung in der Medizin des Mittelalters," *Janus* 37 (1933): 191-92. The English translation is essentially that given in Jacquart and Thomasset, *Sexuality and Medicine*, 172, with only a few words changed.

CHAPTER 3

The (Dis)Embodied Hero and the Signs of Manhood in *Sir Gawain and the Green Knight*

Clare R. Kinney

Recent examinations of the politics of gender in *Sir Gawain and the Green Knight* have resulted in oddly question-begging accounts of this complex romance. In the process of illuminating the "masculinist" paradigms explicitly and implicitly constructed by the Gawain-poet and his twentieth-century critics, feminist readers are quite liable to reinscribe the very categorical imperatives they are interrogating. When, for example, Sheila Fisher argues that the poet represents the plots, games, and contracts initiated or presided over by Morgan and Lady Bertilak as threats to Camelot's "dominant ideologies of feudalism and Christian chivalry,"[1] she takes it for granted that the "dominant ideologies" informing the artist's eventual erasure (or redefinition in "masculine" terms) of all signs of female power are informed by an internally coherent (gendered) system of value.[2] In a more recent study of the critical assumptions that *re*produce the romance as a gendered narrative, "self-evidently" centered upon Gawain's experience, Geraldine Heng shows a similar reluctance to recognize the multiple and contradictory constructions of masculinity to be found within this strikingly heteroglot work.[3] Although both critics offer suggestive reappraisals of *Sir Gawain's* narrative dynamics, they also confer an uninterrogated and monolithic stability upon the master narrative they claim to demystify. It is my own contention that the culturally privileged narrative that appears to marginalize the actions and desires of Morgan and Lady Bertilak does not so much ratify an ideal of "chivalric manhood" as represent its continuous and ultimately equivocal renegotiation.[4] In this essay I will argue that it is not at all clear who has thc last word in defining the proper measure of manhood in *Sir Gawain and the Green Knight*—or what that proper measure might be.

The Disembodied Hero

When the Green Knight appears at King Arthur's New Year's feast, the narrator comments:

> Half etayn in erde I hope þat he were,
> Bot mon most I algate mynn hym to bene,
> And þat þe myriest in his muckel þat myȝt ride;
> For of bak and of brest al were his bodi sturne,
> Both his wombe and his wast were worthily smale,
> And all his fetures folȝande, in forme þat he hade,
> ful clene.[5]

The Gawain-poet's initial construction of manhood is emphatically essentialist. To support his assertion that the Green Knight is as much man as "etayn" (140-41), he describes the stranger's well-proportioned male body, with its broad shoulders, slim waist, and flat stomach (142-46). The Green Knight invokes similarly essentialist, corporeal criteria when he dismisses Arthur's knights as "berdlez chylder" (280), and invites them to prove their manhood by proving their physical recklessness: his opponent in the Beheading Game must be both "brayn in hys hede" and "bolde in his blod" (286). King Arthur, whom the poet has represented from the start as a boyishly restless and "brayn wylde" ruler (87-89), accedes to the Green Knight's definition of masculine worth as soon as he takes up the challenger's ax. But when Gawain asks to replace Arthur as upholder of Camelot's honor, he articulates a different ideal of Arthurian manhood. If we initially see Arthur as a hyperactive and "somquat childgered" (86) reveller who quickly forgets what is due to his own position in grabbing the Green Knight's weapon, Gawain enters the narrative by way of a supremely controlled and tactful speech act (343-61), in the course of which he simultaneously defends the behavior of the Round Table, defers to the judgment of his lord and the whole company, and reduces the challenge to a trifling affair, which the weakest of them all may take upon himself (354).

One reader of the poem has claimed that "Gawain's speech before the court (341-61) often strikes modern students, and some critics, as overly elegant, near paralyzed by etiquette, if not absolutely sissified."[6] His statement revealingly genders verbal dexterity, suggesting that to be gracefully articulate is to be less than a man. But *within* the poem, although the Green Knight derides the "beardless children" of Camelot, for being "Ouerwalt wyth a worde of on wyȝes speche" (314), Gawain makes use of his own word power to insist that, although one may find no "better bodyes on bent þer baret is rered" (353) than his companions, this "nys" enterprise may be easily taken on by the feeblest of them. *Sir Gawain and the Green Knight* opens with a description of a heroic age of British history in which bold men flourished, "baret þat lofden" (21), and the Green Knight directly invokes the supposed "gryndellayk" and the "greme" (312) of the Round Table in kindling some "baret" of his own.

Gawain's speech act not only reasserts the "greme" of his peers but, even more significantly, begins to redefine the testing of Camelot's manhood by way of a paradigm shift that gradually relocates his actions within a quite different value system. This translation is, however, one of genre, not gender. By the time that hero and challenger have formally settled their contract concerning the terms of the Beheading Game, a quasi-epic testing of brute courage privileging deeds over words is transformed by the *speech acts* of both Gawain and the Green Knight into a romance trial of Gawain's pledged word, his "trawthe."

As Arthur's substitute and Camelot's representative in the business of troth-keeping, Gawain has put his body on the line, even as he insists upon that body's irrelevance to his endeavor: "I am þe wakkest, I wot" (354). He does declare that the only bodily power he possesses derives from his kinship with Arthur—"No bounté bot your blod I in my bodé knowe" (357)—but the unfolding romance that contains Gawain does not choose to emphasize the privileged blood tie between uncle and sister's son (which in some Germanic cultures would make Gawain—already his uncle's body double in the Beheading Game—Arthur's heir). Indeed, the narrative presentation of Gawain in the romance's first two fitts encourages us to assume that to represent Camelot's manhood properly is to become disembodied. A. C. Spearing points out that we never get any physical description of Gawain to compare with that of the Green Knight,[7] and we might push this observation further. This poem is full of carefully delineated bodies. The Green Knight is meticulously anatomized on his first appearance, and when he reappears in his human form as Sir Bertilak he is a vivid physical presence, with his high color, ample dimensions, sturdy legs, and beaver-hued beard (844-47). The two ladies at Bertilak's castle are also presented to us in emphatically fleshly terms, as the beautiful body of the hostess is compared with the grotesque ugliness of Morgan. Supernatural champions, alien aristocrats, and alien women are embodied and dissected by the poem as thoroughly as the animals hunted and ritually broken apart in the third fitt, but real men—that is, representative Arthurian heroes—don't have bodies, or at least not while their power to articulate themselves on their own terms remains unchallenged.

Fitt II's lengthy account of Gawain's arming for his journey to the Green Chapel (570-666) hardly fleshes him out for us: in the course of nearly a hundred lines he disappears into (or becomes the disembodied product of) his elaborate accoutrements and knightly insignia. We get all sorts of signs for Gawain's "perfected public self"[8]—the most prominent being the pentangle on his shield, the significance of which is explored at length (623-65). Much of the dramatic tension in the remainder of the poem will derive from the widening gap between the symbolic logic that insists upon the pentangle's absolute and stable betokening of Gawain's "trawthe" and the narrative's subsequent revelation of the gap between the imperfections of the fallible human being and the seamless moral geometry of the "pure pentaungle" 's endless knot of interdependent virtues. Since the Pentangular Knight is constructed only to be undone, it might be worth asking *who* creates this impossible abstraction of Gawain? Who produces the exfoliating gloss of the pentangle and links it to a Gawain who is, *inter alia*, "tulke of tale most trwe" (638), "voyded of vche vylany" (634), "as golde pured" (633). The maker of the poem presumably knows that the superlatives attached to his hero will not be borne out: Gawain will only prove to be comparatively virtuous—better than other knights, according to the final judgment of the Green Knight, in the same way as a pearl is better than white peas (2364-65), but not "as golde pured," not perfect.[9] So whose discourse is the poet re-presenting here?[10]

It is my contention that Camelot itself is "speaking Gawain" in these stanzas, conferring upon him (and, by extension, upon the community he represents) an exemplary character and an exemplary history. The exegeses of Gawain's "pentangular virtues," for instance, suggest that they have been established over a period of time: he "fayled *neuer* . . . in his fyve fyngres," his "clannes and his cortayse croked were *neuer*" (641, 653; emphasis added). This information is all the more remarkable because Gawain has previously presented himself as a mere novice, even among a group of people whom the poet goes out of his way to inform us are in their "first age" (54). Furthermore, each piece of armor he has donned before the arrival of his shield seems to be pristine, shining, unmarked by battle. These discrepancies within the "versions of Gawain" offered by the poem make the last lines of the first stanza discussing the pentangle particularly interesting. We are told that

> þe pentangel nwe
> He ber in schelde and cote,
> As tulk of tale most trwe
> And gentylest knyȝt of lote. (636-39)

The pentangle is "new," I would argue, not because it is newly painted, or a new insignia for Gawain (who in other Arthurian romances bears a golden eagle, a lion, or a gryphon as his device),[11] but because it is a new appropriation of Solomon's token by the community that is putting Gawain's public persona together, bit by bit.

Camelot is *inventing* Gawain-the-pentangular-knight even as his ritual arming takes place. The young warrior's verbal performance before the court and his pledging of his "trawthe" to the Green Knight has certainly given him some claim to the title of "tulk of tale most trwe / And gentylest knyȝt of lote"; the information that he bears his insignia *as* "tulk of tale most trewe" and so on confirms him as its holder even before he has fulfilled the terms of the challenge. The pentangle commentary also completes the process of "disembodiment" begun by Gawain himself. If Gawain's chivalric intervention had displaced Arthur's eagerness to body forth the Round Table's "gryndellayk" and "greme," this new "signifying discourse" threatens to render Gawain even more incorporeal. The pentangle commentary re-presents the hero in terms of a transcendental ideal that plays down his material body and its material connection with other bodies. Gawain's previous insistence that his strength derived only from the blood he shared with Arthur is now contradicted by the information that "*alle* his forsnes he feng at þe fyue joyez / þat þe hende heuen-quene had of hir chylde" (646-47; emphasis added) and that his boldness never failed when he gazed upon the image of Mary painted on the inside of his shield (650). The earlier suggestion of a heroic kin bond between uncle and nephew defers to the abstracted inspiring power of Christian chivalry, focused around a celestial Beloved.

If fitt II's arming sequence figures forth an impossibly idealized, communally constructed, and practically disembodied Gawain, the hero's difficult and lonely journey through the northern wilderness might nevertheless be expected to remind him and us of his corporeality. Certainly the poet's insistence that the cruel winter weather is as inimical to the knight as the adversaries he encounters on his travels speaks to the vulnerability of the flesh:

> Ner slayn wyth þe slete he sleped in his yrnes
> Mo nyȝtez þen innoghe in naked rokkez. (729-30)

But although the metonymic substitution of the term "yrnes" for armor indirectly suggests the chilled skin shrinking from the cold metal, it is the rocks that are ultimately naked to the elements, not the man. When, on Christmas Eve, Gawain prays to Mary that he may find shelter, he makes no mention of his body's needs, insisting that his most pressing desire is to hear mass and matins and to celebrate Christ's birth (754-56). It is, however, Gawain's own incarnation that will be engendered within the castle whose sudden appearance seems to answer his prayers.

The Reembodied Hero

As he enters the elegant stronghold, Gawain is almost immediately stripped of his armor and his insignia, and we even get an indirect look at his face when the poet tells us that it seemed like the spring to his welcomers (866). Nevertheless, Gawain-as-representative-of-Arthurian-manhood continues to be a voice rather than a body: the northern courtiers are primarily interested in his reputation as a wielder of the "teccheles termes of talkying noble" (917). It is his hostess who insists upon reembodying him. Herself an emphatically physical presence—"þe fayrest in felle, of flesche and of lyre" (943)—she traps him naked in his bed on her first morning visit and ambiguously announces that he is "welcum to my cors" (1237). As she bandies words with him, her verbal assaults are aimed from the first at remaking his identity (and redefining his "manhood") in terms of erotic action. When, at the end of that morning's conversation, she scores a palpable hit by doubting his identity, she explains that the real Gawain would have wished to salute her with his lips as well as with his fine speeches (1293-1301). She will eventually rearticulate the chivalric ideal in emphatically secular terms, suggesting that the knight's "lettrure of armes" should be the "lel layk of luf" (1513). Gallant words should be matched with deeds, courtesy enacted in kisses, "luf-talkyng" should be an invitation to other kinds of intercourse. If he is "really Gawain"—really the exemplary representative of the Round Table, the knight whose "worde and . . . worchip walkez ayquere" (1521)—he must be willing to reconstitute himself as a desiring male whose flesh responds to her femaleness. In fitt II, we were told that Gawain bore the pentangle—one of whose five glosses also re-presents him as Mary's knight and another of which insists that his "clannes," his bodily purity, is never "croked"—*because* he is "gentylest knyȝt of lote" (639): the knight of the noblest speech. But his superlative pentangular virtues are open to interpretation: they may encode other values than those of Christian chivalry. From the lady's point of view, Gawain would behave like the "gentylest knyȝt of lote" in employing his perfect speech—and perhaps some other talents—to teach her "sum tokenez of trweluf craftes" (1527); in so doing, of course, he would cease to be the knight whose "courtaysye" *and* "clannes" "croked were neuer" (653). The lady's insistence that Gawain should "body forth" his courtesy does not so much challenge the pentangle's representation of a nexus of spiritualized virtues as draw our attention to its simultaneous over- and underdetermination as an abstract of Gawain's value. The "pure pentaungle" is finally unable to impose clear boundaries between secular social graces and more elevated virtues that share the same signifiers.[12]

Gawain, to be sure, refuses to accede to his hostess's equation of the "lettrure of armes" with the "lel layk of luf." And on the third day of his testing, he rejects both her ring and her girdle when they are offered as love gifts that might signify his surrender to carnal desire. But when he accepts the lady's redefinition of the girdle as a life-preserving talisman, and, in concealing it from his host, contravenes the terms of the Exchange of Winnings game, he nonetheless ends up "reembodied." Having acknowledged the vulnerability of his flesh and privileged his hunger to live over his pledged word, Gawain is no longer "tulke of tale most trwe," and it is thus not surprising that the account of his rearming before his departure for the Green Chapel makes no mention of the pentangle that had designated his "trawthe" (626): we are told instead that he did not leave behind the lady's gift:

> Þat forgat not Gawayn for gode of hymseluen.
> Bi he hade belted þe bronde vpon his balȝe haunchez,
> Þenn dressed he his drurye double hym aboute,
> Swyþe sweþled vmbe his swange swetely þat knyȝt
> Þe gordel of þe grene silke, þat gay wel bisemed. (2031-35)

The last phrase echoes ironically—in the first arming sequence the pentangle shield had also "bisemed þe segge semlyly fayre" (622). Geraldine Heng argues that whereas the pentangle is "an abstract, bodiless sign, the girdle is a sign that is also a fully material object, one that carries . . . the impress . . . of the body itself."[13] It marks the knight with the lady's embrace, especially as the Gawain-poet labels it a "drurye"—love token. One might add that it is in close proximity to hips that are suddenly "balȝe"—swelling, smoothly rounded (967). Gawain's body is not only made visible here, it is also feminized.[14]

The hero's embodiment is reemphasized in the poet's description of the blow that cleaves his naked flesh at the Green Chapel; at the very moment of his chastisement for the sin of privileging his corporeal existence above his "trawthe," Gawain is most visibly a *mere* body:

> Þe scharp schrank to þe flesche þur þe schyre grece,
> Þat þe schene blod ouer his schulderes schot to þe erþe. (2313-14)

Marie Borroff has noted that the phrase "schyre grece"—fair flesh—is employed twice before in the poem—in describing Gawain's own beheading of the Green Knight, when his ax "schrank þurȝ þe schyire grece, and schade hit in twynne" (425), and in describing the "schyree grece schorne vpon rybbes" (1378) of the deer slain and broken by Bertilak and his men.[15] If Gawain's preliminary embodiment, at the hands of the lady, makes his body fleetingly female, his second one, at the hands of the

Green Knight, makes him briefly at one with the hunted animals and the alien male. Readers have regularly observed that Gawain's adventures oblige him to recognize that he is not the superior and singular being he had thought himself to be,[16] and in these passages the diction of the romance quietly insists that he is just like everybody (and every body) else, even though his very identity as representative Arthurian man had seemed to depend on his separation from the condition of mere women, animals, and male exotics.

Gawain's self-condemnation in the wake of his token punishment is revealing; he says to the Green Knight:

> For care of þy knokke cowardyse me taȝt
> To acorde me with couetyse, my kynde to forsake,
> Þat is larges and lewté þat longez to knyȝtez. (2379-81)

Fear of the ax blow led him to value his body's survival above his "lewté"; he has betrayed both the "trawthe" he pledged to his host in the Exchange of Winnings agreement and his faith in the power of God and the Virgin to preserve him against evil. When, however, Gawain insists that he has therefore forsaken his "kynde"—both his true nature and his kinship with the brotherhood of all virtuous knights (2380)—he is begging the question of just what constitutes his "kynde." His sympathetic adversary has already suggested that to be only human, to love one's life a little too much, is not incompatible with being a pearl among knights (2364-65). But Gawain's identity has been constructed by himself and others in terms that will not allow him to reconcile his apprehension of the humanity that is also part of his "kynde" with his more limited definition of knightly worth. Sheila Fisher has argued that in betraying his own notion of "kynde," Gawain necessarily betrays his masculinity, "for in this poem, knighthood and masculinity are in the end the same thing."[17] I would suggest, however, that it is only if we subject ourselves to Gawain's notion of manhood that we must consider him "unmanned." The poem that contains Gawain can also envision a knight-hero who, rather than constructing an exclusive and alienating ideal of chivalric manhood, might reimagine himself in terms of a fallible—if nevertheless admirable—humanity that admits common ground with the Other (whether that Other is female or a male who does not belong to the community of Camelot). The final words of the mysterious figure who now calls himself Bertilak de Hautdesert suggest, furthermore, that the question of what constitutes Gawain's "kynde" is still far from closed. Bertilak asks Gawain to return with him to his castle to celebrate the New Year, and invites him to reencounter his wife's aged companion, who has now been identified as Morgan le Fay and the instigator of the Beheading Game – and who is also, of course, Arthur's half sister and Gawain's aunt. If you're going to speak of "kynde," Bertilak seems to be saying, you should find out more about your kin. You are as much a product of your blood relationship with that enigmatic old woman as of the brotherhood of knights.

The Signs of Manhood

Gawain will not risk another encounter with Morgan. He has, moreover, already complicated his conclusions about his betrayal of his own nature with a further explanation of his failure, a misogynistic denunciation of the wiles of women in the course of which he invokes the exemplary transgressions of Adam, Samson, Solomon, and David (2414-28). These men, says Gawain, were the noblest ("freest") of their time (2422), and "alle þay were biwyled / With wymmen þat þay vsed" (2426-27); he can hardly be blamed for sharing their fate. Tellingly ignoring all the tricky questions that might be raised about the actual moral agency of his heroes, he suggests that the spiritual error into which he has been led by the weakness of *his* flesh is the inescapable condition of all *men* faced with female beguilements. By this definition, of course, Gawain's failure proves him to have been a "real man" all along.

Gawain's bipartite commentary on his performance, which implies that he has both unmanned himself *and*, paradoxically, done what comes all too naturally to men, should not come as a surprise in a poem in which actions, people, and objects are regularly assigned competing identities or made to signify different things, and in whose course both characters and readers must repeatedly reinterpret their experiences. We might note, however, that in generating alternative accounts of his failing, Gawain feels obliged either to insist that he has completely betrayed his *kynde* (i.e. the fellowship of aristocratic male warriors) or to suggest that, if he has kept faith with his *kynde*, that *kynde* is not humankind but *man*-kind. Both of his explanatory narratives represent his fault in gendered terms; and inasmuch as the second one (through its invocation of the worthies who fell to women's wiles) reinserts Gawain within a fellowship of his peers, it does so by shifting the moral focus of his discourse from the failings of a man to the beguilements of a threatening Other.

Gawain's creator, of course, refuses to privilege any one "explanation" of Gawain's fault, and the final lines of his poem complicate rather than fix the significance of Gawain's experience. As he turns back to Camelot, Gawain reembraces the narrative of his unmanning, the regrettable story of his embodiment, insisting that the girdle testifies to the weakness of the "flesche crabbed" (2435). And at Arthur's court he lays bare to his peers the scar that designates his own Christmas incarnation: "þe nirt in þe nek he naked hem schewed" (2498). But despite Gawain's redescription of the girdle as a "token of vntrawþe" (2509), Arthur's followers cheerfully reappropriate it to decorate "uche burne of þe broþerhede" (2516); it will now betoken the "renoun of þe Rounde Table" (2519). Gawain's peers follow the Green Knight in offering an assessment of Gawain's performance that is much more generous than that offered by the quester himself. Their reaffirmation of Gawain's worth is, however, predicated upon an exclusive rather than an inclusive gesture. The Green Knight had suggested that the representative of heroic masculinity might recognize the frailties of the flesh that bore witness to his kinship with every body else and still be a pearl among knights. The Round Table's appropriation of the girdle as a special decoration for each knight of the brotherhood, the exclusive insignia of a group of warrior males, ignores the possibility that to wear the green girdle is to reassert one's ties with *all* of humankind.

In the absence of any authorial commentary on the competing glosses of Gawain's experience, the discrepancy between Gawain's representations and those of his peers remains unresolved. If we read *Sir Gawain and the Green Knight* synchronically, we may reinvoke and choose to privilege the viewpoint of Bertilak, that elusive masculine Other who seems to challenge *both* of these perspectives, but in the work's diachronic unfolding the categories of masculine value, the very signs of manhood, remain subject to change. Camelot's final transformation of the meaning of the green girdle simply reminds us of the power of all elite societies to reconstruct themselves *ad infinitum* in terms that are at once exclusive and restrictive—and utterly provisional.

Notes

A version of this chapter was first delivered as a paper at the 1992 Joint Conference of the South Eastern Medieval Association and the Virginia Medieval Symposium at the College of William and Mary.

1. Sheila Fisher, "Taken Men and Token Women in *Sir Gawain and the Green Knight*," in *Seeking the Woman in Late Medieval and Renaissance Writings: Essays in Feminist Contextual Criticism*, ed. Sheila Fisher and Janet E. Halley (Knoxville: University of Tennessee Press, 1989), 72. See also Sheila Fisher, "Leaving Morgan Aside: Women, History and Revisionism in *Sir Gawain and the Green Knight*," in *The Passing of Arthur: New Essays in Arthurian Tradition*, ed. Christopher Baswell and William Sharpe (New York: Garland, 1988), 129-51.

2. Fisher, "Leaving Morgan Aside," 130-31.

3. Geraldine Heng, "Feminine Knots and the Other *Sir Gawain and the Green Knight*," *PMLA* 106 (1991): 500-514; see 500-502.

4. Recent studies of the poem have emphasized in particular the perpetual (re)negotiations of value in the vocabulary of "pricing and prizing" that attaches itself to assessments of the hero's performance: see, for example, R. A. Shoaf, *The Poem as Green Girdle: Com-*

mercium in Sir Gawain and the Green Knight (Gainesville: University Presses of Florida, 1984); and Jill Mann, "Price and Value in *Sir Gawain and the Green Knight*," *Essays and Studies* 36 (1986): 294-318. My own emphasis here is on some of the less explicitly marked transactions of (masculine) value that take place in *Sir Gawain.*

5. *Sir Gawain and the Green Knight*, ed. J. R. R. Tolkien and E. V. Gordon, 2d ed. rev. Norman Davis (Oxford: Clarendon, 1967), lines 140-46. Further citations from the poem are noted parenthetically.

6. John Plummer, "Signifying the Self: Language and Identity in *Sir Gawain and the Green Knight*," in *Text and Matter; New Critical Perspectives of the Pearl Poet*, ed. Robert Blanch, Miriam Youngerman Miller, and Julian N. Wasserman (Troy, N.Y.: Whitston, 1991), 201.

7. A. C. Spearing, *The Gawain-Poet: A Critical Study* (Cambridge: Cambridge University Press, 1970), 177-78.

8. The term is Fisher's, "Taken Men and Token Women," 88.

9. One might add that the poem's larger portrait of *all* Gawain's insignia offers some contradictions. Although he carries his divine mistress, Mary, on the inside of his shield (649-50), Gawain's harness is elsewhere embroidered with turtledoves and love knots set there by other and earthly women (612).

10. *Sir Gawain and the Green Knight* seems to exemplify M. M. Bakhtin's notion (which he, however, chooses to make a defining characteristic of the *novel*) of "heteroglossia": it repeatedly sets competing language systems in dialogue with one another, most notably in the different "versions of Gawain" produced by different speakers in the poem. I would propose that the arming sequence, although ostensibly rendered in the voice of the omniscient narrator, is ultimately recontextualized by the narrative as a whole as just another of these (often partial and prejudiced) constructions of Gawain. For Bakhtin's discussion of narrative "dialogization," see "Discourse in the Novel," in *The Dialogic Imagination*, ed. Michael Holquist, trans. Caryl Emerson and Michael Holquist (Austin: University of Texas Press, 1981), 262-64.

11. The Gawain-poet had obviously read some of these romances, as he exploits the knight's ubiquitous reputation for courtesy later on in his narrative. On Gawain's other devices, see Tolkien and Gordon's note to line 620.

12. Wendy Clein discusses the alternative "courtly" and "moralist" perspectives offered on Gawain's chivalry in the poem in *Concepts of Chivalry in Sir Gawain and the Green Knight* (Norman, Okla.: Pilgrim, 1987). Britton J. Harwood examines the tension between the Christian ethos and the aristocratic ethos in the poem in "*Gawain* and the Gift," *PMLA* 106 (1991): 483-99; see especially 489-90.

13. Heng, "Feminine Knots," 505.

14. Interestingly, Tolkien and Gordon's textual emendation at line 967 in fitt II would make this the poet's second use of an adjective previously used to describe Morgan's buttocks.

15. Marie Borroff, "*Sir Gawain and the Green Knight*: The Passing of Judgment," in Baswell and Sharpe, *The Passing of Arthur*, 105-28; see 109-10.

16. See, for example, Spearing, *The Gawain-Poet*, 230.

17. Fisher, "Leaving Morgan Aside," 141.

PART II

Men in Institutions

CHAPTER 4

Burdens of Matrimony
Husbanding and Gender in Medieval Italy
Susan Mosher Stuard

If there is received opinion on husbanding as a determinant of gender for men in medieval times, I suppose it was supplied by David Herlihy in 1983 when he argued from art and literature that the last figure set into the constellation of holy child and devoted mother to form the ideal family was the self-denying husband, modeled upon Joseph. Herlihy saw Joseph's entry into iconography as a relatively late medieval phenomenon; Joseph began to figure prominently in urban Italian art in the fifteenth century.[1] Yet Joseph's bent and weary figure, relegated to the periphery of the scene, seems to have held few attractions for men in the vigor of their youth. It is in fact difficult to imagine any success at all for Joseph as a male ideal except in a struggle where age triumphs over youth. Perhaps then, a search for husbanding as a determinant of gender must be undertaken by investigating generational relations among men rather than by studying changing patterns of husband-wife relations.

To turn attention to the early stages of this generational conflict—perhaps I should call it taming men to behave like Joseph—is to take the quest to the twelfth century. In the middle years of that century, at the University of Bologna and in civil and church courts, teaching on a husband's financial obligations to his wife suddenly narrowed to the crucial task of husbanding a wife's natal family inheritance, that is, in Roman law, the wife's Falcidian quarter, or full share of inheritance from her natal family, paid to her upon her marriage in the form of a dowry. It has been generally assumed that this reversal in the direction in which marital gifts moved favored husbands with unencumbered access to their wives' wealth, rather than requiring husbands to pay to marry as had been the case both in Germanic and late Roman customary practice. But, I would argue, men who married did not solely gain at the expense of their wives;[2] instead, elders found legal ways to tie up money flowing to youth, their stated aim being to assure the young couple always had the means on hand to support the "burdens of matrimony." Clearly, marriage changed a man's relationship to his father, uncles, and elder brothers, admitting him to the decision-making body of those who controlled the patrimony, a personal rearrangement of the practical effects of patriarchy. At the same time, however, a wife's dowry established a contractual relation between a new husband and his father-in-law, possibly too the bride's brothers, uncles, and cousins, an acquired kin group the Florentines honored with the name *parentado*. The complexity of responsibilities in a man's life increased substantially with marriage; so did the numbers of persons who looked over a husband's shoulder to see that he behaved responsibly.

Relations between wife and husband were not, of course, left unaltered by such momentous changes. Because gender encompasses the system of social relations between women and men, the tightening of the definition of woman before the law, which was a component of the new legal controls, also restricted, or tightened, gender assumptions about men. Gratian asserted that "it is the natural order among mankind that a woman serves her husband as children do parents; the justice in this is that the lesser serve the greater," and also, "woman should be subject to her husband's rule and has no authority, either to teach, to bear witness, to give surety, or to judge." He defined woman's condition categorically for canon law, basing his case upon a married woman's condition.[3] A woman's resulting "incapacity" before the law mandated certain "capacities" from her husband, first among them being his obligation to preserve her dowry. A husband was answerable before church courts and, in time, before civil courts, if he failed to act for his wife. What a man had to do was as constrained by gender assumptions as were his wife's choices, albeit in opposite ways.

Before the twelfth century, husbands had, by and large, profited from the traditional gift giving prompted by marriage, if we consider men's roles within the orbit of their own natal families. To illustrate this I would like to turn to some important new research by Barbara Kreutz on Lombard charters in tenth-century South Italy. Kreutz cites a charter drawn up in 940 in which a husband declared that if he should predecease his father, his wife was to have her *morgengabe*, a quarter share of any inheritance from the father, over which she was to have complete control.[4] This was generous—a Lombard wife generally expected the *morgengabe*, a *quarta* (one-fourth her husband's estate, which she owned unencumbered).[5] But what I find interesting in this 940 Cava charter is the control of wealth a husband gained from his natal family when he wed. Clearly this husband had already secured sufficient family funds to allow him to marry with the required resources, so his kin had themselves assumed the "burden of matrimony" by sharing out to him part of the family estate well before the death of his father (men generally married in their twenties in this era). This man came from a landowning family, and the charter's provisions are consonant with general practice among propertied families before eleventh-century European society began to enforce the right of primogeniture.

Following Harry Brod's dictum that "traditional scholarship's treatment of generic man as human norm systematically excludes from consideration what is unique to men *qua* men,"[6] I wish to examine how this devolution of wealth to young men at marriage might have affected their masculine identity. First, it effectively marked off youth from adulthood. With the late marrying pattern now applied over most of Germanic Europe,[7] not just the northwest, this was likely an event of the third decade of life for young men. Men were launched into adulthood at this rite through gaining wealth and responsibility simultaneously. Households may have been virilocal, but they were seldom patrilineal. A young couple set up their own modest quarters, perhaps the first of a number of moves if they prospered. Responsibilities came in large, but not overwhelming, measure with marriage; others descended over the course of married life with the birth of children, further inheritances, and age. Marriage did not even deter men from wandering off in search of their fortunes. One explanation for European expansion in this sparsely settled age was that women administered resources at home so effectively that their husbands were freed to seek out new opportunities abroad.[8] This was not to be a lasting feature of European life, however. Footloose adventures tended to cease with marriage by the twelfth century, Georges Duby relates.[9] The wandering years in which young men sought their fortunes terminated with marriage, allowing an advantageous marriage to a propertied widow or an heiress to signify the making of a fortune and an end for youth's caprice, at least among the propertied classes.

When husbanding merely marked a passage in life—that is, until the twelfth century—it lacked the force to define a man in relation to his wife. As a result, the traits that composed identity remained multivalent for men. This was the age of epic, when oral tradition had the power to define. A nickname or epithet often individuated a man according to his physical attributes (Harald Bluetooth), his idiosyncrasies (Notker the Stammerer), or his behaviors (Robert the Crafty), and none too kindly. Honorifics (the Great, the Bold, the Debonair) belonged to a later feudal age, although they were reflected back upon the remembered heroes of this earlier time. Until the end of the first feudal age, the eleventh century in Marc Bloch's chronology, even an ordinary man earned a sobriquet to distinguish him from his fellows, as early charters reveal in plenty.[10] A patronym or a matronym might serve to distinguish a man, but he was not known as a spouse. Foibles, skills, or attributes were encoded in nicknames that stuck like glue even in the formal space of a notary's registers, but marriage lacked such an eponymous role while it merely signified a passage in life.

Marriage Law and New Values

The new set of values associated with marriage law in the twelfth century placed gender distinction at the heart of the matter of a man's definition, fixing him firmly in relation to his wife. Gratian stated, "Woman is subject to her husband," which he explained is the natural order *in hominibus* (among mankind). *Vir* and *homo* took on distinct meanings with the gendered association of husbanding attached to the former – *vir*. Gratian's arguments about a woman's incapacity followed this phrase.[11] Thus the incapacity argument, which held such power for defining women as passive and dependent in subsequent centuries, also established a new identity for a husband by creating a polar interdependence between husband and wife. Because a man was a husband, he bore responsibility for both. Will he or nil he, he must supply the capacity, directing "head," or public *persona*, for both himself and his wife. Context is all in Gratian, and the context of this discussion is the issue of a man leaving his marriage to enter holy orders without his wife's consent. Gratian's answer is, clearly, no, he may not leave. A husband found no escape from the demands a capacity justification placed upon him. As Gratian's argument was applied in ecclesiastical courts and, perhaps more to the point, by civil lawyers in civil courts after the passage of new statute laws in towns that appropriated this capacity argument, husbands, in contrast to their peers who were priests, monks, or unmarried bachelors, were firmly pinned to their responsibilities based upon the gendered understanding that they spoke for their wives according to natural law.[12]

There was no necessary application of this capacity argument to property settlements in marriage, let alone to dowry, but civil lawyers saw a relevance in Gratian's arguments that they linked to property rights arguments. Furthermore, Gratian was studied in schools of law, and his phrase "without dowry there is no marriage" grew famous in time.[13] Later lawyers simply linked what Gratian said about marriage, that it required a Roman dowry, to what he had said elsewhere about married women, that they had no legal capacity. Once these two ideas were joined, control over a woman's dowry and natal inheritance neatly fell to the husband for the span of his lifetime. Women came more and more under legal guardianship with a reimposition of what Roman law had termed the *tutela*, that is, a male right to represent a woman before the law at all times and under all circumstances.[14]

Scholars are of two minds on the implications of the husband's new obligations before the law. Manlio Bellomo sees little here other than a new statutory permission for the *capo di famiglia* to condense a woman's dowry into the patrimony to the benefit of his lineage. Bellomo cites the thirteenth-century laws of cities that eased the way for this strengthening of a husband's financial control.[15] Julius Kirshner is not so certain, and he cites the late medieval Italian jurists who insisted that husbands did not own their wives' dowries but managed them instead, and that a dowry must be intact if a wife predeceases her husband. Other directives in consonance with this principle meant dotal goods always stood in a husband's custody and that he was answerable to a woman's father as donor and a woman's children as heirs.[16] Heaven help the husband found "verging toward insolvency" for, as Kirshner points out, his wife may, nay must, sue him for her dowry. If this principle was enforced in courts, then there was a convergence of husband's financial obligations in marriage and man's authority, or his legal capacity for his wife as Gratian defined it, that has important implications for gender.

Examples from the Archives

It is useful to take this problem to cases. Perhaps Venice, whose late twelfth- and thirteenth-century legal practices are known through surviving records, may shed some light on how husbands' roles came to be understood. The *Procuratoria* of San Marco became a repository for married women's dowries in Venice by the twelfth century. As guardians, the procurators took their responsibilities seriously. They allowed some husbands "authority" over their wives' dowries—that is, husbands could remove amounts of dotal goods—but under stringent restrictions. Reinhold Mueller states:

> Since dowries were often brought to the marriage in the form of real estate [real estate was good as gold in Venice, whereas gold itself was the preferred gift of dowry elsewhere], special provisions restricted the alienation of such property. The doge Pietro Ziani in 1226 saw to the approval of regulations for the sale of real estate [in dowry] *ad usum novum*. After the extent and worth of the dowry had been demonstrated under oath, the husband or seller of the real estate was required to deposit in the *Procuratoria* a sum equal to the appraised value of the dowry. While this provision guaranteed the dowry, it immobilized the capital.[17]

This wrinkle in Venetian law supports Kirshner's contention that the law held husbands liable for the awarded sum or its equivalent.[18] But thinking changed over time in Venice and, in this market-oriented society, practice moved in the direction of increasing liquidity for the sums tied up in dotal gifts. Over the following decades, the requirement to leave sums with the procurators of equal value to the dowry was relaxed. Men might then invest dowry funds, but only in low-risk ventures. They still had to account to the procurators for their investments' success.

Dowries were the cause of constant litigation. In Ragusa (Dubrovnik) in 1319, the Small Council distrained Anna de Bodacio's dowry along with the private wealth of her husband, Petèr Paborra, in order to satisfy foreign creditors. Heedless of the Italian revival of Roman law that forbade this expedient move, the councilors trusted close kin and other members of the affluent aristocratic circle to buoy up these victims of the uncertainties of long-distance trade.[19] Meanwhile, in Venice, Mueller states that in 1338,

> having sold real estate bound in dowry, Andrea Boldu was to deposit the dowry in the Procuratia; instead he lent the 1000 lire to a German count, who deposited jewels in the Procuratia as surety for the dowry. Each year for 17 years he had received 5 per cent plus a "gift" of 12 lire, so that the return totalled 6.2 per cent. When Boldu purchased more real estate, he put a part in his wife's name, and withdrew the jewels.[20]

With such close surveillance of a husband's custodial role, there was little flexibility in Boldu's investment strategy. In Florence, where prosecution before the law made mismanagement of dowry a scandal, Giovanni Morelli could ruin his brother-in-law's name merely by complaining angrily that his sister was too obedient to her husband. As Thomas Kuehn relates, "[The sister's] husband would suddenly appear at home with a notary and witnesses in tow, explaining that she must consent to some deal." Morelli had reason for anger because the obligation to support his sister eventually fell on his shoulders, but not before his hapless brother-in-law was ruined beyond repair.[21] In Italian city-states there was scant opportunity to escape from the capacity argument that the revival of Roman law had pinned on husbands.

The key to what was expected of husbands may lie in how a husband's custodial role reflected current understandings of that newly popular medium of exchange of the twelfth and early thirteenth centuries: silver coin. Here, in preserving dotal wealth, valued and also frequently awarded in good coin, husbands faced an increasingly difficult task as custodians.

This occurred against all received wisdom, because coin—that is, the new medium of currency—was not constant in value but fluctuated, decreasing in purchasing power, often through devaluation, much more commonly than it increased in value. Devaluation was a fact of medieval urban life, as there was never sufficient silver to support the currency needs of the age.[22]

Dowry was awarded in coin whenever possible (although Venice continued to favor real estate). In fact, it became a matter of family honor in most Italian cities to award dowry in the best coin obtainable. Pierre Bonnassie has gone so far as to say that dowry was the first of all intrafamilial exchanges commuted to coin because a woman's kin were loath to divide assets more essential to the patrimony for the purpose of endowing a bride and groom.[23] Furthermore, there is ample proof that then, as now, people thought the newly wed couple should receive the very best gifts. Applied to dowry given in currency, that meant the best coin available: the best groats of silver or, when minted, florins or ducats of gold. By the late Middle Ages in Florence, for example, dowry was paid in special bagged florins guaranteed to be full-weight coin.[24] It is worth suggesting, perhaps, that the movement to gold coinage owes some debt to affluent families' quest for specie that accurately conveyed their prestige and worth in marital exchanges. Good coins were saved up over a lifetime for a dowry, and it is possible that merchants and bankers might recognize a husband verging on insolvency who spent his wife's dowry by the sudden presence of very good coin in circulation. If so, dowry wealth was as marked as the larger influx of coin brought by a visiting ruler from silver-rich Goslar or later, Hungary, whose presence in a big city was broadcast by a marked change for the better in specie in circulation.[25]

In this new cash economy husbands became an accountable personal line of defense against the vicissitudes of a money economy when they were vested with the obligation to preserve the worth of dowry valued in a currency that, understood or not, refused to maintain its own value. The reintroduced Roman law that stood as the foundation for husbands' custodial roles had not been designed to deal with this dilemma. The economy of late Rome had been sufficiently stable, if not static, that dotal wealth had a reasonable chance of maintaining its value over the life of a marriage. The twelfth and thirteenth centuries placed husbands up against expectations at odds with the volatility of money in an emerging commercial economy. Yet, medieval Italian jurists apparently still clung to the outmoded notion of fixed monetary values without modification through at least the fourteenth and fifteenth centuries.[26] Under these circumstances, a husband faced some very difficult choices. As husband, he must invest the dowry in his custody because that was the only way to keep up with the devaluation of money. On the other hand, he must not risk dowry because he was accountable for it, but what was a commercial investment if not risk? Dowry must not sit idle, for it would lose value, but it must not be lost in speculation; by force of circumstances a husband was enjoined to "make" money. Through failure to acknowledge, and very possibly to understand, the proclivities of their own medium of exchange, the enforcers of the law had placed married men in the position of being "in authority" and husbanding a wife's wealth against all realistic expectation of consistent success.

In application to daily life, the law came to mean that a husband kept dowry funds separate from other capital. Often a husband was restrained from investing dowry abroad in long-distance trade, with its inherent risk, but that meant he was also forbidden from investing dowry in the most lucrative ventures open to men in marketing towns and cities. By the late Middle Ages, it was accepted practice that dowry was to be invested near home, that is to say, within the town, in every sense inhabiting a special category of "domestic capital." Efforts to corner this capital source may be seen in Florence, where a *Monte della Dote* was established so fathers might invest in city funds over decades to raise dowry. Husbands were encouraged to leave dowries invested in the fund instead of withdrawing them after marriage. "Pursuing honor while avoiding sin" was touted as a fine reason for investing in the city's debt as the fund's agents became new interested parties in scrutinizing men's performance at preserving their wives', and daughters', wealth.[27]

Over three centuries, the formative influences of the law upon the understanding of a husband's role had gone some distance toward creating a new *persona* for men. The privileged position in which husbands stood before the law, because they possessed legal capacity for themselves and their wives, had been revealed to entail a clear burden. Other features of a man's identity paled before the court-enforced obligation to perform a custodial role in the family.

Implications for Gender Identity

Under the principles of law laid out by Gratian in his *Decretum*, man received his identity in polar opposition to a woman, just as woman received her definition in opposition to man. Note that the singular was used, not the plural. Gratian spoke generically, using categorical imperatives, thus authority of a husband was not equivocal but absolute and the use made in case law, in church law, in civil courts, and in restitution of dowries in cities made an unequivocal, albeit frequently unrealistic, demand on husbands.

Next, this categorization simplified the diverse components of identity for married men to the single issue of a husband's legal capacity and responsibility. Gender often connotes a simplification of understandings, whether applied to women or to men. What was lost in terms of complex understandings, the multivalent nature of personality, was never as complete, I believe, as with the new gendered understanding of woman, nor was gender ever as negatively construed. However, for men as well as for women this change represented a powerful simplifying force in understanding what it was to be a man. Husbanding might come to outweigh all other considerations when a man was judged by his society.

Also, this new gendered understanding was applied to men's lives, or enforced, within an increasingly urban society. Through the actions of civic bureaucracies, the *Procuratoria* of Venice, the *Monte della Dote* of Florence, or their equivalents, and the law courts, both civil and ecclesiastical, married men found new legal definitions affecting their lives. From Italy the concept of Roman dowry spread over most of western Europe in subsequent centuries. It was often accompanied by the justifications originally offered by Gratian and later applied to civil law.

And, in truth, most men in European society were married men. The age of marriage for men rose steadily through the medieval centuries, which may be related in part to the burden marriage had come to represent in the eyes of young bachelors.[28] Because most men did marry eventually, there was a high probability that these gendered arguments were applicable to them at some point. Propertied citizens, the *meliores* or *sapientes*, as they were called—the better sort, wise or grave—were men who could not, in matter of fact, escape marriage often as not because marriage signified that they had become the responsible, mature adults the community demanded to shoulder the burdens of governing and overseeing the welfare of others.[29] The dialectic of privilege and burden had become an institutionalized feature of men's lives. It comes as no surprise then that when Francesco Barbaro condemned marriage he attacked it as an institution bringing unsupportable personal burdens to men. His quarrel lay with his elders rather than with women.[30]

Changes in gender assumptions about men figured in the secularization of European society. Increased consequence of the married estate accompanied the spread of the ideals of humanism in the early Renaissance centuries. The gradual transition from an ideal based upon celibacy to an ideal based upon a life solidly lived "in the world" carried with it, in most instances, the assumption that a man marry. In matter of fact, the man who married and carried off his gendered husbanding role well was often the man most in possession of dignity as Renaissance ideals defined dignity. As Stanley Chojnacki notes in his essay in this volume, "The dynamic driving [Venetian] patrician culture from generation to generation can thus be seen as the fusion of patriarchal, patrilineal, and patrimonial objectives into a triptych of gender principles that guided, by blending, the domestic and official worlds of the governing class." This was the bargain struck between privilege and burden. It ascribed a narrow hierarchical pyramid of ascent, where few aspirants achieved a level near the ideal.

For these reasons we need to take a second look at the power over and access to money men gained through the award of their wives' dowries and the complex laws that grew up about this marital assign. Through them, gender came to restrict men's lives. The perception of what it was to be a man, and in time men's identities, began to change, just as surely here as did the identities of women in the Middle Ages. Joseph had taken up his background pose, an icon of responsibility.

Notes

1. David Herlihy, "The Making of the Medieval Family: Symmetry, Structure, and Sentiment," *Journal of Family History* 8 (1983): 116-30; see especially 127-28.

2. For the analogue of this argument featuring gender and married women, see Susan Mosher Stuard, "From Women to Woman: New Thinking about Gender, c. 1140," *Thought* 64 (1989): 208-19.

3. Gratian, *Decretum*, *Causa* 33, *Questio* 5, *Corpus juris canonici*, ed. E. Freidburg (Graz: Bernard Tauchnitz, 1911), vol. 1, cols. 1254-55. This is my translation from the Latin; the original is as follows: "Est ordo naturalis in hominibus, ut feminae serviant viris, et filii parentibus, quia in illis hec iusticia est, ut maiori serviant minor"; and "Mulierem constat subiectam dominio viri esse, et nullam auctoritaten habere; nec docere potest, nec testis esse, neque fidem dare, nec iudicare."

4. Barbara Kreutz, "Lombard Women, Lombard Law, Lombard Reality in the Ninth and Tenth Centuries," paper presented at the Medieval Academy of America, Madison, Wis., April 1988; to be published in expanded form as "The Twilight of *Morgengabe*" in a festschrift for David Herlihy, forthcoming. See notes 36 and 49. The author cites *Codex Diplomaticus Cavensis*, 8 vols. (Milan: 1873-93), 1:166 (940).

5. See Diane Owen Hughes, "From Brideprice to Dowry in Mediterranean Europe," *Journal of Family History* 3 (1978): 263-96.

6. Harry Brod, ed., *The Making of Masculinities* (Boston: Allen & Unwin, 1987), 2.

7. David Herlihy, *Medieval Households* (Cambridge, Mass.: Harvard University Press, 1985), 109-111.

8. David Herlihy, "Land, Family and Women in Continental Europe, 700-1100," *Traditio* 18 (1962): 89-120.

9. Georges Duby, "The Youth Culture of Twelfth Century France," in *Social Historians of Contemporary France*, ed. Marc Ferro, trans. the staff of Annales, Paris (New York: Harper, 1972), 87-99.

10. Marc Bloch, *Feudal Society*, trans. L. A. Manyon (New York: Harper, 1972); for nicknames in charters, see Robert S. Lopez and Irving I. Raymond, *Medieval Trade in the Mediterranean World* (New York: Columbia University Press, 1955): "Malfiliastro" (Genoa) (181); also "Porchetto Streiaporco"—the surname was a long-standing name for a prominent

family of the Genoese merchant aristocracy (172); in Venice the patrician Giovanni Loredan was called merely *vacca* (cow) in the body of a contract – no other name was supplied (283).

11. Gratian, *Decretum, Causa* 33, *Questio* 5, c. 12, *Corpus juris canonici*, vol. 1, cols. 1254-55. "Mulieres viris suis debent subesse."

12. See, for example, the *Constitutem Legis: Constitutum Usus*, Pisa. Ms. 415, Beinecke Rare Book Library, Yale University. Comparable changes occurred in the law in Siena; see Eleanor Riemer, "Women in the Medieval City: Sources and Uses of Wealth by Sienese Women in the Thirteenth Century," Ph.D. diss., New York University, 1975, 71-73. For change to Roman dowry in Genoa, see Hughes, "From Brideprice to Dowry," 290ff.

13. Gratian, *Decretum, Causa* 33, *Questio* 5, c. 6, *Corpus juris canonici*, vol. 1, col. 1106. "Sine dote non facit coniugium."

14. Gigliola Villata di Renzo, *La tutela: Indagini sulla scuola dei glossatori* (Milan: Giuffre, 1975).

15. Manlio Bellomo, *Ricerche sui rapporti partrimoniali tra coniugi* (Milan: Giuffre, 1961), 8-25.

16. Julius Kirshner, "Wives' Claims against Insolvent Husbands," in *Women of the Medieval World*, ed. Julius Kirshner and Suzanne F. Wemple (London: Basil Blackwell, 1985), 256-303. *Vergere ad inopiam* was the legal phrase.

17. Reinhold C. Mueller, "The Procurators of San Marco," *Studi Veneziani* 13 (1971): 176.

18. The phrase is *dos estimata*.

19. *Libri Reformationes, Monumenta spectantia historiam slavorum meridiolium*, ed. Fr. Racki (Zagreb, 1879-97), vols. 10, 13, 27, 28, 29, known consecutively as *Monumenta Ragusina*, 1-4, vol. 5, 93.

20. Mueller, The Procurators of San Marco," 178-79, n. 141.

21. Thomas Kuehn, " '*Cum Consensu Mundualdi*': Legal Guardianship of Women in Quattrocento Florence," *Viator* 13 (1982): 322. Kuehn cites Giovanni Morelli, *Ricordi*, ed. Vittore Branca (Florence, 1956), 187-88.

22. Peter Spufford, *Money and Its Uses in the Middle Ages* (Cambridge: Cambridge University Press, 1988), 240-88.

23. Pierre Bonnassie, "A Family of the Barcelona Countryside and Its Economic Activities around the Year 1000," in *Early Medieval Society*, ed. Sylvia Thrupp (New York: Appleton-Century-Crofts, 1967), 103-123; see especially 120-21.

24. Mark Phillips, *The Memoir of Marco Parenti* (Princeton, N.J.: Princeton University Press, 1987), 23, 150-68. Phillips gives one detailed example of how two families in Florence felt about the quality of wedding gifts.

25. See Spufford, *Money and Its Uses*, 240ff.

26. Kirshner, "Wives' Claims," 266-75.

27. See Julius Kirshner, " 'Pursuing Honor while Avoiding Sin': The Monte della Dote of Florence," *Quaderni de Studi senesi* 87 (Siena, 1977): 177-258.

28. David Herlihy and Christiane Klapisch-Zuber, *Tuscans and Their Families* (New Haven, Conn.: Yale University Press, 1985), 202-31.

29. As Stanley Chojnacki notes in chapter 5 of this volume, some prominent men began to resist marriage by the late Middle Ages.

30. See Francesco Barbaro, "De re uxoria," ed. A. Gnesotto, *Atti e Memorie della R. Accademia di Scienze, lettere ed arti di Padova*, n.s. 32 (1915), 23-27, 62-100; translated by Benjamin Kohl as "On Wifely Duties," in *The Earthly Republic*, ed. Ronald Witt and Benjamin Kohl (Philadelphia: University of Pennsylvania Press, 1978), 189-228.

CHAPTER 5

Subaltern Patriarchs
Patrician Bachelors in Renaissance Venice

Stanley Chojnacki

Gender Roles, Feminine and Masculine

In a landmark article of the mid-1970s, Natalie Zemon Davis observed:

> We should be interested in the history of both women and men. . . . Our goal is to discover the range in sex roles and in sexual symbolism in different societies and periods, to find out what meaning they had and how they functioned to maintain the social order or to promote its change.[1]

Endorsing Davis's suggestion, this essay explores the connection between two aspects of sex-role relationships in the governing patriciate of fifteenth-century Venice. The first aspect concerns the impact on gender roles of changes in the "social order," specifically in the patriciate's social and political structures, which early in the Quattrocento were modified in ways that implicated gender differentiation among patricians (or nobles, as they called themselves). The other aspect concerns the relationship between the "range in sex roles and in sexual symbolism" among the women and that among the men of the patriciate. The hypothesis advanced is that the two aspects are closely connected: that changes in the social order led to changes in the range of gender identity among both women and men.

The principal focus of the investigation is upon differentiation among men, specifically between those who married and those who did not. Out of this focus emerge the two points advanced in the essay. The first is that patriarchal principles refined during the early Quattrocento as part of the self-definition of the ruling class underscored the anomalous masculine position of bachelors. The second is that the position thus occupied by bachelors overlapped in social practice with that of their married sisters—though within a structure that clearly favored men of whatever marital status. The ambiguous gender placement of unmarried male patricians illustrates the nuance and plasticity to be found along the "range in sex roles and in sexual symbolism" in concrete, evolving historical contexts.[2]

It is important to mention at the outset some ideas that inform the discussion. A critical one is the relativity (or "relationality") of gender: the status and roles of women cannot be understood without concurrent attention to those of men, and the reverse; they are constructed vis-à-vis one another.[3] These reciprocal influences work on two levels, the institutional and the personal; they can be configured in terms of the dynamic between structure and practice.[4] In the view advanced here, men and women tailor their practical actions with reference not only to structural definitions of gender behavior but also to their particular flesh-and-blood experience of the opposite sex. Laws and customs officially prescribed the elements of masculine and feminine identity in Venice. In practice, however, conformity with those prescriptions was mediated by the manifold contingencies in the interactions of individual men and women, with each other and with the laws and customs. It was through this double experience of gender that Venetian patricians constituted, or had constituted for them, their gender identities.[5]

Because both the institutional and the personal dimensions of gender were shaped by the circumstances of a specific historical context, they were subject to change as the context evolved over time. The laws and customs that prescribe how men and women are to act are constantly being revised in response to changes in the political, economic, social, and religious environment.[6] The revisions in turn lead men and women to adapt their actions and relationships to the altered gender structures—whether in conformity with or in deviation from them.[7] This sequence seems likely to occur most dramatically in moments of major cultural change, such as the Renaissance is traditionally considered to be. Historians are still in the early stages of formulating a periodization of gender principles and relations in European history, and there is much disagreement among them. But that the status of women, the touchstone of gender, went through different stages from the Middle Ages through the early modern period is a matter of consensus.[8] In this chronological exploration, the Renaissance, not surprisingly, is actively contested terrain, with the question first posed in 1976 by Joan Kelly, whether women had a Renaissance, still the pivot of discussion.[9] A useful approach to that encompassing question is to inquire, in inseparable complement to investigation of the experiences of women, whether, which, and how men had a Renaissance.

The Patrician Patriarchal Ideal

Early Renaissance Venice is an auspicious context for probing these conceptual and historiographic issues. During the first half of the fifteenth century, a body of legislation was enacted that elaborated with unprecedented precision the structures that defined the ruling class's political and social identity. These laws profoundly affected sex roles and sexual symbolism by prescribing new behavior and qualifications for both the men and the women of the class.[10] Central to this new articulation of patrician culture was reinforcement of the formal dominance of the father in public and private life. The roles and relationships of all the age and gender groups in patrician society were reconstituted on the basis of officially enhanced paternal authority over wives and children. Space limitations permit only a few samples of this legislation, but they convey its flavor. Fathers were now expressly preferred as sponsors of their sons' formal introduction into political life, were specifically charged with responsibility for their sons' behavior in public forums, and were officially recognized as the parties responsible for providing dowries for daughters.[11] Men elected to office were to be identified with their patronymic.[12] Fathers and husbands were held responsible for restraining sumptuary excesses by their daughters and wives.[13]

The intensification of formal paternal authority in the fifteenth century built on a centuries-old tradition.[14] Yet, although they were the supreme figures in public and private life, fathers were only the most prominent participants in a broader structure of patriarchy that encompassed all patrician men, whose privileges as hereditary nobles were inseparable from those that accrued from their maleness.[15] These two dimensions of privilege were integral to one another. Nearly every aspect of patrician status celebrated masculinity, starting with its essential entitlement, that of participating in government, an activity reserved to men. Membership in the political class thus entitled depended legally upon one's birth to a father who possessed the same privilege, inherited in turn from *his* father. Locking it all together was the blending of the paternal legacy and paternal direction in public life with the *patria potestas* in the domestic environment. The dynamic driving patrician culture from generation to generation can thus be seen as the fusion of patriarchal, patrilineal, and patrimonial objectives into a triptych of gender principles that guided, by blending, the domestic and official worlds of the governing class.

The pivotal role of fathers in this dynamic had been crucial to patrician politics and society from the first official articulation of the hereditary principle in 1323.[16] However, the enforcement of the principle in administrative practice appears to have occurred only gradually, in response to changing historical circumstances and reaching maturity only around 1400.[17] The definitive steps in the functional implementation of heredity were laws enacted in 1414 and 1430, which instituted procedures for checking the genealogical credentials of claimants to noble status and enjoined the officials charged with conducting the procedures thenceforward to keep careful records of them. From these laws, which expressly required that young men claiming noble status be presented by their fathers for the official scrutiny, derive the first official lists of the patriciate's membership, based on uniform tests of qualification, and inscribing the father-son link in the public documentation of the regime.[18]

These laws also mandated notation of the names of the mothers of the young claimants to noble status, as part of a campaign against liaisons between patrician men and women from the lowest classes. Indeed, mothers are identified, by given name and natal surname, in the records from this time forward. The emphasis on maternal status shows that married patrician women also were acquiring a new symbolic importance as part of their class's effort to achieve a castelike distinctiveness in the early Quattrocento.[19] The formal effect, however, was to reinforce the status of their husbands and sons: wellborn wives and mothers were means of enhancing the dignity of the men entitled to govern Venice today and those who would inherit the government tomorrow, by patrimonial and patrilineal succession. Thus, the institutional reformulation of the patriciate's public status was achieved by increased governmental direction of private behavior, by means of the enlarged authority officially bestowed on fathers to enforce the conformity of their womenfolk and children to the requirements of the class regime.

All these elements made the patriarchal husband and father the ideal type in patrician culture. The symbolic grandeur of patrician husbandhood was vividly displayed every year on Ascension Day in the feast of the *Sensa*. With lavish pageantry, the doge renewed Venice's "eternal dominion" over the Adriatic by ritually marrying it, thereby underscoring the authority of the patriarchal father in the blending of public and private life that was the essence of patrician culture.[20] The redoubtable image of the patrician father is beautifully rendered in the treatise *De re uxoria*, written in 1415-16 by the young patrician humanist Francesco Barbaro, and recently elucidated by Margaret King.[21] In brief, Barbaro held that the ultimate purpose of marriage among nobles was the continuance and prosperity of the regime. The excellence of the individual patrician, what gave him, or her, moral identity as a noble, lay in the integration of individual pursuits and family purpose into the broader aims of the nobility as a whole. Both fathers and mothers played important roles in the lofty enterprise of raising their children into this ideal, but it was the father specifically who, in Barbaro's words, should command and his wife who should cheerfully obey.[22] Barbaro thus invested patriarchal authority with a moral dignity carrying powerful sociopolitical resonance, which paralleled and complemented the legislation then refining the public culture of the noble regime. Fatherly primacy in public and private life was conveyed with special pointedness to the young men whose disciplining in the present and whose preparation for the patriarchal responsibilities of the next generation constituted one of the foremost duties of paternal authority.

The symmetry between Francesco Barbaro's ideal formulation of fatherhood and the principles of official patrician culture is attested in reverse in a treatise written six decades later by his grandson, Ermolao Barbaro. Consciously written as a mirror image of Francesco's *De re uxoria*, Ermolao's *De coelibatu* praised not the married state that merged with public duty but rather an ideal of bachelorhood that rejected it.[23] Ermolao preferred bachelorhood—strict celibacy, in fact—in the first instance because family responsibilities distracted the scholar from his learning. But equally important was his recognition, like that of his uxorious grandfather, that husband- and fatherhood in patrician reality entailed the relentless demands of public service as part of the seamless structure of patriarchal duty.

The Bachelor Exception

Ermolao Barbaro's unwillingness to conform to the ideal of the male noble ultimately led him to put his personal conviction on the score into practice by casting off his Venetian birthright. His dissent directs us to the matter of an alternative masculine identity among nobles.[24] Ermolao dramatized his choice by associating an apatriarchal manhood with a non-Venetian manhood. But there were other patrician men who, like Ermolao, did not marry, head households, or propagate and educate the next generation of noble patriarchs—but who, unlike him, remained in Venice living active lives as nobles. What was the relationship of these bachelors to the patriarchal paradigm? Were they denied it? Did they themselves deny its dignity by rejecting it? Or were they able to break the Barbaros' linkage by taking a productive part in the public and private life of the noble regime? These questions have implications for more than just the matter of masculine gender identity in a culture that celebrated the integrated private and public roles of the patriarch. Assessing the male periphery of patriarchy inevitably carries over into the significance of female identity in the unified structure of patrician gender relations. The pages that follow make a start in grappling with the seeming paradox of patriarchal bachelorhood by exploring it with specific reference to the chief locus of public life for patrician men in Venice, government service, from which all women were excluded absolutely.

A compelling reason for studying unmarried men is that there were so many of them: nearly half of male nobles who reached adulthood in the fifteenth century appear to have remained bachelors. To be precise, of 952 men from sixteen clans whose entry into adulthood can be documented, 412 (43.3 percent) apparently never married.[25] That is a striking percentage in a culture that assigned great dignity and importance to fatherhood, and it raises the first question: What accounts for such widespread deviation from a norm tied so eloquently and with so many practical advantages to the well-being of family and regime? The first part of an answer must be that some men did not marry because they did not live long enough to do so.[26] But among those who lived, some undoubtedly chose not to marry. There was only one Ermolao Barbaro, but in the fifteenth century growing numbers of lesser lights were similarly drawn to undistracted study and contemplation.[27] Another likely motive for elective bachelorhood was a disinclination to marry for sexual reasons. In addition to evidence of homosexual activity and suggestions of a gay culture disclosed by the research of both Patricia Labalme and Guido Ruggiero, we should allow also for the choice of heterosexual alternatives to the duty-laden role of patrician husband and father.[28] There can be little doubt that some male nobles simply did not want to be patriarchs.

Nevertheless, in view of the celebration, in law, politics, cultural tradition, and new intellectual fashion, of husband- and fatherhood as the culmination of male identity for nobles, the large incidence of bachelorhood must have been the result chiefly of force of circumstance rather than choice. There is reason to see as the principal circumstance the sharpening of patrician self-consciousness around 1400, given force in the legislation noted above. In addition to widening the gap between nobles and the populace, the heavy emphasis that the new laws put on genealogy increased sensitivity to status and advantage within the ruling class. A major consequence was the attachment of heightened importance to intraclass marriage alliances, and thus to marriage settlements, featuring large and growing dowries. At a time when many noble families were confronting shortages of disposable wealth, the rise in dowries propelled by intensified matrimonial ambition took an increasingly heavy bite out of family patrimonies. A Senate act in 1420 aimed at limiting dowries specifically mentioned the hardships that large marriage settlements for daughters were causing the other potential heirs, namely, the sons, of the fathers amassing them.[29]

Some of the severest hardships hit the marriage prospects of sons from the patrician rank and file. James C. Davis reported that by the mid-sixteenth century, patricians followed the practice of restricted marriage, limiting the number of marriages in a sibling group in order not to disperse the collective patrimony among too many brothers with conjugal families.[30] The same calculus was likely at work in the fifteenth century, applied both to sons and to marriageable daughters. As fathers poured their families' substance into dowries with which to marry their daughters into wealthy and influential families, they thereby reduced the marriage prospects of their sons, because the funneling of the sons' prospective inheritance into their sisters' dowries made them commensurately less appealing as recipients of large dowries in their turn. The effect built upon itself. As the language in the dowry-limiting law of 1420 noted, dowry inflation eroded the chances of marriage for some girls even as their sisters' marriage prospects were being enhanced.[31] Diminishing the pool of potential brides, this tendency also made the girls who remained in the pool harder to attain for male nobles of modest circumstances. Outside of the richest and most prestigious families, whose sons were likely to receive the most extravagant marriage settlements, a potential groom's eligibility seems to have rested in part on his brothers' bachelorhood – on, that is, their avoidance, willing or unwilling, of the patrimony-reducing burdens of heading families themselves.

The economics of dowry restitution also worked toward the same end. Because all the members of a fraternal group that had not been legally dissolved were liable for the restitution of the dowry of the wife of any one of them, brothers unencumbered with their own wives assured the fathers of potential sisters-in-law that the husband's family possessed resources adequate to guarantee eventual restitution of the dowry. With so much family treasure going into dowries, fathers of brides not surprisingly sought every assurance that their daughters would recover them at the ends of their marriages. For their part, men sought to allay this concern by explicitly pledging their goods toward the restitution of the dowries of their brothers' wives.[32] To the economic motive should be added a potent political one. At a time when many if not most noble families depended materially upon the remunerative government posts filled in Great Council elections, parents seeking in their daughter's husband a political ally were likely to regard as especially attractive a potential groom with unmarried brothers. Without wifely affines of their own, these bachelor brothers-in-law might be counted on to lend their supportive votes in the Council to the alliances into which their marrying brother had entered.[33]

Bachelors in Marriage Strategies and Government

Unfortunately, Venetians have not left much information describing their marriage strategies regarding men. Parents occasionally provided "dowries" for their sons, by which they meant property to guarantee restitution of the dowries brought by their wives. But we do not have much beyond such testamentary wishes to go on in reconstructing parental expectations for their sons' marriages.[34] It is possible, however, to make a rough reconstruction of the matrimonial activity of brothers. The following information is based on examination of ninety-one fifteenth-century sibling groups from six clans; I concentrate especially on the seventy-three groups that included at least two brothers.[35]

A couple of features are worth noting that bear upon the circumstances of bachelorhood in the nobility.[36] One is the unsurprising information that size influenced marriageability. The twenty-three fraternal groups in which all the brothers married were small, averaging 2.6 members.[37] By contrast, the forty-five groups in which some brothers married and others remained single averaged a whole brother larger, 3.7 compared with 2.6. This suggests a practice of ensuring the continuation of the line by getting one or two brothers married, then permitting (or requiring) additional brothers to marry as circumstances allowed.[38] The other and, I believe, more interesting feature is that in sixteen (more than one-third) of the forty-five groups consisting of both bachelors and husbands, the eldest brother was not among the ones who married. Although this surprising circumstance needs to be explored in greater prosopographical detail, it suggests that some families observed a discipline in which the firstborn son undertook (or was directed by a living *paterfamilias*) to work toward favorable marital circumstances for his siblings. At the very least, such a practice suggests nuance and complexity in the implementation of the patriarchal ideal among patrician sibling groups – never mind what it says about primogeniture. What is clear is that in nearly 69 percent of the families with several sons, one or more remained unmarried. This is strong evidence that the fraternal collaboration that, according to James Davis, fostered the patrimony-preserving strategy of marriage limitation among patrician sibling groups in the sixteenth century was already serving the same objective in the fifteenth. The cultural-psychological implications of this division of functions are considerable. In the century in which the patriciate fully formulated and enforced its identity as a genealogically precise, hereditary ruling class, in more than two-thirds of fraternal groups some brothers were fated to be nonpropagating instruments of domestic patriarchy.

However, if brothers met opposite destinies in the domestic environment, the divisions were not so clear-cut in political life. Unmarried men took an active part in the governmental activity that was the hallmark of their status as nobles and, according to the articulators of patrician culture, the symmetrical public counterpart to domestic patriarchy.[39] An examination of the political careers of fifty-eight men, members of fraternal groups from three clans, reveals that the 69 percent who married held an average of 4.8 offices. We might expect that of the sons-in-law of families that invested large dowries in their daughters' marriages and that expected a return in the form of support in the councils of government, where the material benefits of patrician status were distributed. What is more intriguing in the patriarchal environment is that the bachelor brothers of these married men averaged 2.7 offices.[40] To look at it from another angle, of the 239 offices accounted for by all the brothers in the sample, one-fifth (48) were held by men who never married. The sample cannot be taken as either representative or unrepresentative, but at least the officeholding record shows that as many as one-fifth of the political posts that were the distinguishing monopoly of this patriarchal governing class may have been assigned to men who did not themselves perpetuate their lines or hand a patrimony on to their own sons.[41] Bachelors constituted an important element in patrician government.

Officeholding bachelors, like all nobles, were conscious of their privilege as members of the ruling class, and they surely welcomed the stipends they received from their positions. However, in a parallel of their role in the strategy of the fraternal group, officeholding by bachelors may also have savored of instrumentalization on behalf of the larger community of which they were a second-echelon element. Indeed, their function as government officials may have been an extension of their role within the family: the function, namely, of holding government jobs and casting electoral votes in line with a family interest supervised by their fathers and married brothers. The context of the officeholding of bachelors (as of all male patricians) in the fifteenth century is the growing eagerness of families to get their sons into government jobs. The eagerness is evident in an increase of more than 50 percent in the number of young men registered as patricians between the first and second halves of the Quattrocento.[42] Bachelors in the council chambers and in remunerative office may have been especially valuable to their marrying brothers, whose wives' natal relatives likely regarded unmarried male in-laws as potential political allies unburdened with affinal obligations of their own.

Encouraging this instrumental characterization of the governmental role of bachelors is its confinement to the lesser offices in the governmental apparatus. Subordinate contributors to patriarchal domestic strategies, unmarried men were also locked into the lower echelons of the patriciate's official activity. At the most influential levels, the patriarchal paradigm uniting domestic with governmental authority held overwhelming sway. Among seventy-four men from fourteen clans who served between 1438 and 1455 in the Ducal Council, the Senate and its annex, the *Zonta*, or the Council of Ten, only one was a lifetime bachelor.[43] This stark contrast between a husbandly monopoly of the important posts and the sturdy presence of bachelors in the lesser offices may owe something to the possible coincidence of bachelorhood and early death speculated upon earlier; as Robert Finlay has demonstrated, a man had to be mature and seasoned to gain election to the highest offices.[44] It may also owe something to the coincidence of powerful government position and family wealth: Finlay and other scholars have argued that political power in Quattrocento Venice was the preserve of a small oligarchy of wealthy families, of the kind that might have had the means to marry more sons than their rank-and-file counterparts.[45] Yet, even discounting for these factors, the nearly complete confinement of bachelors to posts of modest prestige and power points to bachelorhood as a double liability, signifying a lesser, nonauthoritative male status in both the domestic and the official environments of ruling-class patriarchy.

Bachelors as Subaltern Patriarchs

However, from the perspective of "the range in sex roles and in sexual symbolism" across gender lines, the evidence of bachelors' involvement in patrician government encourages a more nuanced reading. Certainly, with its suggestion of the instrumental inscription of bachelors in family strategy supervised by their married brothers, the seeming exclusion of unmarried men from high office suggests different layers of patriarchal privilege. Here, given the exiguousness of the sample at hand, I can only raise issues to be explored more thoroughly elsewhere. But it is worth recalling that, although as many as two-fifths of adult patrician males may have been bachelors, they accounted for only one-fifth of the offices in the government: not an insignificant proportion, but smaller than their overall presence within male society. The inescapable uncertainty about the mortality of the unmarried men cautions against making too much of these proportions. But the discrepancy seems to lend plausibility to the idea that, just as some men consciously rejected domestic patriarchy, some also had a lesser commitment to its official counterpart – to their class's political vocation – than did their married brothers. Many more men than just Ermolao Barbaro likely elected not to share in either the public or the private dimension of noble patriarchy.

These initial findings suggest that in both the domestic and the governmental arena of patriarchal authority, the experience of bachelors covered a variety of choices and restrictions, from intense commitment to the interests of family and regime to cool (or assertive) aloofness from them. The unmarried male population ranged from men with active political careers to office-fleeing contemplatives like Ermolao Barbaro. As Guido Ruggiero has suggested, it also included both homosexuals cultivating a subculture of their own and sexual exploiters of the women of the populace.[46] And it probably ran the psychological gamut from economically disqualified patriarchs manqué to men who willingly declined the responsibilities of husband- and fatherhood. More than for the husbands who realized, and were defined by, the patriarchal ideal in domestic and public spheres, for bachelors the denial (or rejection) of patriarchy could loosen the tethers of conformity to the requirements of mainstream patrician manhood in the same degree that it closed off the highest rewards that the culture reserved for men.

So from the perspective of normative patriarchy, newly articulated in the Quattrocento as the fulcrum by which the patrician regime intensified its identity as an exclusive elite, permanent bachelors may be seen as resembling in certain respects their marrying sisters more than their marrying brothers.[47] Like noble wives, noble bachelors participated in, benefited from, were essential to, but occupied a lesser status in their class's official and domestic culture. Deprived of patriarchal authority—and indeed subordinated instruments of its objectives—bachelors and married women alike had less inducement than married men to identify themselves psychologically with the discipline of its requirements. Both categories could therefore construct nuances of identity along a range of possibilities not restricted by the responsibilities of dominance—albeit within parameters enjoined by a patriarchal regime and enforced by individual patriarchs.[48] For women, the junctions of choice lay between loyalty to natal and to marital family, and in at least some cases between marriage and religious profession.[49] Although the early findings presented here barely scratch the surface of the experience of bachelors, they encourage the hypothesis that it too ran a gamut, from active contribution to the purposes of family and regime to token or outright nonparticipation in the domestic and official life of the patriciate.

This is not to say that the agency of either patrician wives or bachelors threatened to subvert or even to deviate significantly from the blended purposes of family and regime. On the contrary, members of both categories could find reasons to associate themselves with their class's values and aims. Mothers especially recognized the great advantages for their children's prospects that derived from adherence to the collective interest and its discipline; bachelors characteristically directed their beneficence toward their families.[50] Nonetheless, both groups deviated from the patriarchal mainstream in sometimes convergent ways; anecdotal evidence, for instance, shows unmarried men sharing the bilineal social orientation of their married sisters as well as supporting the patrilineal aims of their married brothers.[51] Taking it all together, we may ponder the idea that bachelors shared with married patrician women a perpetually liminal status in, and at the same time an instrumental indispensability to, the social, political, and cultural order of the patrician regime.[52]

Yet in the end the similarity must not be overstated. Legal dispositions and customary values had over the centuries dug a yawning gender gulf between women and men whether married or unmarried, a gulf that deepened from around 1400 as public and private life came to be increasingly regulated by official prescriptions, obligations, and definitions, the principal purpose of which was the entrenchment of the noble regime and the families that, benefiting from inclusion in it, accepted the obligation to sustain it.[53] As male participants in this culture, bachelors were obliged to accept some measure of the discipline imposed on all the men in noble lineages, but—in contrast with even the most economically and socially influential women—they also shared in its privileges, material and moral, which legislators and humanist commentators alike reserved to men alone. Serving in government, thereby contributing to the purposes that benefited themselves, their kinsmen, and their regime, these unmarried brothers can be seen as subaltern participants in patriarchy precisely by reason of the uncertain boundary between the public and private dimensions of the culture of the hereditary nobility. By their activity in government, their instrumental inscription into a familial marital strategy, and their mentoring and economic contributions to the vocations of nieces and nephews, they shared in the patrician masculine identity associated with the integrated values and objectives of the patriarchal lineage in the patriarchal regime.[54]

Notes

An earlier version of this essay was read at the annual meeting of the American Historical Association in December 1989. It was written in the peerless scholarly environment of the National Humanities Center, with the support of fellowships from the Andrew Mellon Foundation and the National Endowment for the Humanities, to both of which I express my deep gratitude. I also gratefully acknowledge my indebtedness to Laura M. Noren for research assistance and to Judith M. Bennett, Monica E. Chojnacka, and Barbara J. Harris for valuable suggestions on earlier drafts.

1. Natalie Zemon Davis, " 'Women's History' in Transition: The European Case," *Feminist Studies* 3 (1976): 90.

2. The specific issue addressed here, namely, differentiation among males within patriarchal structures, has importance for gender in all historical contexts. However, the factors I discuss are inseparable from the peculiar social and political character of Venice's patrician regime as it developed in the fourteenth and fifteenth centuries. I propose to address

elsewhere the relationship of Venice's patrician culture to that of Florence with regard to gender practices in the two Renaissance republics. For now, the conclusions presented here must be considered in their Venetian context. On the importance of attending to the distinctiveness of different contexts, see Clifford Geertz, "Local Knowledge: Fact and Law in Comparative Perspective," in *Local Knowledge: Further Essays in Interpretive Anthropology* (New York: Basic Books, 1983), 167-231.

3. For varied approaches to gender, see Sherry B. Ortner, "Is Female to Male as Nature Is to Culture?" in *Woman, Culture, and Society*, ed. Michelle Zimbalist Rosaldo and Louise Lamphere (Stanford, Calif.: Stanford University Press, 1974), 67-87; Joan W. Scott, "Gender: A Useful Category of Historical Analysis," *American Historical Review* 91 (1986): 1053-75; R. W. Connell, *Gender and Power* (Stanford, Calif.: Stanford University Press, 1987).

4. On the interplay of structure and practice (or agency) in a process labeled "structuration," see Anthony Giddens, *Central Problems in Social Theory: Action, Structure and Contradiction in Social Analysis* (Berkeley: University of California Press, 1979), especially 1-48. For an application to gender issues, see Connell, *Gender and Power*, 61-64.

5. See Stanley Chojnacki, " 'The Most Serious Duty': Motherhood, Gender, and Patrician Culture in Renaissance Venice," in *Refiguring Woman: Perspectives on Gender and the Italian Renaissance*, ed. Marilyn Migiel and Juliana Schiesari (Ithaca, N.Y.: Cornell University Press, 1991), 134-38.

6. For an excellent illustration of changes in conceptions of what constituted marriage in Florence as a result of statutory adjustments regarding property claims between husbands and wives, see Julius Kirshner, "Maritus Lucretur Dotem Uxoris Sue Premortue in Late Medieval Florence," *Zeitschrift der Savigny-Stiftung für Rechtsgeschichte Kan. Abt.* 108 (1991): 111-55.

7. For a consideration of how human agents' consciousness of the structures in which they act works to change those structures, see Giddens, *Central Problems in Social Theory*, 198-225. For the way specific structures helped shape individual identity in sixteenth-century France, see Natalie Zemon Davis, "Boundaries and the Sense of Self in Sixteenth-Century France," in *Reconstructing Individualism: Autonomy, Individuality, and the Self in Western Thought*, ed. Thomas C. Heller, Morton Sosna, and David E. Wellbery (Stanford, Calif.: Stanford University Press, 1986), 53-63.

8. Useful summary comments can be found in Judith M. Bennett, *Women in the Medieval English Countryside: Gender and Household in Brigstock before the Plague* (New York: Oxford University Press, 1987), 3-9. See also the essays in Renate Bridenthal and Claudia Koonz, *Becoming Visible: Women in European History* (New York: Houghton Mifflin, 1976); and Renate Bridenthal, Claudia Koonz, and Susan M. Stuard, *Becoming Visible: Women in European History*, 2d ed. (New York: Houghton Mifflin, 1987).

9. Joan Kelly, "Did Women Have a Renaissance?" in Bridenthal and Koonz, *Becoming Visible*, 137-64 (reprinted in Bridenthal et al., *Becoming Visible*, 2d ed., 174-201). The continuing influence of her essay is apparent in the introductions and various essays in Margaret W. Ferguson, Maureen Quilligan, and Nancy J. Vickers, eds., *Rewriting the Renaissance: The Discourses of Sexual Difference in Early Modern Europe* (Chicago: University of Chicago Press, 1986); and in Migiel and Schiesari, *Refiguring Woman*. For examples of its heuristic application to specific contexts, see Judith C. Brown, "A Woman's Place Was in the Home: Women's Work in Renaissance Tuscany," in Ferguson et al., *Rewriting the Renaissance*, 206-24; and Nicholas Terpstra, "Women in the Brotherhood: Gender, Class, and Politics in Renaissance Bolognese Confraternities," *Renaissance and Reformation / Renaissance et Réforme* 26 (1990): 193-212.

10. Stanley Chojnacki, "Political Adulthood in Fifteenth-Century Venice," *American Historical Review* 19 (1986): 791-810; idem, "Marriage Legislation and Patrician Society in Fifteenth-Century Venice," in *Law, Custom, and the Social Fabric in Medieval Europe: Essays in Honor of Bryce Lyon*, ed. Bernard S. Bachrach and David Nicholas (Kalamazoo, Mich.: Medieval Institute, 1990), 163-84.

11. A law of 1414 required fathers, if alive and in Venice, personally to register their sons for government service; Archivio di Stato, Venice (henceforth abbreviated ASV), Maggior Consiglio, Reg. 21, Leona, ff. 241v-242r; a law of 1443 authorized fines and the loss of officeholding privileges for fathers whose sons misbehaved during meetings of the Great Council; ibid., Reg. 22, Ursa, f. 148v. A law imposing a limit on marriage settlements identified fathers as the agents of a ruinous rise in settlements; ASV, Senato, Misti, Reg. 53, f. 70rv.

12. ASV, Maggior Consiglio, Reg. 21, Leona, f. 127rv.

13. A fine authorized in 1463 for excessive expenditure on dress by women was to be imposed on the "husbands, fathers, or others with authority over the offending women [maritis, sive patribus, vel illis sub quorum potestate contrafacientes mulieres essent]"; ASV, Senato, Terra, Reg. 5, f. 46r.

14. See Giorgio Zordan, "I vari aspetti della comunione familiare di beni nella Venezia dei secoli XI-XII," *Studi veneziani* 8 (1966): 127-94.

15. The formative phases of Venice's hereditary patrician regime are the subject of a book I am currently writing. For orientation to the establishment and chronology of the regime, see Frederic C. Lane, "The Enlargement of the Great Council of Venice," in *Florilegium Historiale: Essays Presented to Wallace K. Ferguson*, ed. J. G. Rowe and W. H. Stockdale (Toronto: University of Toronto Press, 1971), 236-74; Stanley Chojnacki, "In Search of the Venetian Patriciate: Families and Factions in the Fourteenth Century," in *Renaissance Venice*, ed. J. R. Hale (London: Faber & Faber, 1973), 47-90; idem, "Political Adulthood"; John Easton Law, "Age Qualification and the Venetian Constitution: The Case of the Capello Family," *Papers of the British School at Rome* 39 (1971): 125-37. For a dissenting view, see Guido Ruggiero, "Modernization and the Mythic State in Early Renaissance Venice: The Serrata Revisited," *Viator* 10 (1979): 245-56.

16. Lane, "Enlargement of the Great Council," 258.

17. The long evolution of effective enforcement of heredity is traced in my book in progress. See, meanwhile, Law, "Age Qualification and the Venetian Constitution."

18. ASV, Maggior Consiglio, Reg. 21, Leona, ff. 241v-242r (1414); Reg. 22, Ursa, f. 88r (1430). The officials charged with conducting the tests were the state attorneys, the Avogadori di Comun. The official records of the tests begin in 1408; ASV, Avogaria di Comun, Balla d'Oro, Reg. 162/1. See Chojnacki, "Political Adulthood," 798-99.

19. Chojnacki, "Marriage Legislation," 167-71.

20. Edward Muir, *Civic Ritual in Renaissance Venice* (Princeton, N.J.: Princeton University Press, 1981), 119-22.

21. Francesco Barbaro, *Francisci Barbari liber de re uxoria in partes duas*, ed. Attilio Gnesotto (Padua: Randi, 1915). See Margaret L. King, "Caldiera and the Barbaros on Marriage and the Family," *Journal of Medieval and Renaissance Studies* 6 (1976): 31-35; idem, *Venetian Humanism in an Age of Patrician Dominance* (Princeton, N.J.: Princeton University Press, 1985), 92-98.

22. Barbaro, *De re uxoria*, 63.

23. Ermolao Barbaro, *De coelibatu, De officio legati*, ed. Vittore Branca (Florence: Olschki, 1969). See King, *Venetian Humanism*, 197-202; Vittore Branca, "Un trattato inedito di Ermolao Barbaro: il *De coelibatu libri*," *Bibliothèque d'Humanisme et Renaissance* 14 (1952): 83-98.

24. On Barbaro's rejection of his Venetian identity, see King, *Venetian Humanism*, 198-205. Branca states that Ermolao fully accepted the dignity of the married state for men other than himself; "Un trattato inedito," 86.

25. This information is derived from two sources. The first is the records of the Balla d'Oro or Barbarella, the exercise by which patrician youths established their credentials for adult membership in the ruling class, providing proof of legitimate patrician birth and attainment of age eighteen. A total of 952 young men from sixteen clans who presented their credentials from 1410 to 1490 constituted the basic population for this analysis; their acts of presentation are in ASV, Avogaria di Comun, Balla d'Oro, Regs. 162, 163, 164. Their marital activity was then tracked in the most complete available list of patrician marriages, the

"Libro di nozze patrizie," compiled in the sixteenth century by Marco Barbaro; Barbaro's autograph manuscript is in the Biblioteca Nazionale Marciana, Venice, Codici italiani, classe VII, 156 (=8492). It is important to note, however, that the Barbaro compilation includes marriage notices for 132 men who did not register for the Barbarella. Adding these men would enlarge the population to 1,084, making it more complete, but it would also add disproportionally to the percentage of husbands, as there is no comparable source identifying men who failed to register for the Barbarella but remained single. For that reason, I have limited the analysis to Barbarella registrants. The sixteen clans examined are as follows: Arimondo, Balbi, Da Canal, Lando, Loredan, Morosini, Muazzo, Da Mula, Navagero, Pisani, Polani, Priuli, Ruzzini, Vitturi, Zane, Zulian. My test of the accuracy of Barbaro's compilation of marriages will be presented elsewhere. On this manuscript, see Emmanuele Antonio Cicogna, *Delle inscrizioni veneziane*, 6 vols. (Venice: G. Orlandelli, 1824-53), 6:24; on the Barbarella, see Chojnacki, "Political Adulthood," 801-4.

26. To note this is to recognize that the entire inquiry rests on a basic uncertainty, deriving from the impossibility of determining the percentage of men who reached documented "political" adulthood but died before attaining the normal marriage age of around thirty; on men's age at marriage, see Stanley Chojnacki, "Measuring Adulthood: Adolescence and Gender in Renaissance Venice," *Journal of Family History* 17 (1992): 378-79. Although it is unwarranted to assume in all cases that men who died in their twenties would have married had they survived into their thirties, the bachelorhood of many of them may indeed have been the result not of the choices or forces examined here, but simply of premature (i.e., prenuptial) death. Some support for this conclusion comes from the fact that many more "bachelor" brothers than "husband" brothers fail to appear in the officeholding records; the complexities of interpreting this information are discussed below. However, because the great majority of bachelors did, like husbands, hold office at one time or another, it is necessary to account for their persistent adult presence and their bachelorhood. In the absence of any sure means of determining who among the bachelors were prevented from marrying by death, I treat bachelors as an undifferentiated category.

27. The valuable "profiles" of Venetian humanists in King, *Venetian Humanism*, 315-449, show that most either married or embraced clerical careers. The choice of the latter vocation may reflect a desire, like that of Ermolao, to avoid familial entanglements. In addition, as King notes, the prominent humanists came from the wealthiest and most influential tier of the patriciate (277); on the greater frequency of marriage among this tier, see below. For one prominent patrician humanist's ambivalence about the tension between the desire for study and the duty of public service, see the references to Leonardo Giustinian in Patricia H. Labalme, *Bernardo Giustiniani: A Venetian of the Quattrocento* (Rome: Edizioni di Storia e Letteratura, 1969), 9-10.

28. Patricia H. Labalme, "Sodomy and Venetian Justice in the Renaissance," *Tijdschrift voor Rechtsgeschiedenis (The Legal History Review)* 52 (1984): 217-54; Guido Ruggiero, "Sodom and Venice," in *The Boundaries of Eros: Sex Crime and Sexuality in Renaissance Venice* (New York: Oxford University Press, 1985). Michael J. Rocke, studying homosexuality in Florence, has noted an age-specific, temporary homosexual experience turning into a heterosexual alternative as men grew to full maturity; Rocke, "Il controllo della omosessualità a Firenze nel XV secolo: Gli *Ufficiali di Notte*," *Quaderni storici*, n.s., no. 66 (1987): 708-9.

29. "Divitum substantia attenuatur in maximum damnum et preiuditium suorum heredum" ("The economic substance [of dowry-providing fathers] is reduced, entailing severe damage and prejudice for their heirs"); ASV, Senato, Misti Reg. 53, f. 70rv. The preamble of the act is reprinted in Giulio Bistort, *Il Magistrato alle Pompe della Repubblica di Venezia* (Venice, 1909; reprint Bologna: Forni, 1969), 107. This legislation is discussed at length in Chojnacki, "Marriage Legislation," 164-66 and passim. In her will of 1391, Pellegrina Venier Basadona acknowledged with loyal gratitude that "my father took so little account of his need to provide for his many children that he gave me a marriage settlement worth more than half his worldly goods [mio pare non aver respeto a la so condizion de tanti fioli et fie ch el me de tanta de dota et coriedi plu de la mitade de zo che lo avena al mondo]." She there-

fore made him her residuary heir, entreating her husband not to be aggrieved. ASV, Notarile, Testamenti, Bu. 364, Darvasio, no. 44. See other evidence of daughters' dowries favored over sons' inheritance in Stanley Chojnacki, "The Power of Love: Wives and Husbands in Late Medieval Venice," in *Women and Power in the Middle Ages*, ed. Mary Erler and Maryanne Kowaleski (Athens: University of Georgia Press, 1988), 129.

30. James C. Davis, *A Venetian Family and Its Fortune, 1500-1900: The Donà and the Conservation of Their Wealth* (Philadelphia: American Philosophical Society, 1975), 93-106.

31. The preamble to the law of 1420 noted that fathers of richly endowed wives were consequently "forced to imprison their [other] daughters in convents, amid the latters' well warranted tears and wailing [coguntur in monasteriis carcerare, cum dignis lacrimis et plantibus ipsarum]." Bistort, *Il Magistrato alle Pompe*, 107.

32. An example of brothers committing themselves and their property toward the restitution of the dowry of their brother's wife: "The noble lords Nicolò and Piero da Mosto, with their heirs, declare that they have received their sister-in-law, Isabetta, and her entire dowry, pledging all their property, movable and immovable, present and future. [Manifestum fecerunt viri nobiles domini Nicolaus et Petrus de Musto . . . cum suis heredibus quod receperunt eam dictam dominam Isabetham cognatam suam et totam suam repromissam predictam super omnibus et singulis bonis suis mobilibus et immobilibus presentibus et futuris.]" ASV, Giudici del Proprio, Vadimoni, Reg. 4, f. 25. On the other hand, some brothers who married sought to keep their wives' dowries separate from the substance shared with their brothers in the *fraterna*, or collectively held patrimony. In a *divisio*, or agreement dissolving the shared fraternal inheritance, by which in 1416 Piero Soranzo was economically separated from his brothers Donato and Jacopo, the three brothers explicitly excepted marriage portions from the goods that they were dividing: "dowries, trousseaux, and other marital assigns are and should remain the property of him or them who now possess them [que dos sive repromissa, correda, et provissiones sint et esse debeant illius et illorum nostrum qui habuit, habet, aut habuerunt vel habent]." ASV, Cancelleria inferiore, Notai, Bu. 71, Dotto, prot. ff. 21v-22r.

33. The marriage ties of brothers could also be knotted together in more complex coalitions. That is more likely to have happened in made marriages than in the calculations of fathers of daughters with large dowries. For cases of brothers-in-law from different families combining, see Stanley Chojnacki, "Kinship Ties and Young Patricians in Fifteenth-Century Venice," *Renaissance Quarterly* 38 (1985): 262-68. On widespread patrician dependence upon political office, see Donald E. Queller, "Welfare Jobs for the Nobles," in *The Venetian Patriciate: Reality versus Myth* (Urbana: University of Illinois Press, 1986).

34. In a will of 1469 (?) Ermolao Pisani made his two sons his residuary heirs, "with the understanding that before the distribution of my estate, my son Giovanni is to have one thousand gold ducats, since his brother had more than that for his dowry [hoc declarato quod Ihoannes [*sic*] filius meus primo et ante omnia et super partem habeat ducatos mille auri eo quod plus habuit in doctem . . . frater suus]." ASV, Notarile, Testamenti, Bu. 1238, Tomei, Pt. 1, no. 15. In a rare instance of a father requiring his son to marry, Nicolò Muazzo, testating in 1420, conditioned his son Piero's share in his state and inclusion among his executors upon the young man's marrying. ASV, Notarile, Testamenti, Bu. 1255, Zane, Protocollo, f. 184v (11 February 1419/20).

35. The fraternal groups were reconstituted using the Barbarella registration records in ASV, Avogadori di Comun, Balla d'Oro, Regs. 162, 163, 164. Their matrimonial experience was taken from Marco Barbaro, "Libro di nozze patrizie" (see full reference above, note 25). The fraternal groups ranged in size from two to nine; the average was 3.26 brothers, the median, 3, and the most frequently encountered (modal) size was 2 brothers (twenty-three of the seventy-three groups). The information available on these men is not precise enough or extensive enough to warrant a lot of reporting, and it proved impossible to get an adequate grip on the variables of numbers of brothers, presence of sisters, and family wealth and influence to be able to come to any sensible conclusions about any one of these with reference to the others. Thus, of the five cases in which no brother married, four (80 percent) had

sisters who married, which might be expected as an influential circumstance of wholesale male bachelorhood. But any conclusions along those lines are undercut by the fact that of the twenty-three cases in which all brothers married, seventeen (73.9 percent) had sisters who married, close to the same percentage as in the nonmarrying groups. Among the forty-five fraternal groups that included both bachelors and husbands within the group, the proportion with marrying sisters was 71.1 percent ($n = 32$). These percentages seem too close to warrant any conclusions, especially in the absence of consistent information about family wealth and prestige. Finally, the lack of complete information on brothers who did not marry, and of any consistent information at all on sisters who did not marry, keeps us in ignorance of the total composition of the sibling groups.

36. The information may be schematically displayed as follows:

Marital Activities in 73 Fraternal Groups

All brothers marry	23	(31.5%)
Eldest marries; at least one other a bachelor	29	(39.7%)
Eldest a bachelor; at least one other marries	16	(21.9%)
None marries	5	(6.9%)
Total	73	(100%)

37. The information in tabular form:

Average Sizes of Categories among 73 Fraternal Groups

All brothers marry	2.6
Eldest marries; at least one other a bachelor	4
Eldest a bachelor; at least one other marries	3.3
None marries	2.2

38. We should note, however, that six of these forty-five divided groups consisted of two brothers, only one of whom married.

39. This information comes from reconstruction of the governmental careers of fifty-eight men who came of age in the 1460s and 1470s, members of seventeen multiple-brother groups from the Arimondo, Balbi, and Da Canal clans. The nucleus of the sample is the men from those clans who registered for the Barbarella from 1465 to 1475; to this core were added their brothers, older and younger. The governmental activity of these men was reconstructed from the following sources, all in the ASV: Segretario alle Voci, Universi, serie antica, Reg. 6; Avogaria di Comun, Prove di Età, Regs. 169, 170, 171. Marriages were compiled from Barbaro, "Libro di nozze," and from ASV, Avogaria di Comun, Balla d'Oro, Regs. 164, 165.

40. The forty men who married (69 percent) were collectively elected to office 191 times, averaging about 4.8 offices per husband. The eighteen bachelor brothers (31 percent) accounted for forty-eight offices, an average of 2.7 per man.

41. Many of the offices held by husbands were of course entered into before marriage. I do not mean to suggest that the marital state as such was either a qualification for or a disqualification from office, but precisely the reverse: that participation in the government was a consequence of patrician male birth rather than of marital vocation.

42. In the sixteen sample houses, 417 young men registered between 1408 and 1450; between 1451 and 1497 the number rose to 648, a 55 percent increase. ASV, Avogaria di Comun, Balla d'Oro, Regs. 162, 163, 164.

43. ASV, Segretario alle Voci, Universi, serie antica, Reg. 4. This register was used for this examination because, unlike Reg. 6, which was examined above, it includes the high offices. To the seventy-four whose marital status could be identified should be added three whose identities or marital status remain uncertain. Only fourteen rather than sixteen clans appear, because the Muazzo and the Navagero clans had no men elected to the offices

considered. Many of the men encountered held two or all three of the offices considered, sometimes for many terms.

44. Robert Finlay, "The Venetian Patriciate as a Gerontocracy." *Journal of Medieval and Renaissance Studies* 8 (1978): 157-78. However, many of the politically active bachelors held posts reserved for men in their thirties, that is, well into the normal age of marriage for men.

45. Indeed, evidence seems to bear this idea out: of thirteen holders of high office from six clans examined in detail, ten belonged to fraternal groups in which all brothers married, only three having bachelor brothers. The clans are the Arimondo, Balbi, Da Canal, Lando, Da Mula, and Vitturi. It was impossible to reconstruct the sibling groups of an additional three men from these clans. Note that the five Balbi men belonged to only two groups. On the presence of an oligarchy at the patriciate's center, see Gaetano Cozzi, "Authority and the Law in Renaissance Venice," in Hale, *Renaissance Venice*, 293-345; Giorgio Cracco, "Patriziato e oligarchia a Venezia nel Tre-Quattrocento" in *Florence and Venice: Comparisons and Relations*, ed. Sergio Bertelli, Nicolai Rubinstein, and Craig Hugh Smyth, 2 vols. (Florence: La Nuova Italia, 1979) 1:71-98; Robert Finlay, *Politics in Renaissance Venice* (New Brunswick, N.J.: Rutgers University Press, 1980), 59-81 and passim.

46. Ruggiero, *The Boundaries of Eros*, passim.

47. For discussions of the informal power of married patrician women in Venice, see Chojnacki, "The Power of Love" and "The Most Serious Duty"; and Dennis Romano, *Patricians and Popolani: The Social Foundations of the Venetian Renaissance State* (Baltimore: Johns Hopkins University Press, 1989), 131-39.

48. On the capacity of members of nondominant groups to construct identities on the basis of their relationships with the constraints imposed on them, see the comments regarding women in Davis, "Boundaries and the Sense of Self," 61-63.

49. Chojnacki, "The Most Serious Duty," 148-51.

50. On mothers, see Chojnacki, "Kinship Ties and Young Patricians," 255-60; idem, "The Most Serious Duty," 144-48 and passim. On the family orientation of bachelors, one example may stand for many: in his will of 1502 the unmarried Francesco Morosini, who, having registered for the Barbarella in 1471, was then probably approaching age fifty, divided his estate between his married sister, to whom he willed fifty ducats, and his brother, whom he designated as his residuary heir. ASV, Notarile, Testamenti, Bu. 66, Busenello, no. 160. His Barbarella registration is in ASV, Avogaria di Comun, Balla d'Oro, Reg. 164, f. 218r.

51. Scattered evidence shows unmarried men supporting the political careers of their sisters' sons and contributing to the dowries of their sisters' daughters. On the other hand, see the words of a bachelor who took responsibility for fraternal nieces: Antonio da Canal, testating in 1519, named as his executors and universal heirs the three daughters of his late brother, Girolamo, "whom I have always regarded as my own daughters [le qual o sempre tenute et reputate mie fie proprie]." ASV, Notarile, Testamenti, Bu. 66, Busenello, no. 43. For the effects of the bilineal social orientation of patrician wives, see Chojnacki, "Kinship Ties and Young Patricians," 259-68.

52. The role of liminal age and gender groups in the articulation of the political and social culture of Florence's patrician regime is a central theme in Richard C. Trexler, *Public Life in Renaissance Florence* (New York: Academic Press, 1980). On liminality in Venice, see Chojnacki, "Political Adulthood," 807-10.

53. The acceptance by patricians of discipline as a means of securing benefits is discussed in Chojnacki, "Political Adulthood" and "Marriage Legislation."

54. In a useful formulation, they can be seen as achieving a kind of publicly defined, encouraged, and rewarded generativity, in Erik Erikson's notion of a person's "interest in establishing and guiding the next generation." Erik H. Erikson, "Growth and Crises of the Healthy Personality," *Psychological Issues* 1 (1959): 97. See also Daniel J. Levinson et al., *The Seasons of a Man's Life* (New York: Random House, 1979), 196ff.

CHAPTER 6

Friars, Sanctity, and Gender
Mendicant Encounters with Saints, 1250-1325

John Coakley

In the late thirteenth and early fourteenth centuries, the mendicant orders had a major interest in making saints. In addition to sponsoring several successful candidates for papal canonization, they promoted literally scores of the new cults that attracted more purely local followings in Mediterranean, especially Italian, cities.[1] In those cities, as André Vauchez has shown, "the selection of saints conformed approximately to the composition of society," in contrast to the model in northern Europe, which favored the ruling classes.[2] Thus the friars, uncloistered and committed to pastoral work, found their saints among the urban population with whom they had contact.[3] We are fortunate to have evidence of those contacts from many mendicant authors who wrote vitae of recent saints for which they could rely on either themselves or others as eyewitnesses.[4] Such vitae give us a fairly close look, through friars' eyes, at their encounters with the people they would call saints, within the social world they shared with them. Moreover, those saints included persons of both sexes: fellow friars and laymen but also a comparatively large number of women.[5] This fact in turn enables us by comparison to consider the role of gender in the sanctity that emerged from those encounters; this essay is about that role, specifically in its religious aspects.

A word is in order about the phenomenon of "sanctity" as I am understanding it here, namely, as a function of the interaction between a particular extraordinary person and those who, on the basis of that interaction, decide to call him or her a "saint." "To be a saint," as Pierre Delooz has written, "is finally to be a saint *for others*, to acquire the reputation of saint from others and to play the role of saint for others."[6] Thus venerators are as intrinsic to the phenomenon of sanctity as saints themselves, in the sense that it is they who create the saints. Sanctity is often discussed in terms of "ideals," that is, various "harmonious ensembles of virtues" that characterize saints in given historical settings.[7] Indeed, articulating an "ideal" can be a useful way of summarizing the virtues implicitly valued by the venerators of a given saint. But an ideal itself does not tell us much about the meanings that the saint's virtues (or other attributes or actions) held for the venerators, or the concerns that these elicited in them or helped them to articulate. It does not, in other words, tell us about that encounter between venerator and saint that lies at the heart of the phenomenon of sanctity. We need therefore to penetrate beyond ideals, to discern more directly the meanings of saints for venerators, and consequently to bring the latter, as essential actors, out of the shadows and into our field of vision.

The question of the significance of gender in mendicant sanctity illustrates the usefulness of moving venerators into view. It has become clear that friars had a particular interest in female saints. Thus André Vauchez has made the intriguing observation that mendicant influence in this period had two effects on local urban sanctity, one a "clericalization," in the sense of a favoring of the cults of male clerics, particularly fellow friars, and the other precisely a "feminization."[8] The feminization consisted in a favoring of the cults of laywomen over those of laymen, such that it was certain of the laywomen, including Margaret of Cortona and Angela of Foligno (both to be discussed here), who acquired the greatest reputations, and laymen were in general "second-rank figures."[9] The women in question tended to have reputations as contemplatives, and the ideal of sanctity that they embodied was that of a "flight from the world," in contrast to the "charitable action and desire to pacify and moralize society" that had been characteristic of lay saints in the early thirteenth century, before the friars' influence was strongly felt.[10] They offered no competition to the friars' ministry in the cities. Consequently, both "clericalization" and "feminization," in Vauchez's view, served effectually a common end, namely, to support the friars' own dominance, as distinct from lay dominance, of urban religious activity.[11] That both were compatible with this end seems clear enough. Yet it is not self-evident why, in the case of lay saints, women should have been preferred over men. As Vauchez acknowledges, the friars also had models at hand (some of whom I shall discuss below) of laymen who had similarly fled the world.[12] Why then did they apparently accord the women greater prominence? Calling attention to the friars' ideal of female sanctity, that is, to the particular ensemble of virtues of the women they venerated, does not itself answer the question.

In this essay I shall attempt to answer to that question, in part, by going beyond the friars' "ideals" of sanctity to examine their encounters with the saints they venerated, as witnessed by the vitae. More specifically, I am concerned with the religious meanings the friars attached to female and male saints, respectively. I ask: What do the encounters suggest about the role that gender played in the language (so to speak) of the friars' religious concern, and what light do they thus shed on the friars' reasons for cultivating female sanctity? The answers will, it is true, fall short of a comprehensive analysis of the role of gender in mendicant sanctity; a fuller study would need to examine not only the explicitly religious concerns of the friars but also other aspects of the cults, for instance, whether the economic gains friars might have hoped to realize in individual cases varied according to gender. Nonetheless, the friars' religious concerns have much to tell us about the role of gender here.

In the first place, we get a sense of what aspects of sanctity were *not* gender specific. Thus comparison of vitae will indicate that flight from the world was something friars perceived and valued in male as well as female saints. More precisely, in the accounts of both, the flight is undertaken simultaneously with an embrace of the world—in the sense that the saint renounces the world and yet remains in active service within it—and therefore the theme carries a similar inherent tension. Such simultaneous flight and embrace were of the essence of mendicant spirituality, in the sense that by their very vocation friars attempted to pursue monastic ideals of perfection without the separation from secular society that such ideals had once presupposed. And like the friars, the world-fleeing women who fascinated them also remained uncloistered and thus unseparated from society even while renouncing the world. So in the saints' portraits, neither flight from the world nor the ambivalence of the terms on which it was undertaken was itself specific to gender.[13]

What *was* specific to gender, I shall argue, was the mode of interaction between mendicants and their saints. In the case of the women, the combination of their own flight from the world and the mendicants' pastoral calling propelled saint and mendicant witness toward each other; the women came under the intense pastoral care of the friars, in which the latter became expert observers of the women's inner life. That inner life constituted a capital theme in friars' writings about women, in which descriptions of the saint's dreams, visions, temptations, spiritual wisdom, and in general her relationship with God were standard fare. But in the case of the saints who were men, mendicant witnesses did not in general encounter them as subjects or beneficiaries of pastoral or evangelical work, but typically as colleagues in that work, taking an active role in civic life. It was a role about which the saints often displayed an apparent ambivalence and a tendency to retreat—a stance admired by the witnesses, who seemingly shared the ambivalence. All of this had the effect, not of propelling saint and witness toward each other, but rather of maintaining a distance between them. To be resolutely shirking attention, and eluding one's admirers, was part of the male saint's very saintliness.

Consequently, the witness tended to remain a stranger to the saint's inner life, and thus the men's vitae have little to say about the personal spiritual matters so important in the women's.[14]

The essential condition for the gender distinction that thus appears in the religious meanings of saints for friars was their very calling as friars, a calling that involved them by definition in an uncloistered life of evangelical activity such as preaching and pastoral work. It was a calling that shows them to be heirs of that cultural change a century earlier from which had issued the "public sphere that belonged to men alone," described by Jo Ann McNamara in chapter 1 of this volume. For the friars, occupying that sphere appears to have carried the price of a certain alienation from an interior life of intimacy with God; accordingly, it heightened for them the importance of women, who, not pursuing the friars' activity, came to epitomize the divine contact from which that activity seemed to distance them.

Portrayals of Women

To begin with friars' accounts of women: how a friar could construe flight from the world as also an act of service in the world may be illustrated by one of the earliest of mendicant accounts of laywomen, the vita of the Franciscan tertiary Humiliana dei Cerchi of Florence (d. 1246) by the Franciscan friar Vito of Cortona (d. ca. 1250). There we learn that Humiliana married at sixteen, but that when her husband died after five years she returned to her family's home and resisted their attempts to see her remarried. Her father eventually took back her dowry, and she resolved to live, according to Vito, "as a servant and handmaid [*ut famulam et ancillam*]" in her father's house.[15] There at first she continued her ministrations to the poor, but after a year, she "sprang higher [*altius evolavit*]," became more reclusive, devoted herself to prayer and ascetic practices, and took the habit of a tertiary.[16] Vito left no doubt about her renunciation of the world. He reported, for instance, that she kept her eyes half closed at home, and downcast abroad, so as literally not to have to see the world, and after she had once reflexively looked up when endangered by a runaway horse, was so distraught at betraying her own resolve that she prayed for blindness.[17] But significantly, she did not leave the world; Vito explained that God had specifically not permitted her to leave her home, which would presumably have meant entering a cloister. Whereas "others flee to solitude by leaving the world and their fathers' houses to fight for the Lord, she found her solitude in her father's house, and fighting nobly, she conquered the world and its vices in the midst of worldly things."[18] Why not "flee to solitude"? Because of her potential effect on others in that very world to which she was closing her eyes—an effect caused by her "preaching" through example:

> What of her preaching? It was through works more than words that she preached, and she has not stopped preaching now that she is dead, and she will keep on preaching. If she did not leave the house of her father and her widowhood, it was not of herself that she stayed on, since with a willing mind she gave up everything under the sun. It was God who did not permit [her to leave]: for he wanted by her example to draw from the world lazy folk who, whether held back by curiosity or pusillanimity, or even by not being able to find the discipline [*religionem*] of their heart and be received in it, wallowed in the worst vices: so that no one from the least to the greatest might have any excuse from the possibility of serving God at home and in secular dress, and that there might be no one who could hide from the warmth of his love.[19]

So her very renunciation of the world, inasmuch as she accomplished it at home, constituted an evangelistic act.[20]

It was this same act of taking on ascetic discipline while staying out of the cloister that brought lay holy women into close association with the friars who often became their venerators. Thus Humiliana's vita makes continual reference to a Franciscan named Michael who came to her as her confessor and "her teacher in the way of devotion."[21] Another example is Margaret of Cortona (d. 1290), who, having been a mistress of a nobleman until his violent death, repented of her past life, became a tertiary, and began to receive revelations from Christ. Her vita, by her Franciscan confessor Giunta Bevignati, stresses her renunciation of the world; Giunta reported, for instance, that if obliged during the day to have conversation "pertaining to secular business," Margaret would then cry all night in penitence.[22] Nonetheless, according to Giunta, Christ denied her request for total seclusion and told her to attach herself instead to the friars.[23] This was for reasons of evangelism, as Christ explained to her when she complained that the friars denied her the solitude she wished: "You are a star for the world, newly given for bestowing sight on the blind. . . . You are a new banner, by which sinners are rallied back to me."[24] It was her status as a former spectacular sinner that fitted her for the role, making her an example for other sinners, and it was the friars who would admonish and protect her for the task.[25] They were to be her access to the world, and her doings were to be intertwined with theirs.

The intertwining is particularly striking in Margaret's relationship with Giunta himself. His descriptions of his relationship with her convey considerable detail. They show him, on the one hand, exercising authority over her. Thus, when she contemplated deforming her face as penance, he commanded her not to; when she undertook to say six hundred paternosters daily, he directed her to shift her energies to mental prayer; when she wandered from her cell in extrasensory raptures, he brought her back.[26] But on the other hand, she could also put him on the receiving end of the relationship, and even in a certain sense take the upper hand. Thus, he reported her receiving oracles that criticized or admonished him, for instance, telling him not to impede her when she moved the location of her cell, and to take his confession of penitents more seriously.[27] He also reported oracles exhorting him to preach fervently and comforting him for receiving little recognition.[28] And he sometimes pictured himself acting in concert with her, as when she received revelations of the sins of certain persons whose confession he would then solicit.[29] All in all, Giunta made himself an active principal figure in the vita.

Not all women's vitae by friars feature a male witness or confidant as prominently as does the vita of Margaret of Cortona. But even in vitae in which few male witnesses appear, the ones who do are often portrayed in interaction with the saint. This could even be true when the woman was cloistered. Thus, the Franciscan Peter of Florence who wrote a vita of the nun Margaret of Faenza (d. 1330) was not her confessor, nor did he have much of a place as a character in the narrative of the vita, which was set in her cloister. Yet Peter managed to explain how he had importuned the abbess and nuns of the monastery for permission to interview her for the vita, and then how he labored long and hard to persuade her to reveal the hidden things of God that she had experienced, and how finally she agreed, partly because of the familiarity he claimed to have had with her in his own childhood.[30] Further, he reported some of the substance of their conversations.[31] Peter seems indeed to have made a point of his own interactions with the saint.

Such weaving of male mendicant witnesses into the vitae of female saints frequently reveals something of those witnesses' own personal spiritual concerns. This was especially the case when the witness relied on the saint for some supernatural service. Thus Vito's description of Humiliana's favors to her confessor and another friar reveals their own desire for devotion:

> Friar Buonacorso of Todi of the Order of Minors, well known and a familiar of hers, desiring to taste something of God, frequently commended himself to her, begging of her that he might obtain some gift of devotion from God through her. On a certain day, as though having been heard [by God] she said to him, dearest brother, I believe that my God will give you consolation with regard to that which you

> have often asked through me. Wonderfully, just as she said, after a few days, when the said friar was alone in church, he was infused with such grace, that by tasting so much divine sweetness he was made so drunk, full of the wine of divinity, that, put outside of himself, he could not support the fullness of grace inside himself, and it seemed to him that his bodily senses had left him for the most part. This also happened when she was praying in his presence at a certain place near the city. Similarly Friar Michael, praying on a certain day in her presence, and not having devotion, said to her as though inwardly moved, "My daughter, pray for me, because I am all dry." The daughter of obedience obediently lifted her eyes to heaven and prayed to the Lord. And he was immediately infused with such grace, that it appeared very obvious that he could not receive the fullness of the grace that was infused.[32]

Or again, in the vita of Margaret of Cortona, several stories of friars who ask for the saint's prayers expose personal concerns that occasioned the requests. One friar, for instance, wanted frequent communion but doubted his worthiness:

> A certain friar dear to God wanted to communicate daily, but he held back from fear, such that he did not dare to communicate even rarely, nor did he make any approach to receive the sacrament of the body of Christ. For which reason, seeking out the servant of God Margaret, he begged of her to beseech God by her prayers for the gift of frequent communication [for him]. To her prayer the Savior agreed, saying, "Tell the friar, whom I have made to be of the elect, and love as a son, that although the purity of his innocence is such that I would concede myself to him daily, his use of his tongue is not. Let him therefore constrain his tongue until he speaks with great zeal: and then let him receive me with my benediction whenever he wants."[33]

Such exposure of personal concerns tends, moreover, to show us what the friars in question perceived as their own deficiencies or shortcomings. Typically these involved some sense of distance or separation from God, contrasting precisely with the women's apparent closeness or contact with God.[34] The book of revelations of the laywoman Angela of Foligno (d. 1309) written down by her Franciscan confidant and kinsman, "Friar A.," illustrates the point. In trying to report the revelations of Angela as precisely as possible, Friar A. described as a matter of course the process by which he arrived at some clarity about them, and thus, like other hagiographers of women, made his own interaction with the saint a part of the subject matter of the work. In describing the interaction, he tended to highlight his own inadequacy or ineptness as her scribe. Thus, in explaining his role, he wrote:

> And this may reveal something of how incapable I was of grasping any except the most obvious of [her] divine words: one time, when I was writing exactly what I was able to grasp from her mouth, I read back to her the things I had written so that she might tell me what else to write, she told me in amazement that she did not recognize them. And another time when I read to her so that she could see if I had written well, she responded that I was speaking dryly and without any flavor; and this surprised her. And another time she explained, "Through these words I remember the ones that I spoke to you; but the writing is very obscure, because these words that you read to me do not explain what they contain. Therefore the writing is obscure."[35]

Friar A.'s interaction with Angela also involved a steady stream of questions on his part that demonstrate a sort of driving curiosity about what she had experienced. How could she attribute a certain revelation simultaneously to the Holy Spirit and the crucified Christ? How could she recognize the body of Christ in the host? How had she dispelled a doubt whether tribulation was good for her? What happened to her inwardly when she made the sign of the cross? Did she shed tears when she was in an exalted state of love of God?[36] The obsessiveness of his questions suggests a certain continuing lack of comprehension, even as he strained to take in what she told him.[37]

In the case of female saints, therefore, the vitae written by mendicants show the women, especially laywomen, coming into close interaction with the friars who then served as witnesses to their sanctity. Mendicant hagiographers were disposed to describe their interactions in such a way as to suggest in the witnesses, in effect, a longing for a divine contact that they found elusive, and an assumption that what eluded them did not elude the women. Vitae of women served these men therefore as a means for exploring and exploiting the women's unique experience.

Portrayals of Men

Just as in the women's vitae, so also in men's, mendicant hagiographers portrayed saints as resolutely in flight from the world even while they remained uncloistered. The hagiographer of the Franciscan tertiary John Pelingotto of Urbino (d. 1304), for example, pictured that saint as eschewing the world around him in a way that reminds us of Humiliana. Thus when he walked through the city square on the way to church he deliberately avoided looking at people, and otherwise, "remaining at home, he desired to serve only the true and living God."[38] Or again, in the case of a saint who was himself a friar: the four Dominicans who wrote the vita of the famous Dominican preacher Ambrose Sansedoni shortly after the saint's death in 1287 were at pains to show Ambrose avoiding the fame that his success at preaching brought him. They noted that, in his days as a scholar at Paris, when his preaching had begun to attract crowds, he petitioned his superiors to relieve him of such public duties.[39] They also reported that he refused the pope's offer to make him a bishop after he had reconciled the Sienese to him when they were under interdict, and that later, as lecturer at Rome under the pope's auspices, he once again attracted crowds and once again retreated, and finally that it was from a deliberate cloistered seclusion that the pope recalled him for diplomatic preaching errands.[40] The overall picture suggests someone who drew away from his own public achievements, successful in spite of himself.

A combination of renunciation of the world and involvement in it was therefore a common denominator of men's and women's vitae. Nonetheless, as the foregoing examples may already suggest, the logic and emphasis of the portrayal of renunciation and involvement were different in men's vitae, whose authors were not as intent on showing how renunciation of the world could constitute an act of service. Their central point was rather how the men's evident presence in the world fell short of compromising their renunciation of the world; this was what Pelingotto and Ambrose proved, for instance, in their different ways. Thus, whereas in women's vitae their renunciation constituted a given and their active service had to be demonstrated, in men's vitae it was active service that could be assumed, and it was renunciation that required the demonstration.

The anonymous vita of Elzear of Sabran (d. 1323), a pious Provençal nobleman whom the Franciscans championed as a saint, illustrates how a hagiographer might thus make the point of a saint's ascetic renunciation against the background of an ongoing involvement with the world.[41] There, in the story of one of several similar events that appear to have been decisive for his subsequent life, Elzear is shown conducting a conversation with God concerning his way of life, in which God directed him not to leave his station in life, but nonetheless to maintain a high level of chastity and devotion:

> He began to beseech God from the bowels of his heart that he might not disdain to open the door and show him the way by which [God] wanted him to live in this world. For he wanted very much to leave all such temporal things, and flee to some desert place where un-

> known to anyone he could give himself totally in service to God, under the sole expectation and confidence of divine protection. And after that supplication he was inspired in spirit, as though a person were speaking to him in his heart, that he should not give up his current state, nor leave it, nor give up the temporal goods he had, nor make any external change in himself. And when he responded to that mental inspiration and speech, that because of his fragility he could not thus live, nor persevere, in the ardor of divine love, then the inspiration spoke to him saying: I know how much you can do; and whatever you will not be able to do, I will do, and supply the lack; and the inspiration strongly indicated that he would persevere in virginity.[42]

Afterward, according to the hagiographer, Elzear no longer wanted anything temporal, and never desired to consummate his marriage to his wife Delphine, which in any event the vita represents as completely chaste.[43] Yet he retained throughout his life all the duties of a great nobleman. One episode pictures him at a family wedding that lasted several days; unable to extricate himself to engage in his customary prayer and contemplation, he nonetheless awoke at night to find himself soaked with tears of devotion.[44]

The very stress that mendicant hagiographers laid upon male saints' renunciation of the world suggests an uneasiness on the writers' part with the daily interaction with the world that was nonetheless part of the friars' own calling, and therefore not only unavoidable but also in some sense to be embraced. One suspects ambivalence. Indeed, in the vita of Ambrose, there are some prominent temptation stories that in effect suggest inner tensions underlying his avoidance of honors. When, before entering the order, the young Ambrose was on his way to a monastic retreat to avoid participating in some neighbors' wedding celebrations, a demon in the form of a friar advised him to stay and "spend more time with your companions and beautiful girls, dancing, and playing and singing," as a means of resisting temptation and acquiring merit.[45] He also pointed out the pridefulness of Ambrose's presumption to "spurn the society" of his neighbors.[46] Ambrose dispelled the demon, but worried about the message; he "remained among the said monks for some days, continually turning over in his mind the dark words of the tempter, and strongly fearing lest he fall into the vice of pride."[47] Later, after he had refused the bishopric, another demon appealed to his evangelical zeal and his reformist inclinations, telling him that if he tried he could become pope himself and remedy matters in Christendom.[48] He dispelled this demon too, but the reader is left to wonder whether the terms of the temptation might not be apt. Ambrose is not shown confronting him, but rather saying, "If it is on behalf of God that you are exhorting me to such things, then let him ordain of me as he shall please."[49]

Male saints as pictured in the vitae typically, at any rate, displayed reticence about their virtuous activity, attempting to hide their sanctity in a way that I do not find characteristic of female saints. An example is the Augustinian friar and later Augustinian Master General "Augustine Novello" (Matthew of Taormina, d. 1309), who had been a famous jurist and official in the court of King Manfred of Sicily. Augustine's anonymous biographer, a fellow Augustinian, wrote that "he hid the fame of his knowledge, the nobility of his birth, and the exaltation of his previous status" when he entered the order, and indeed was thought by his previous associates to have died in battle.[50] He was to hide his identity so successfully that, when after many years he asked for writing equipment and penned some virtuosic legal advice for the Sienese Augustinian house to which he belonged, the steward of the house at first ridiculed him, assuming him to be illiterate. What he then wrote, however, came to the notice of a layman who had been his fellow student at Bologna. Recognizing the stamp of the latter's mind, the man revealed Augustine's identity, much to Augustine's distaste:

> Seeing the one whom he had thought to be dead [Augustine], and amazed at his humility, he rushed to embrace and kiss him, not being able to contain his tears of devotion. And when the venerable Father begged him not to disturb his peace by exposing him, he would not agree, but said to the brothers: brothers, you have a hidden treasure, for this is the best man in the world; hold on to him as is fitting; and your dispute is also resolved in your favor. The friars therefore began to venerate [Augustine], and show him reverence. But he, firm in true humility, spurned honors and all reverence, and not ceasing his servile work, he remained altogether as he was.[51]

This reticence of male saints often made them, in effect, unhelpful as sources for their own vitae, in contrast to the women, whose vitae, as we have seen, relied heavily on what they told their confidants. The vita of Elzear stands apparently as an exception, narrating the events of his personal interaction with God (as in the example given above) in such terms that the hagiographer's source, if he had one, must have been a close confidant or confessor. Nonetheless, no such source is identified, and in general men's vitae lack named confidants. In most cases, indeed, the men's hagiographers relied heavily instead on public witnesses. Ambrose Sansedoni's hagiographers, for example, related how he began once to tell his confessor of a revelation that certain pilgrims he had helped were angels in disguise, but found himself unable to come to the point, apparently out of humility. The hagiographers claimed to know the details of the incident only because the saint gave them anonymously in a sermon heard by witnesses.[52] Or again, Ambrose's hagiographers had it on the authority of a witness (a friar, Vincent of Arezzo) that many persons saw Ambrose levitate while preaching, and responded with loud emotion, while the saint himself wondered what the commotion was about:

> The said friar Vincent witnessed that very many religious as well as secular people claim to have seen him raised in the air twice while he was preaching with great fervor of spirit. When they would see this they would kneel and with compunction in their hearts they would begin to cry out loudly, amid great outpouring of tears: Jesus, Jesus, our Lord! By thus crying out, God willing, they would make known to the people what to see, and the people themselves would cry aloud the same words in tears – on account of which, the man of God, astonished at where such words were coming from, began to think back to the source of the shouts. The aforesaid persons affirm moreover that they saw a dove at the ears of the servant of God Ambrose, while he would preach.[53]

Such stories from witnesses gave Ambrose's hagiographers much of the substance of the vita.

Such more or less public witnesses played various prominent roles in men's vitae. They could serve a hagiographer, for instance, as foils for the saint's sanctity, obliging him to display it; thus, the vita of the Sienese Servite saint Joachim Piccolomini relates that when Joachim's fellow friars discovered that he was suffering an alarming deterioration of the skin, they urged him to pray for himself. But he refused, saying that the sickness was given him for his sins, and quoting St. Paul to the effect that infirmity brings strength.[54] Or witnesses could be adduced as interpreters of events to point out the saint's sanctity. The vita of the Dominican James Salamoni of Forlì (d. 1314), for example, tells how the saint, visiting the church of St. Sebastian at Rome with other friars, was unable to get the door to the catacomb open until he prayed. When it then opened, one of the friars attributed the event to James's merits, before the saint could enjoin him to secrecy.[55] In both instances the picture of the saint emerges not from his own confidences, as in so many cases of women, but rather only from what others were able to witness, even to the saint's displeasure.

Moreover, like the witnesses whom they mentioned and upon whom they depended, the male saints' hagiographers generally did not claim confidences from the saints they wrote about, or, if they did, made no conspicuous use of them; and here the contrast between men's and women's vitae comes most clearly into focus. The men's hagiographers were most often anonymous, even when they had apparently been eyewitnesses. In the latter case, they might occasionally make reference to themselves in conjunction with the saints, but only to establish on what authority they spoke; they revealed nothing of the character of their interactions. An example is the anonymous author of the vita of John of Alvernia (d. 1322). This author wrote in his prologue that "the few things I tell about, I either found out from his [John's] own mouth, albeit at much insistence and confidentially, or else from persons worthy of faith, or else I saw them myself."[56] Thus he claimed to have heard details from the saint of his ascetic rigors, he vouched for his thankfulness for the Franciscans' abundance of alms and for his lack of concupiscence, and he declared himself to know more of the saint's visions and spiritual consolations than he was telling.[57] Such references to himself are enough to establish the author's connection with the saint. But the kind of information he attributed to himself makes him no different from the other witnesses in these vitae. He does not appear in the vita as the saint's companion or familiar; it would seem to have been as unnatural for him to describe his interaction with the saint as it was natural for Margaret of Faenza's hagiographer to do so, even though John's was very likely better acquainted with his subject personally.

Thus the male saints' renunciation of the world went hand in hand with a reticence about their virtue, and what appears, in comparison with female saints, as a detachment from their mendicant venerators. They were typically observed and admired in a public manner, on a pedestal as it were, and their stories were largely the stories of witnessed deeds; and in the few instances in which this was not the case—that is, when the vitae did treat their subjective experience—still the subjectivity of their witnesses did not enter into the picture. Therefore, whereas for the female saint renunciation of the world meant coming into close personal interaction with her mendicant witnesses, for the male saint it brought a certain distance from those witnesses. What made the female saint appear in an intimately revealing way made the male saint appear elusive.

Conclusion

What do the friars' encounters with saints tell us about the religious meanings of gender for them, as an aspect of sanctity? In the first place, when we view friars' portrayal of men against the contrasting background of their portrayal of women, it becomes apparent that men's own inner life is, if not a completely taboo subject of investigation, at least one approached with a good deal of reticence. The terms of men's relationships with God and of their life of prayer, the shapes of their temptations, and the matters of their dreams and visions are either not conveyed to the reader at all or conveyed in a way that comparison with the women's vitae points up as notably indirect. This does not imply that the friars lacked interest in such matters or did not value them; their very undetached fascination with the fecund inner life they found in women vividly demonstrates the contrary. Nor does it mean simply that, for themselves, the men placed action above contemplation and thereby relegated the inner life, however esteemed, to a level of secondary importance. It may be that, in effect, this is what they did, yet they seem not to have experienced themselves as doing so deliberately. Rather, their writing communicates a sense of defensiveness about their embrace of an active life of service in the world, as they protested themselves to have maintained the high standard of ascetic renunciation nonetheless. To be sure, they did embrace the active life, and yet with a persistent undercurrent of reluctance or ambivalence. If a commitment to a public, active life of evangelical and pastoral work entailed an alienation from their own inner life, in such a way that the embrace of activity distanced them from an intimate sense of relationship and interaction with God, this was not for them a matter to be affirmed. But at any rate, such distancing does appear to have been a particularly male matter.

Of course, in these sources as elsewhere, what is distinctively male becomes clear only by means of comparison with what is distinctively female, and vice versa; and as I have already implied, the particularity of the portrayals of men comes into view only in relief against the portrayals of women. The women in those portrayals were anything but alienated from the inner life of interaction with God. And the abundant interest of the hagiographers and other mendicant witnesses in investigating the women's inner life suggests that women's special significance for them had to do with the women's possession of precisely the treasure that, by themselves, they found elusive. Oppositeness of gender was a powerful symbol for what the friar encountered as other, as fascinating but absent from himself. Women accordingly became available repositories of an experience of God that somehow eluded the men otherwise. Only in encountering women, it would seem, did they find the opportunity to explore such experience without reservation; and this made women's possession of it loom all the larger and more fascinating. The cultural language of gender therefore served the men both to express and, although only vicariously, to transcend the divide between a life of evangelical action and a life of experiential contact with God—a divide that was given an aura of inescapability precisely by being linked with the most inescapable of human distinctions, namely, the distinction between the sexes.

Notes

Earlier versions of this essay were presented at the Berkshire Conference on the History of Women in June 1990 and the University of Pennsylvania Conference "Creative Women in Medieval and Early Modern Italy" in September 1991. I am especially grateful to Caroline Walker Bynum, Jo Ann McNamara, and Thelma Fenster for comments and criticism.

1. André Vauchez, *La sainteté en occident aux derniers siècles du moyen age, d'après les procès de canonisation et les documents hagiographiques* (Rome: École française de Rome, 1981), 133-42, 243-56; Donald Weinstein and Rudolph Bell, *Saints and Society: The Two Worlds of Western Christendom 1000-1700* (Chicago: University of Chicago Press, 1982), 167-81.

2. Vauchez, *La sainteté en occident*, p. 219.

3. On the cities as the friars' milieu, see Jacques Le Goff, "Apostolat mendiant et fait urbain dans la France médiévale: l'implantation des ordres mendiants," *Annales: Economies, Sociétés, Civilisations* 80 (1968): 335-52; Lester Little, *Religious Poverty and the Profit Economy in Medieval Europe* (Ithaca, N.Y.: Cornell University Press, 1978), 146-217; *Les ordres mendiants et la ville en Italie centrale (v. 1220-v. 1350). Actes de la Table Ronde (Rome, 27-28 avril 1977)*, ed. André Vauchez, in *Mélanges de l'École Française de Rome. Moyen Age-Temps Modernes* 89 (1977): 557-773; Daniel R. Lesnick, *Preaching in Medieval Florence: The Social World of Franciscan and Dominican Spirituality* (Athens: University of Georgia Press, 1989), especially 35-85. On the urban origins and social status of saints associated with the mendicants, see Michael Goodich, *Vita Perfecta: The Ideal of Sainthood in the Thirteenth Century* (Stuttgart: A. Hiersemann, 1982), 147-72.

4. Useful for assaying the scope of mendicant hagiography and its place in the broader hagiographic literature of the time is the list of vitae compiled by Félix Vernet, which groups these by chronology and saints' religious affiliations, and also identifies authors' affiliations. Vernet, "Biographies spirituelles. IV. Le moyen age," *Dictionnaire de spiritualité, d'ascétique et de mystique*, vol. 1 (Paris: Beauchesne, 1936), cols. 1646-79. See also Goodich, *Vita Perfecta*, 59-68, for a brief overview of "hagiographers and their intentions" in the period. Specifically on mendicant hagiographers of women, see John Coakley, "Friars as Confidants of Holy Women in Medieval Dominican Hagiography," in *Images of Sainthood in Medieval Europe*, ed. Renate Blumenfeld-Kosinski and Timea Szell (Ithaca, N.Y.: Cornell University Press, 1991), 222-46.

5. Weinstein and Bell's statistical study of 864 saints from 1000 to 1700 indicates the relative importance of women in mendicant sanctity. They found that 23.5 percent of saints associated with the mendicant orders (none of whom, of course, predated the early thirteenth century) were women, and these in turn accounted for about a third (50 of 151) of all the female saints in the sample. The period of the present study, moreover, falls within the authors' "era of female sanctity," namely, the thirteenth, fourteenth, and fifteenth centuries, in which, respectively, 22.6, 23.4, and 27.7 percent of the saints in the sample were female, as distinct from 11.8 percent in the twelfth century and 18.1 in the sixteenth. Weinstein and Bell, *Saints and Society*, 224, 220.

6. Pierre Delooz, *Sociologie et canonisations* (Liège: Faculté de droit, 1969), 7.

7. The phrase is Hippolyte Delehaye's; he characterized sanctity as "un ensemble harmonieux des vertus Chrétiennes pratiquées à un degré qu'une rare élite est en mesure d'atteindre." *Sanctus: essai sur le culte des saints dans l'antiquité* (Brussels: Societé des Bollandistes, 1927), 240.

8. Vauchez, *La sainteté en occident*, 243-54.

9. "A l'exception de S. Elzéar qui fut canonisé en 1369, il s'agit cependant de personnages de second plan." Ibid., 245. Richard Keickhefer has observed in the same vein that among extant thirteenth-century saints' vitae, "brief lives of men vastly outnumber those of women, but the genders are more or less equally represented in the longer vitae," and in the fourteenth century the list of longer vitae is "almost exclusively a catalogue of holy women." Kieckhefer, "Holiness and the Culture of Devotion: Remarks on Some Late Medieval Male Saints," in Blumenfield-Kosinski and Szell, *Images of Sainthood*, 292.

10. The women had in common "leur spiritualité axée sur la fuite du monde et le refus du mariage, l'extrême ascétisme et la dévotion aux souffrances du Christ." Vauchez, *La sainteté en occident*, 248. In the earlier thirteenth century, lay saints "l'esprit de prière allait de pair avec l'action charitable et le souci de pacifier et de moraliser la société dans laquelle ils vivaient. Désormais les valeurs proposées à l'imitation des fidèles seront purement spirituelles. Seule importe la recherche de l'union à Dieu par la méditation solitaire des mystères du salut." Ibid., 249.

11. Ibid., 242-43, 248-49, 254.

12. Ibid., 244-45.

13. On the importance of such simultaneous involvement with and withdrawal from the world for the spirituality of the period generally, see Richard Kieckhefer, *Unquiet Souls: Fourteenth-Century Saints and Their Religious Milieu* (Chicago: University of Chicago Press, 1984), 85-88.

14. Richard Kieckhefer has also noticed this phenomenon. Kiekhefer, "Holiness and the Culture of Devotion," 292-93.

15. *Vita* [Umilianae], *Acta Sanctorum* (hereafter *AA SS*) May, vol. 4 (Paris, 1866), 385-400, parr. 1-8; par. 8 (hereafter cited as *Vit. Um.*, followed by paragraph number). On Humiliana, see Anna Benvenuti Papi, "Umiliana dei Cerchi. Nascità di un culto nella Firenze del Dugento," *Studi Francescani* 77 (1980): 87-117.

16. *Vit. Um.* 10-11. She now, in any event, lacked substance of her own to give; ibid., 10.

17. "Utinam essem caeca et surda, ut deinceps talia non audirem." Ibid., 35. (On the importance of terminology related to sight, see note 23.) Humiliana also wanted to be violently martyred or "at least to be gravely ill, so that she might be vouchsafed by the love of God to suffer, and feel Christ's pains in the pain of her body [saltem infirmari graviter, ut Dei amore pati mereretur, et Christi dolores in sui corporis dolore sentiret]." Ibid., 36.

18. "Alii relicto seculo et paternis mansionibus, ad solitudinem fugientes, Domino militarunt; haec in domum patris solitudinem adducens, militando nobiliter vicit mundum, et vitium in medio mundanorum." Ibid., 11.

19. "Quid de praedicatione, qua magis opere praedicavit quam verbo, et corpore mortua praedicare non cessat, et in perpetuum praedicabit? Si domum patris et vestes viduales non dimisit, non per ipsam stetit: quoniam cuncta quae sub coelo sunt liberali mente deseruit. Sed Deus non permisit: voluit enim exemplo ejus seculi otiosos trahere, qui vel curiositate vel pusillanimitate detenti, vel etiam non valentes invenire religionem secundum cor suum, in qua recipi potuissent, jacebant in infimis vitiorum: ut nullus a minimo usque ad magnum viam excusationis haberet, quod Deo servire non posset juxta possibilitatem suam in domo propria et habitu seculari, et jam non sit qui se abscondit a calore caritatis suae." Ibid., 13.

20. Marie-Humbert Vicaire has shown that the early Dominican friars and cloistered women saw the cloistered women's prayers specifically as part of the Dominican evangelical enterprise. Vicaire, "L'action de St. Dominique sur la vie régulière des femmes en Languedoc," in *La femme dans la vie religieuse du Languedoc (XIIIe- XIVe s.)* (Toulouse: Privat, 1988), 234-35.

21. "Doctor ejus in via devotionis fuit." *Vit. Um.* 13; see also ibid., 24, 25, 28, 31, 40, 42, 51, 53, 66, for other references to Michael.

22. "Nam si praecedenti die quicquam dixerat vel audierat cum aliquo seculari, ad secularia negotia pertinens, assuetas Christi dulcedines nullatenus praesumebat in orando nocturnis horis repetere. Sed cum interna moestitia lacrymando noctem ducebat insomnem."

Vita [Margaritae], *AA SS* February, vol. 3 (Paris, 1865), 302-63, par. 14 (hereafter cited as *Vit. Marg. Cort.*, followed by paragraph number). On Margaret and Giunta in the context of events in Cortona, see F. Cardini, "Agiografia e politica: Margherita da Cortona e le vicende di una città inquieta," *Studi francescani* 76 (1979): 127-36; and Anna Benvenuti Papi, " 'Margherita Filia Ierusalem.' Una visione mistica della terrasanta nella spiritualità femminile Francescana," in *Toscana e Terrasanta nel medioevo*, ed. F. Cardini (Florence: Alinea, 1982), 117-32.

23. She was, however, to attach herself *only* to the Franciscans; Christ would otherwise draw close to her in direct proportion to her separation from secular persons. *Vit. Marg. Cort.* 27-30.

24. "Tu es stella mundo, concessa noviter ad caecos illuminandum. . . . Tu es vexillum novum, quo reducentur peccatores ad me." Ibid., 196. Catherine Mooney, in an analysis of Tuscan and Umbrian hagiography in this period (including many of the works I am discussing here), has noted that there is more thematic emphasis on sight, and more terminology related to sight, in women's vitae than in men's—a fact that corresponds with the comparatively greater emphasis in women's vitae on visions as a means of supernatural knowledge. Mooney, "Women's Visions in Fourteenth-Century Italian Spiritual Texts," paper presented at the Berkshire Conference on Women's History, June 1990.

25. *Vit. Marg. Cort.* 65, 21.

26. Ibid., 40, 89, 106, 186.

27. Ibid., 31-32, 144.

28. Ibid., 217, 242.

29. Ibid., 58, 214-15.

30. *Vita* [Margaritae Faventinae], *AA SS* August, vol. 5 (Paris, 1868), 847-51, par. 1 (hereafter cited as *Vit. Marg. Fav.*, followed by paragraph number). On Margaret, see Gian Domenico Gordini, "Margherita da Faenza, beata," in *Bibliotheca Sanctorum*, vol. 8 (Rome: Istituto Giovanni XXIII, 1967), cols. 773-74.

31. *Vit. Marg. Fav.* 14.

32. "Frater Bonacursus de Tuderto de Ordine Minorum, valde notus et familiaris ejus, cupiens de Deo aliquid degustare, frequenter commendabat se ei, rogans ut per eam a Deo devotionis donum aliquod obtineret. Cui die quadam velut exaudita dixit: Frater carissime, credo, quod Deus meus consolabitur te in proximo de illo, quod a me saepius postulasti. Mirum in modum, sicut dixit, post paucos dies, cum esset praedictus Frater solus in ecclesia, tanta sibi superinfusa est gratia, ut abundanter divina dulcedine degustata ita ebrius effectus est, plenus divinitatis vino, quod extra se factus plenitudinem gratiae suscipere non poterat stricto sinu, et sensus corporeos in parte maxima sibi visus est amisisse. Hoc etiam ei contigit orante ipsa eo praesente in quodam loco juxta civitatem. Similiter Fratre Michaele orante quadam die praesente ipsa, et non habente devotionem, quasi motus intrinsecus dixit ei: Filia mea, roga pro me, quia ego sum totus siccus. Cui obediens obedientiae filia, levatis oculis in coelum oravit ad Dominum. Cui statim tanta infusa est gratia, quod evidentissime appareret quod, recipere non posset infusae gratiae plenitudinem." *Vit. Um.* 24. Vito then cites an instance in which she similarly procured an experience of devotion for a matron.

33. "Quidam carus Deo Frater quotidie communicare desiderans, tamen retrahebatur timore, ita quod etiam raro communicare non audebat, nec accedebat ad Christi corporis sacramentum suscipiendum. Qua ex re Dei famulam Margaritam requirens, rogavit eam, ut impetraret a Domino suis precibus donum saepe communicandi. Cujus orationi Salvator annuens, dixit: Dic Fratri, quem feci de numero electorum, et diligo ut filium, quod quantum ad ejus innocentiae puritatem ipsi me concederem omni die, sed non quantum ad linguae usum. Suam igitur prius linguam coerceat, quantumcumque loquatur ex magno zelo: et cum benedictione mea me recipiat, quando volet." *Vit. Marg. Cort.* 226. The vita includes a series of such stories of interactions (mostly involving oracles) between Margaret and friars who had problems or requests; ibid., 226-41.

34. For an exploration of this theme in early mendicant hagiography, see John Coakley, "Gender and the Authority of Friars: The Significance of Holy Women for Thirteenth-Century Franciscans and Dominicans," *Church History* 60 (1991): 445-60. The notion of God's special accessibility to women appears indeed to have been widespread and deeply rooted in the period. Daniel Bornstein, "The Shrine of Santa Maria a Cigoli: Female Visionaries and Clerical Promoters," *Mélanges de l'Ecole Française de Rome – Moyen Age, Temps Modernes* 89 (1977): 557-73, gives a late fourteenth-century local case of interest in a female visionary that suggests a widespread "conviction that the privileged conduit for divine revelation was young, poor and female" (573). Thus, too, supernatural visions were particularly associated with women, as shown for instance by Elizabeth Petroff, *Medieval Women's Visionary Literature* (New York: Oxford University Press, 1986), 5-20. The very association of femaleness with the body suggested, moreover, a connection between women and Christ as incarnated divinity; see Caroline Walker Bynum, "'. . . And Woman His Humanity': Female Imagery in the Religious Writing of the Later Middle Ages," in *Gender and Religion*, ed. Caroline Bynum, Stevan Harrell, and Paula Richman (Boston: Beacon, 1986), 257-89; and idem., and *Holy Feast and Holy Fast: The Religious Significance of Food to Medieval Women* (Berkeley: University of California Press, 1987), 277-96.

35. "Et hic potest aliqualiter patere quod ego non poteram capere de verbis divinis nisi magis grossa, quia aliquando, dum ego scribebam recte sicut a suo ore capere poteram, relegenti sibi illa quae scripseram ut ipsa alia diceret ad scribendum, dixit mihi admirando quod non recognoscebat illa. Et alia vice quando ego relegebam ei ut ipsa videret si ego bene scripseram, et ipsa respondit, quod ego sicce et sine omni sapore loquebar; et admirabatur de hoc. Et alia vice exposuit ita dicens: Per ista verba recordor illorum quae dixi tibi, sed est obscurissima scriptura, quia haec verba quae legis mihi non explicant illa quae portant, ideo est obscura scriptura." *Il libro della beata Angela da Foligno* (hereafter *Il libro*), ed. Ludger Thier and Abele Calufetti (Rome: Editiones Collegii s. Bonaventurae, 1985), pt. 1, ch. 2, 172. On Angela's book of revelations, see Paul Lachance, *The Spiritual Journey of the Blessed Angela of Foligno According to the Memorial of Frater A.* (Rome: Pontificium Athenaeum Antonianum, 1984); *Vita e spiritualità della beata Angela da Foligno*, ed. C. Schmitt (Padua: Serafica Provincia di san Francesco, 1987); and Ulrich Köpf, "Angela von Foligno. Ein Beitrag zur Franziscanischen Frauenbewegung um 1300," in *Religiöse Frauenbewegung und Mystische Frömmigkeit im Mittelalter*, ed. Peter Dinzelbacher and Dieter R. Bauer (Cologne: Böhlau Verlag, 1988), 225-50.

36. *Il libro*, pt. 1, ch. 7, 320; pt. 1, ch. 4, 226; pt. 1, ch. 6, 272-74; pt. 1, ch. 7, 310; pt. 1, ch. 7, 320.

37. He duly noted, but apparently could not quite take to heart, Angela's assertion that "the more people feel of God, the less they can talk of him, because from the very fact that what is being sensed is infinite and inexpressible, they can say less about it [illi qui magis sentiunt de Deo, minus possunt loqui de eo; quia eo ipso quod sentiunt de illo infinito et indicibili, de eo minus loqui possunt]." Ibid., pt. 1, ch. 7, 322.

38. "Sed in sua manens domo, soli Deo vivo et vero servire cupiebat." *Vita* [Pilingotti], *AA SS* June, vol. 1 (Paris, 1867), 145-51, par. 7 (hereafter cited as *Vit. Pil.*, followed by paragraph number). On Pelingotto, see Silvino da Nadro, "Pelingotto (Pelino Goto), Giovanni, beato," in *Bibliotheca Sanctorum*, vol. 10 (Rome: Istituto Giovanni XXIII, 1968), 449-50.

39. *Vita* [Ambrosii], *AA SS* March, vol. 3 (Paris, 1865), 181-200, par. 25 (hereafter cited as *Vit. Amb.*, followed by paragraph number). A prologue and a prefatory epistle belonging to the vita are to be found in "Un legendier dominicain peu connu," *Analecta Bollandiana* 58 (1940): 37-40. On Ambrose's preaching, as illustrated by an extant sermon, see T. Kaepelli, "Le prediche del b. Amrogio Sansedoni da Siena," *Archivum Fratrum Praedicatorum* 38 (1968): 5-12.

40. *Vit. Amb.* 34, 38, 39-40.

41. *Vita* [Elzearii], *AA SS* September, vol. 7 (Paris, 1867), 539-55 (hereafter cited as *Vit. Elz.*, followed by paragraph number). On Elzear, see G. Duhamelet, *St. Elzéar de Sabran et la bienheureuse Dauphine* (Paris: Éditions Franciscaines, 1944).

42. "Incepit ex cordis visceribus Deum rogare, ut sibi dignaretur ostium aperire, et viam ostendere, per quam vellet eum vivere in hoc mundo. Nam relinquere omnia ista temporalia, et fugere ad aliqua loca deserta, ubi a nemine cognitus sub sola spe et divinae praetectionis confidentia Dei servitio se totaliter dedicaret, tunc nimium affectabat. Et post ipsam supplicationem inspirabatur sibi in mente, quasi si una persona sibi loqueretur in corde quod non dimitteret statum suum, nec se absentaret, nec dimitteret bona temporalia, quae habebat, nec de seipso exterius faceret mutationem. Et cum ipse tali responderet inspirationi et locutioni mentali, et propter suam fragilitatem non posset in ardore divini amoris sic vivere, nec perseverare, tunc inspiratio loquebatur sibi dicens: Scio, quantum potes; et quod tu non poteris operari, ego faciam, et supplebo: et quod in virginitate perseveraret, illa inspiratio sibi fortiter suggessit." *Vit. Elz.* 10-11.

43. Ibid., 12.

44. Ibid., 22.

45. "Nec divinam crede te posse adipisci gratiam, nisi contra inimici fallacias fortiter dimicaveris: quod utique melius efficies, si saepius cum sodalibus tuis formosisque puellis in choreis et ludis et cantibus conversatus fueris." *Vit. Amb.* 13.

46. "Nonne in superbiae vitium incidere videris, si propinquorum tuorum nuptiis interesse renuis, et societatem eorum qui te honorare cupiunt aspernaris? Non vides quod scandali ocasionem das ex murmuratione ob superbiae tuae vitium?" Ibid., 14.

47. "Permansit autem Ambrosius apud praefatos monachos per dies aliquos, colorata tentatoris verba jugiter ruminans, et fortiter timens ne in superbiae vitium rueret." Ibid., 15.

48. Ibid., 34-35.

49. "Si tu ex parte Dei ad talia me hortaris, quantum sibi placuerit de me disponat." Ibid., 36.

50. "Occultavit suae scientiae claritatem, generis nobilitatem, et prioris status sublimitatem." *Vita* [Augustini], *AA SS* May, vol. 4 (Paris, 1866), 616-21, par. 6 (hereafter cited as *Vit. Aug.* followed by paragraph number). On Augustine, see Agostino M. Giacomini, "Agostino Novello, beato," in *Bibliotheca Sanctorum*, vol. 1 (Rome: Istituto Giovanni XXIII, 1961), cols. 601-7.

51. "Et videns quem mortuum existimabat, admirans ejus humilitatem, ruit in amplexus et oscula ejus, lacrymas devotionis continere non valens. Et cum rogaret eum idem venerabilis Pater, non perturbare pacem suam eum manifestando; nullatenus acquievit, sed ait Fratribus: Fratres, habetis thesaurum occultum; hic enim est melior homo mundi; teneatis ergo eum ut decet; sed et quaestio vestra est terminata pro vobis. Coeperunt ergo Fratres eum venerari, et sibi reverentiam exhibere. Ipse autem vera humilitate fundatus, honores et omnem reverentiam respuebat; operaque servilia non dimittens, omnino sic permanebat." *Vit. Aug.* 12.

52. *Vit. Amb.* 10.

53. "Testatus est etiam praefatus F. Vincentius, quod quamplures alii religiosi et seculares [dixerint] dum beatus vir populo cum magno spiritu fervore praedicaret, bis in aera elevatum se vidisse: quod ut viderunt, genibus flexis et corde compuncti, magna cum lacrymarum effusione alta voce clamare coeperunt: Jesus, Jesus, Dominus noster. Dum autem sic clamarent, Deo volente, populo quid viderant nuntiarunt: populus autem ipse cum lacrymis eadem verba inclamarunt: ex qua re vir Dei admirans unde talia procederent verba, coepit mente revolvere unde tales procederent clamores. Affirmant etiam praefati, columbam ad aures servi Dei Ambrosii se vidisse, dum praedicaret." Ibid., 51.

54. Peregrinus Soulier, ed., "Vita ac Legenda Beati Ioachimi Senensis Auctore Coaevo Fr. Christophoro de Parma (?)," *Analecta Bollaniana* 13 (1894): 383-97, par. 9. Peter Crisci of Foligno similarly refused urging of his cohorts that he receive medical attention; see (as completing the text published as *Acta Mutila* in *AA SS* July, vol. 4 [Paris, 1868], 665-68) Michael Faloci Pulignani, "Beati Petri de Fulgineo Confessoris Legenda Auctore Fratre Joanne Gorini Ordinis Praedicatorum," *Analecta Bollandiana* 8 (1880): 365-69, ch. 11. Another example of friar-as-foil, from the vita of John of Alvernia (*Acta* [Joannis], *AA SS* August, vol. 2 [Paris, 1867], 459-69 [hereafter cited as *Acta Jn.*, followed by paragraph number]): one

day when John was walking along "with his eyes raised to heaven [oculis elevatis in coelum]" and obstacles injured his feet, the accompanying friar admonished him to watch out, but the saint replied, "Brother, we must not distract the spirit just to avoid cutting our feet [Non debemus, Frater, ut caveamus pedum laesionem, deserere mentem]." *Acta Jn.* 11. On John, see note 56.

55. *Vita* [Jacobi], *AA SS* May, vol. 7 (Paris, 1866), 452-66, par. 16. On James, see Sadoc Bertucci, "Salomoni, Giacomo, beato," in *Bibliotheca Sanctorum*, vol. 11 (Rome: Istituto Giovanni XXIII, 1968), cols. 592-93.

56. "Pauca, quae narro, vel ab ejus ore percepi, licet cum magno conatu et sub secreto, dum viveret, vel a personis multum fide dignis audivi, vel ego a me ipso perspexi." *Acta Jn.* 2. On John, see Giacinto Pagnani, "Giovanni della Verna (detto anche di Fermo), beato," in *Bibliotheca Sanctorum*, vol. 6 (Rome: Istituto Giovanni XXIII, 1965), cols. 919-21; and L. Oliger, "Il B. Giovanni della Verna (1259-1332). Sua vita, sua testimonianza per l'indulgenza della Porziuncula," *La Verna* 11 (1913): 196-235.

57. *Acta Jn.* 6, 12 (John's affirmation of abundance suggesting a moderate or anti-Spiritual stance on the author's part in the Franciscan controversies over poverty then current), 19, 27.

CHAPTER 7

The Male Animal in the Fables of Marie de France

Harriet Spiegel

The Medieval Fable and Its Origins

From its beginnings, the fable genre has been almost exclusively a masculine one—a means of transmitting patriarchal wisdom and culture. From classical times through the Middle Ages, the fable features prominently in the formal education of young males, and the fable itself presents narratives of parent instructing child, typically directed toward the proper behavior of those in power. It is remarkable then to find a woman fable writer in the Middle Ages; indeed, aside from Marie there are no known female fabulists from classical times through the eighteenth century. With Marie de France, writing in twelfth-century Anglo-Norman England, the conventional and conventionally male fable form becomes not only a way to question the male hierarchy but also a way to explore the gender roles inherent in this order.

The *Fables*, or *Ysopet*, of Marie de France are, as she announces in the prologue, a continuation of the Aesopic tradition. Yet they are also distinctly her own, one woman's personal, compassionate, clever, caustic, and sometimes even despairing, critical view of her world, the world of women and men. The fable genre, a satirical blurring of human and animal worlds, allows us to view men and women from the outside, as "other," and thus to be better able to see the relationship between our civilized trappings and our natural world. Accordingly, Marie's fables are particularly concerned with systems of power, authority, and class, for in her fables the questions of "maleness" and public power are often closely connected or interrelated. Marie thus offers not only a twelfth-century woman's view of men and manhood, but also a view of the ways our human world constructs and establishes our senses of gender.

The classical fable was for the Middle Ages a basic element in the education of schoolboys. Medieval Europe knew the classical fables through the two main branches of the Aesopic tradition: the first-century Latin iambics of Phaedrus and the second-century Greek verses of Babrius. Babrius's version was put into Latin elegiac verses by Avianus in the fourth century; this version, known as the Avionnet, was the source of numerous school texts for young students, studied in the *trivium* as part of the rhetoric; more than a hundred of these manuals survive. As for Phaedrus, although his name was apparently not well known to medieval Europe, his fables were popularized through a fourth-century prose collection called *Romulus*. The fables of this classical tradition are thus also a part of the patriarchal tradition, from Babrius, who presents his fables as instruction for his son, to the medieval schoolboy learning his lessons in Latin rhetoric as well as in political and social responsibility.

Because Marie places her fables within this tradition, modestly (and conventionally) claiming that she is but translating from a purported English text, it is when Marie's fables are compared with possible sources and analogues that her individual contributions become dramatically clear. Marie uses the very form that establishes and supports the male hierarchy both to endorse it and to challenge it, even as she makes clear that she, and all women, are excluded from it.

Marie's collection includes 103 fables. Like other fables, hers are short narratives, often witty and wry, and each with a moral – in Marie's collection, the moral follows each narrative as an epimythium. Many of her fables are of animals acting like human beings (or like the beasts we really are); some include human beings in the animal world, others are exclusively of human beings. Marie's first forty fables can be clearly connected to written classical tradition, specifically, three manuscripts of the Romulus branch of Phaedrus called the Romulus Nilantii.[1] But many of the other sixty-three fables have no known written sources; many have analogues in widely diverse oral traditions from England to the Middle East. A comparison of Marie's fables to these analogues can only be suggestive.

Marie's Medieval World: Female and Male

It has been noted elsewhere that one way Marie adapts traditional fables to make them her own is by medievalizing them, providing commentary on feudal social structure, on the mutual obligations of serfs and seigniors, and on questions of social order and justice.[2] Yet Marie's vision of a better society looks not only at institutions but also at the individuals who constitute this society; especially striking is her revisioning of gender characteristics and social hierarchies. Whereas sometimes Marie's exploration of traditional gender roles results in acceptance, at other times the presentation of male and female behavior is unsettling and even subversive, suggesting what feminine theorists have identified as a distinctly female problem of voicing, the question of how can a woman speak in a positive female voice in a genre that, as male, defines her negatively, as "other." This issue is especially germane to the fable, a genre directed toward the public behavior of young men and thus, by definition, excluding females, noble or not. Although Marie's fables do not challenge the conventional distinction between private and public, male and female spheres, they do endorse and even redefine particular responsibilities and possibilities inherent in each.

Marie's particular interest in women is bold and dramatic.[3] The females in her fables are more compassionate than the males; their responses are personal rather than formulaic—a goddess who offers comfort to her petitioners instead of silence, or a raped female bear who cries out in pain and despair. The female animal world is likewise personal, defined perhaps by biology—the females are engendering and nurturing creatures in a domestic setting, rather than, as in the male world, ruling and serving. Domesticity, however, does not necessarily result in passivity or subservience. In fable 3, for example, Marie's mouse, as *dame de la meisun*, rules with the *seignurie* and largesse of a gracious medieval lord (Marie's addition to this Romulus fable). And female human beings in Marie's collection are clever. In two fabliau-type fables (44 and its variant, 45), for example, when a peasant discovers his wife in bed with her lover, it is the quick-witted wife who dupes her husband and wins our admiration. In only one case—that of the rich man's daughter who spills her father's blood that had been collected for the doctor, replaces it with her own, and inadvertently reveals that she is pregnant (fable 42)—is the woman not clever enough (though cleverer than her father, who assumes that *he* must be prcgnant). Marie's most notable assertion of female strength is right at the top—with the deity, who in the animal world is always distinctly female—*la Destinee* (fables 6 and 18), *la Sepande* (fables 75 and 97), and *la Crïere* (fable 23). Curiously, whenever this animal world includes human beings, Marie safely sticks with the masculine *Dieu*. Marie's females are not only distinctly different from her male characters, they are also considerably stronger and more individualized than their counterparts in contemporary analogues.[4]

The Male Hierarchy

Marie's commentary on the male world, although just as much her own as her views of the female world, is perhaps more problematic, especially in its ambivalence. If the female animal world is generally domestic and compassionate, the male world is usually outside the home, embracing the public world of hierarchies and politics. And whereas the intimacy of the home offers sociability, the public world depends on power. Marie's male world is defined by social class—there are lords and peasants, seigniors and villains; lions and hedgehogs, eagles and frogs. Marie seems to accept and thereby to endorse the established social hierarchy: serfs are naturally and incurably stupid and boorish; seigniors and kings (or their animal equivalents) – though they may abuse their positions of power, authority, and wealth – rule by right. This is the male world (animal and human); there are no females in this social and political hierarchy, no females empowered by title or position, though there are many female victims. So exclusively male is the realm of public authority that even when grammatical gender is feminine, though the animals themselves are nondistinctive and presumably male, the animals have no public titles. Marie's fable 11 illustrates this well. Following Romulus Nilantii, Marie presents two versions of this fable, one right after the other. In the first account, "The Lion, the Buffalo, and the Wolf," the animals are futilely arguing with the lion king over distribution of their spoils. These animals are grammatically masculine and each has a title: the buffalo (bugle), is seneschal; the wolf is provost. The second version, "The Lion, the Sheep, and the Goat," has, instead, two gramatically female animals, *la berbiz* and *la chevre*. While nothing else about the sheep and goat seems feminine, neither animal is given a public position or title. This distinction is of course not Marie's but one she inherited from Romulus Nilantii. It is, nevertheless, a specifically medieval distinction; in the classical Greek of Babrius the wild ass and lion are partners; the ass, although male, has no public position or title.

Marie seems to accept not only the natural appropriateness of males to rule, but also the internal hierarchy, which is established at birth and cannot be assumed or pretended. In fable 41, "The Rich Man and the Two Serfs," Marie tells of two peasants huddled together in a field, seemingly in close consultation. Their seignior rides by and, seeing the two, criticizes them for foolishly trying to look like important men. Marie's audience may have been particularly interested in this seignior-serf distinction – more so than later audiences, for in several later Continental manuscripts the scribe unwittingly substituted a cerf (stag) for serf, and in one manuscript (BN fr 2173) the fable is even illustrated with two stags talking – which may look as if it belongs in a collection of animal fables, but quite misses Marie's point – serfs (peasants) are not senators and should not act as if they are.

Marie's hierarchies are traditional – her lions and eagles are always regal in position and character – but her concerns are often personal. Even when the conclusion is that the eagle, by nature, deserves to be king, it is because of what he does, rather than who he is, that he deserves to rule. Marie challenges moral behavior, but not the other factors determining authority: male gender and social and political rank. In "The Birds and the Cuckoo" (fable 46), the birds hold a convention to select a king. (It is typical of Marie's concern for the mutual obligation of ruler and ruled that she frequently has animal conventions in which the general populace, by democratic process, selects a ruler—sometimes wisely, sometimes foolishly, sometimes tragically.) In this fable the birds agree that what they should look for in choosing a ruler is someone who "should govern and be just and true," someone who would rule *par dreite fei*. They go first for the cuckoo, a bird they do not know well but who impresses them with his clamorous voice that can be heard throughout the woods, a useful quality in a king, they reason. Before they settle on him, however, they wish to find out a bit more about his character, and the titmouse, a small and female bird, flies over to investigate. She finds that he is not so regal after all:

> She perched in close proximity
> And gave him careful scrutiny.
> His manner gave her no delight:
> He was indeed a dreadful sight.
> Yet higher still she wished to settle
> So she could verify his mettle.
> She jumped up to a higher limb
> And defecated over him.
> The cuckoo did not say a word
> And did not seem the least disturbed.
> The titmouse to the rest returned;
> The cuckoo bird she cursed and spurned—
> Never should he be made seignior!
> She told them of his dishonour
> And how, by her, he'd been disgraced:
> "He did not seem to mind the least!
> Were a large bird to do him wrong,
> This bird's revenge would not be strong—
> Considering that he has not stirred
> Against the very smallest bird." (31-50)[5]

Marie's choice of titmouse is suggestive and even subversive, for the titmouse is not merely the smallest and least consequential of the birds (*de tuz oiseus la mendre*), but she is also female. The closest analogue to this fable, in the Romulus Roberti, slightly later than Marie, also has a titmouse, but it is male! (Perry 652) In an analogue by Odo of Cheriton (5), also slightly later than Marie, the messenger is omitted altogether; the inappropriate king, here a dove, is deposed by his subjects, who find him too meek.[6] Marie is presumably not suggesting that defecating upon a ruler, however unqualified, is appropriate female behavior; however, this fable does indicate Marie's interest in gender characteristics: the little female titmouse can be bold and insulting when necessary—albeit in the intimacy of the home. The male cuckoo's response is then evaluated according to male standards: what is hurt is his honor—he has been disgraced, never mind that his head must be uncomfortably dirty. And the conventional male recourse for dishonor is the standard by which the cuckoo cinches his unworthiness—he fails to take revenge, the necessary response, or even to realize that he must.

But Marie is not merely critical; she also believes in the qualities of a good ruler, and the fable instructs us accordingly. In rejecting the cuckoo, the birds realize:

> We ought to choose one stout of heart,
> Who's noble, valorous, and smart.
> A king should be one very righteous
> Who's firm and stern in dealing justice.[7] (51-54)

And so they make the eagle their king, the fable continues:

> And I'll give you the reasoning:
> The eagle's grand and glorious
> And he's especially valorous
> And very staid and dignified.
> And once the eagle's satisfied,
> He fasts again quite easily
> And does not lust too much for prey.[8] (58-64)

And then, while emphasizing the importance of moderation in both personal and public behavior, the fable generalizes to all rulers:

> A prince should be well-rested, too;
> In his delights not overdo;
> Nor shame himself or his domain
> Nor cause the poor folk undue pain.[9] (65-68)

Marie seems to accept and even endorse the male hierarchy—rulers are male, and of proper social class; they are strong of body and character, yet humble and moderate. And when those of lesser birth attempt to rule, their behavior is but an unenlightened parody of wise judiciousness. The Monkey King (fable 34) is but a silly simian mimic of human regality. Her endorsement, however, is not a passive one, but an assertive reminder of the proper behavior incumbent upon those in positions of power. Marie does not see justice as a natural or inevitable consequence of the authority established by gender and social class. Indeed, in medievalizing these fables, Marie is sometimes harshly critical of contemporary male rulers and their corrupt systems. The moral to "The Wolf and the Lamb" (fable 2), a fable of a wolf who accuses a lamb of polluting his drinking water by drinking upstream from him (the lamb points out that it is the wolf who is in fact upstream), speaks directly to the male hierarchy, the lords, viscounts, and judges (*li riche seignur, li vescunte, e li jugeür*) who abuse the rights of those under their rule:

> And this is what our great lords do,
> The viscounts and the judges too,
> With all the people whom they rule:
> False charge they make from greed so cruel.
> To cause confusion they consort
> And often summon folk to court.
> They strip them clean of flesh and skin,
> As the wolf did to the lambkin.[10] (31-38)

Unlike the brief and general moral pointing to the greed of malicious prosecutors (*calumpniantor*) in Romulus Nilantii (1:2), Marie's address is directly to those who abuse their authority and the judicial process.

Even more broadly than this fable, which speaks to the titled hierarchy, in fable 4, "The Dog and the Ewe," in which a ewe has been wrongly accused of stealing a loaf of bread and is forced to sell her woolen coat, Marie sees society as sharply divided between the rich and the poor:

> This example serves to tell
> What's true for many men [*meint hume*] as well:
> By lies and trickery, in short,
> They force the poor to go to court.
> False witnesses they'll often bring
> And pay them with the poor folks' things.
> What's left the poor? the rich don't care,
> As long as they all get their share.[11] (35-42)

Marie's moral, addressed to the men who victimize the poor, is much more specific than the brief Romulus Nilantii moral, which warns of *insidiatores* (plotters, conspirators) who make false accusations (Romulus Nilantii 1:4). Although critical of individual behavior, Marie here, as in "The Wolf and the Lamb" and several other fables, endorses the power structure and its judicial system, which, given proper due process, can serve the public good.

If Marie accepts the male hierarchy as a given, it is not without ambivalence about its inherent justness. While she does at times support its natural rightness, at other times she envisions a society happily free of any such structure, a society in which the people rule and women have equal voice. In "The Sun Who Wished to Wed" (fable 6), the animals as a group assemble to decide what to do to oppose the sun's plan to marry. Marie's fable, unlike Romulus Nilantii and the earlier classical versions, sees this debate as potentially significant, for only in Marie's fable does the animals' petition receive a positive response. Although the animals in Marie's fable are unspecified as to kind or gender (and in Latin versions are male), Marie uses the feminine pronoun when referring to the wise spokesperson. This pronoun may well be simply in grammatical agreement with the antecedent *creature*, but it is worth noting that the accompanying illustration to this fable in ms BN fr 2173 presents two petitioners, both young women, an indication that a contemporary reader recognized both the female and the human qualities that mark Marie's contribution to this fable. In this fable the animals are right and they serve themselves well; they decide communally on appropriate action to oppose the imminent danger of the sun's marriage. Marie's moral advises all under evil rule to behave similarly:

> Thus everyone should cautioned be
> When under evil sovereignty:
> Their lord must not grow mightier
> Nor join with one superior
> To them in intellect or riches.
> They must do all they can to thwart this.
> Stronger the lord, the worse their fate:
> His ambush always lies in wait.[12] (25-32)

But not all communities are so wise. The frogs who request a king, receive a log, and wrongly—and vilely—abuse it, get nothing but contempt from Marie, who seems more sympathetic with the ruling sovereign than with the boorish peasants ("The Frogs Who Asked for a King," fable 18):

> This is what many folks have done
> To a good lord (should they have one):
> They always want to stamp their lord;
> His honor they don't know to guard.
> If they're not kept in stressful plight,
> They'll do him neither wrong nor right.[13] (45-54)

Marie's fable, unlike analogues in Phaedrus (1:2) and Romulus Nilantii (2:1), presents the frogs in open discussion, trying to decide where they will live; they wish to leave their muddy pond and seek dry land—a foolish idea because it goes against nature. In Phaedrus and Romulus Nilantii, the frogs have no discussion; they seek a king who will control their lax morality. They are at least smart enough to know that they are unworthy creatures. Marie seems to want to believe in the value of a public, democratic process, but she also knows that not everyone is worthy of it. Debate and public consent suggest an interest in a democratic process, as does Marie's concern about the ability of the populace to make informed, enlightened decisions. Yet these debates are not presented as potentially revolutionary; rather, they generally confirm the truly aristocratic male's natural right to rule. Nor does Marie grant that all lords are necessarily good (*quant il l'unt*—should they have one [a good lord]), although she does support here the sovereign's right to keep firm control over the masses (*s'il nes tient aukes en destreit*).

Limitations of the Male Hierarchy and the Victims

Thus, although Marie sees the male world as one of public power and authority, she sees this power as "other," as "them" abusing "us"; and the "us" includes females as participating, and often essential, members of the community. In this fable (fable 18), as in "The Sun Who Wished to Wed," it is the female speaker whose advice and participation in a community decision are crucial to the survival of the community.

If Marie is ambivalent about males in the public world, supporting the hierarchy but not the individuals, she has but little hope to offer concerning males in the more private world of male-female relationships. Several fables are quite explicit and shocking in their depiction of the cruelty females suffer at the hands of males. The wolf threatens the pregnant sow about to give birth and demands that she deliver immediately so he can gobble up her tender little piglets ("The Wolf and the Sow," fable 21); the male bear tricks the proud mother monkey into showing off her darling babe—only to snatch it and gobble it up in front of her ("The Monkey and Her Baby," fable 51); the fox cruelly tricks and traps a female bear so he can rape her—taunting her all the while, in spite of her tears ("The Fox and the Bear," fable 70). These are gender-specific situations—males victimizing females because of their sex.

There are no loving husbands or happy families in Marie's *Fables*. There are six fables of a parent instructing a child (fables 32, 80, 87, 90, 92, 93); only one parent is male, and this is but a grammatical designation (in fable 93). Unlike analogues and possible sources, Marie presents the other nurturing, instructing parents as distinctly female.[14] Yet whereas Marie generally renders as female those parents who in classical analogues are gramatically male even if otherwise not gender specific, there is one curious exception. In "The Fox and the Eagle" (fable 10), Marie presents both the anguished parent and the eagle who has just snatched away the baby fox as male. But in Phaedrus (1:28) as well as in Romulus Nilantii (1:12) both fox and eagle are grammatically as well as distinctly female (the fox is referred to as a mother; the eagle is seen as nurturing, concerned about providing food for her fledglings). Marie's fox, male, is outside playing with his cub; her eagle seems to have snatched the cub from meanness, not for her concern for feeding the young eaglets. Perhaps Marie could not consider as female a parent who would let a child be snatched away (even though the fox gets his vengeance by burning the eagle's nest). And perhaps Marie could not allow a kidnapping eagle to be female. At any rate, this is the only fable with distinctly female characters in classical analogues that Marie presents as male.

What seems to be lacking in Marie's males is the ability to work together with others, most fundamentally in partnership. As creatures of power, they establish their identities publicly and alone. The females, in contrast, are community creatures; they nurture their young, and share their hearths and their hearts.

There are of course many traditional fables in Marie's collection of professed male partnerships, of one creature attempting to trick the other with a false offer of aid and fellowship. But Marie also presents fables in which the commitment is mutual; the two are, in Marie's word, companions. In two fables of a wolf and a hedgehog (fables 72 and 78), the two pledge to be companions but readily abandon each other when danger is near. In "The Fox and the Cat" (fable 99), the two, walking together in a field, decide together to be companions:

> Un gupil e un chaz alerent
> Par mi un champ, si purparlerent
> Qu'il sereient cumpainun. (1-3)

But they, too, readily abandon each other when endangered. In "The Bat" (fable 23), the bat's pledge of loyalty is worthless, as he switches sides as soon as he feels the other side winning. Surprisingly, in all of these fables, Marie holds back and does not point to companionship and loyalty as the desired qualities exemplified; in the epimythia she sees just the more traditional plot of one character trying to outsmart the other, only to entrap himself instead. Marie does not see her males as capable of forming mutual bonds; the best she can expect is that they make only those promises they intend to keep.

There is little room for new and significant friendships in a society defined by rigid hierarchies. It is equally difficult for Marie's males to define themselves in any new and desired way; they find they must remain where they must be. Marie sees males who try to be what they are not as vain—a quality in her fables typically medieval yet unique to her males. Marie's presentation of vanity is apt to her time in that it includes both those who are vainglorious and who misunderstand true physical beauty and, more significant, those who do not understand the natural hierarchy and their appropriate position. Marie's crow, for example, foolishly thinks he can adorn himself in peacock feathers and be as beautiful (fable 68); in another fable, the peacock complains that his voice is not as lovely and melodious as the nightingale's (fable 31). The hare wants antlers so he can be as well adorned as the deer, but finds they are much too heavy for him to carry on his head (fable 97). Another male animal, the vole, a creature that Marie says resembles a mouse, is so vainglorious (*enorguilliz*) that in looking for a potential wife, he wrongly thinks his own kind unworthy (fable 74):

> . . . he'd not of his lineage,
> Of his own kind or heritage,
> Look for or choose a wife to wed.
> He'd never have a wife, he said,
> Unless he found one very pleasing—
> The daughter of a most high being
> Was what the vole thought he should seek.[15] (3-9)

The vole's terms, "lineage," "kind," "heritage" (*parage, semblant, lignage*), are those of the male hierarchy, defining identity and status by birthright.

The vole learns that there is no better match for him than the little lady mouse (*la soricette petite*). The lesson is clear; the wall, the last place the vole goes to ask about finding a wife, tells him:

> Go home, and keep in mind for aye
> That you should never, come what may,
> Your nature ever again despise.
> Whoever thinks that he can rise
> Beyond his rightful situation
> Must come back to a lower station.
> Never should one his birthright scorn
> Whate'er he knows (unless baseborn).[16] (83-90)

Here too vanity, either for personal beauty or public prestige, characterizes the male world of Marie's fables, and is indeed exclusively male, as is the rigid hierarchy that establishes each creature's proper position.

The Impossible Solution: Marie's Social Vision

Marie's collection is framed by a pair of fables that makes clear the vanity of the public world of male animals as distinct from the intimacy of the social world of the females. Both the first and final fables of Marie's collection are of a fowl (cock, hen) searching, scratching for food. In Marie's first fable, a cock, scratching in a dung heap in hopes of finding something good to eat, finds instead a precious gem, which he rudely and disdainfully rejects: "Since I have no desire for thee / No honor will you have from me" (15-16). The cock's contempt is based on his vanity and his sense of public image; he believes that he is more worthy than this inedible pebble and cannot therefore see its intrinsic beauty. Yet the fable supports male hierarchical values: true beauty here is in the value and sparkle of the jewel, like the richness and prestige that define social position in the male world. The fact that the cock fails to appreciate the gem merely instructs us to the contrary – we should appreciate its beauty and worth. As the moral to this fable points out, the cock's values are self-centered, self-serving, and shortsighted.

By contrast, the fable that concludes Marie's collection is of a hen (*geline*), not a cock, but likewise scratching for food. As the females in Marie's world are community creatures, and nurturing ones, too, it is appropriate that this hen is in female company, here a loving peasant woman who *par grant amur* offers the hen some of her own grain and some rest from her henly labors. A poor and humble peasant woman, she is outside the male world of wealth, power, and public prominence, the cock's world. Nor is she boorish and stupid, like peasant men, but generous and loving. She is content with her lot and generous with her humble provisions, unlike the arrogant cock. The hen must refuse her offer, but not, like the cock, from arrogant presumption and vanity, but because of her nature – she is supposed to scratch all day for food; such is her nature and custom, she says to the dear peasant woman: "sulunc ma nature, sulunc mun us." This is a kind and loving world lacking in vanity and foolish ambition.

This tranquil conclusion is all the more striking when compared with a Latin analogue, in Perotti's Appendix, a branch of Phaedrus (11, Aesopica 539).[17] Here too the world is female, but the fable begins with the goddess Juno praising her own chastity, and then challenged by Venus, who offers the hen as an example. The hen, Venus says, never ceases from scratching, her hunger is never satisfied, just as the lust of women never ceases and is never satisfied. Unlike Marie's fable of an intimate female world, this is a woman's world seen from a male perspective, publicly laughing at Juno's false pride in her chastity.

The focus of Marie's fable thus differs from analogues; hers is not a fable of men laughing at women who do not see themselves for what they are (incessantly lusty creatures), but of women who do indeed see each other in a distinctly female setting. Her fable then becomes a fitting female counterpart to the cock fable, highlighting the qualities that define both male and female. The cock is alone, the hen is in female company. The cock thinks about his public image, the hen is content with her own nature. The cock is arrogant and rude; the hen, humble and polite. The cock is alone, at the top—of a dung heap; the hen is in loving company by the front door of a farmhouse. The cock is at odds with his environment, the hen is at peace. The cock has the first word in Marie's collection; the hen, the last.

But the hen's world, while a countervision of the cock's, is no more than that; it remains "other," outside the hierarchies of power, title, and wealth. And it seems destined to stay that way. Marie seems to accept the traditional lesson of "The Cock and the Gem," that the cock was wrong to despise the gem for its gustatory unworthiness (even if a small part of our practical minds must agree with the cock that a worm would make a more welcome meal).

In her fables as a whole, Marie seems to hold on to a set of values that endorses the very system her fables often criticize, supporting a male hierarchy even as the fable admonishes those empowered by it. In part this is the world of the fable. As satire, it is a conservative genre, criticizing the individuals to the extent that they do not measure up to expectations or ideals. But Marie also separates herself from this tradition, professing to adopt the classical voice of father/king instructing his young son/heir, but also speaking as a woman. Marie's ambivalence about proper authority of the male hierarchy suggests the kind of language problems identified by Luce Irigaray, Hélène Cixous, and others—that of finding a distinctly female voice in the language of the patriarchy, and here, in a conventionally male literary form as well.[18] Marie's exploration of democratic alternatives—including female speakers and leaders—ends up endorsing, perhaps for lack of alternative, the patriarchal system. The close attention to gender as a quality of character distinguishes Marie's fables from sources and analogues. Her males are not the "us" of traditional fables but the "other" of a female artist looking at her world, defined by a male hierarchy she accepts at least in the abstract. If Marie's "otherness' makes her an outsider, denied any significant position of public power, it also gives her an especially strong voice as a satirist and fabulist, able to look at her world simultaneously from both within and without, and seeing the populace as both "them" and "us," as both male and female, as both beast and (hu)man.

Notes

An earlier version of this paper was presented at the International Congress on Medieval Studies, Kalamazoo, Michigan, May 1990. I am grateful to Thelma Fenster, Benjamin Hoover, Jo Ann McNamara, Christine Rose, and especially Clare A. Lees for their helpful suggestions.

1. For Romulus Nilantii, see Leopold Hervieux, ed., *Les Fabulistes latins, depuis le siècle d'Auguste jusqu'à la fin du moyen âge*, 2d ed., vol. 4 (Paris: Firmin-Didot, 1893-90), 173-250. For Phaedrus, see Ben Edwin Perry, ed., *Aesopica* (Urbana: University of Illinois Press, 1952), trans. Ben Edwin Perry, *Babrius and Phraedrus*, LOEB Classical Library (Cambridge, Mass.: Harvard University Press), with the same fable numbering.

2. See Harriet Spiegel, *Marie de France: Fables* (Toronto: University of Toronto Press, 1987), 6-7.

3. For a discussion of Marie's *Fables* as a product of the twelfth century, see E. A. Francis, "Marie de France et son temps," *Romania* 72 (1951): 78-99; and Erich Köhler, *Ideal und Wirklichkeit in der Höfischen Epik*, 2d ed. (Tübingen: Max Niemeyer, 1970), translated by Eliane Kaufholz as *L'aventure chevaleresque: Idéal et réalité dans le roman courtois* (Paris: Gallimard, 1974), 29-32. For a discussion of the medieval quality of the morals, see Arnold Clayton Henderson, "Medieval Beasts and Modern Cages: The Making of Meaning in Fables and Bestiaries," *PMLA* 97 (January 1982): 40-49.

4. See Harriet Spiegel, "The Woman's Voice in the *Fables* of Marie de France," in *A Marie de France Tapestry*, ed. Chantal Marechal (New York: Edwin Mellen, 1991).

5. Mut s'esteit pres de li asise,
Si l'esgarda par grant quointise.
Ne preisa gueres sa manere,
Kar il feseit mauveise chere.
Uncore vodra plus haut munter,
Sun curage volt espruver.
Sur une branche en haut saili,
Desur le dos li esmeulti.
Unc li cuccu mot ne dist
Ne peiur semblant ne l'en fist.
Arere s'en vet la mesenge;
Le cuccu leidist e blastenge—
Ja de lui ne ferunt seignur!
As autres dist la deshonur
E la hunte qu'il li fist grant:
"Unc ne mustra peiur semblant!
Si uns granz oiseus li mesfeseit,
Mauveisement s'en vengereit—
Quant envers li ne se osa prendra,
Ki est de tuz oiseus la mendre.

Texts and translations of Marie's fables are from Spiegel, *Fables*. All line numbers are cited parenthetically.

6. For Odo of Cheriton, see Hervieux, *Les Fabulistes Latins*, vol. 4, 173-250; John C. Jacobs, trans., *The Fables of Odo of Cheriton* (Syracuse, N.Y.: Syracuse University Press, 1985).

7. Eslisent tel ki seit vaillant,
Pruz e sage e enpernant.
Reis deit estre mut dreiturers,
En justise redz e fiers.

8. E si vus sai bien dire pur quei:
Li egles ad bele grandur,
Si est asez de grant valur;
Mut est sobres e atemprez.
Si une feiz est bien saülez,
Bien repeot juner aprés,
Qu'il n'est de preir trop engrés.

9. Prince se deit bien reposer,
Ne se deit mie trop deliter,
Lui ne sun regné aviler,
Ne la povre gent eissilier.

10. Issi funt li riche seignur,
Li vescunte e li jugeür,
De ceus qu'il unt en lur justise:
Faus acheisuns par coveitise
Treovent asez pur eus confundre;
Suvent les funt a pleit somundre.
La char lur tolent e la pel,
Si cum li lus fist a l'aignel.

11. Par ceste essample nus veut mustrer,
E de meint hume le puis prover,
Ki par mentir e par tricher
Funt les povres suvent pleider.
Faus tesmoines sovent traient,
De l'aveir as povres les (a)paient.
Ne lur chaut que li las devienge,
Mes que chescun sa part tienge.

12. Issi chastie les plusurs
Que sur eus unt les maus seignurs,
Que pas nes deivent esforcïer
N'a plus fort de eus acumpainer
Par lur sen ne par lur aveir,
Mes desturber a lur poeir.
Cum plus est fort, pis lur fet:
Tuz jurs lur est en mal aguet.

13. Issi avient, plusurs le funt
De bon seignur, quant il l'unt:
Tuz jurs le veulent defuler;
Ne li seivent honur garder.
S'il nes tient aukes en destreit,
Ne frunt pur lui tort ne dreit.
A tel se pernent, quis destruit;
De lur aveir meine sun bruit.

Lores regretent lur bon seignur,
A ki il firent la deshonur.

14. See Harriet Spiegel, "Instructing the Children," *Children's Literature* 17 (1959): 25-46.

15. . . . il ne voleit en sun parage,
En sun semblant, en sun lignage,
Femme quere, qu'il preisist.
Jamés n'avera femme, ceo dist,
S'il ne la treve a sun talent—
Fille al plus haut element
Vodra li mulez demander.

16. Va a meisun, e si te retien
Que ne voilles pur nule rien
Ta nature mes despiser.
Teus se quide mut eshaucer
Utre sun dreit e relever,
Que plus estut bas returner.
Mespreiser ne deit nul sun dreit
(Si ceo n'est mal) ki k'il seit.

17. Fable 539 in Perotti's Appendix, included in Perry, *Aesopica*, 539.

18. Luce Irigaray, *Speculum of the Other Woman*, trans. Gillian C. Gill (Ithaca, N.Y.: Cornell University Press, 1985); and Hélène Cixous, "The Laugh of the Medusa," trans. Keith Cohen and Paula Cohen, in *The Signs Reader: Women, Gender and Scholarship*, ed. Elizabeth Abel and Emily K. Abel (Chicago: University of Chicago Press, 1983), 279-97.

PART III

Epic and Empire

CHAPTER 8

Men and *Beowulf*

Clare A. Lees

He is a man, and that for him and many is sufficient tragedy.
J. R. R. Tolkien, "*Beowulf*: The Monsters and the Critics"

We certainly do not need feminist theory to tell us that Beowulf *is a profoundly masculine poem.*
Gillian R. Overing, Language, Sign and Gender in "Beowulf"

Beowulf is an Anglo-Saxon poem about men—male heroes, warriors, kings—and yet the vision and limits of this world as a masculine one have rarely been examined. From the perspective of either feminist or nonfeminist criticism, the question of what it means to call the poem masculine, or its hero male, seems too obvious to merit attention. The foregoing comments from J. R. R. Tolkien and Gillian R. Overing invite assent, not investigation.[1] The masculinity of *Beowulf*, in other words, forms a point of departure—a beginning—that is rarely factored into our interpretations.[2] I wish to turn our critical gaze back onto this beginning and pose two related questions: First, how does *Beowulf* criticism use masculinity as a beginning for interpretation? And second, in what ways can the poem's masculinity be understood?

The insight that informs my own perspective is one fundamental to theories of gender: that the categories of "man," "maleness," and "masculinity" need to be deconstructed in ways similar to those of "woman," "female," and "femininity" (even "feminist"). Gender studies addresses the demystification of the social, cultural, and historical relations between the sexes in order to lay bare the ideological workings that underpin the terms *man* and *woman* at any given historical moment. Neither category exists outside history or culture as a timeless universal, and both are subject to continual redefinition and reinterpretation. Theories of gender, in tandem with much recent materialist criticism, lead me to examine the assumptions of a view that is presented as natural and consensual, and to question whether a particular ideology might be operating instead.[3] In the case of *Beowulf*, we can investigate its so-called self-evident masculinity by inquiring whether "masculinism," as Arthur Brittan usefully puts it, that is to say the "ideology of male power that justifies and naturalizes male domination" has created this effect of self-evidence in its critical reception.[4]

I begin this project of demystification in relation to *Beowulf* and its critical reception by examining in some detail J. R. R. Tolkien's "*Beowulf*: The Monsters and the Critics." First published in 1936, Tolkien's essay remains justifiably influential, and offers an example of how ideologies of masculinism empower and promote a New Critical view of the poem. By contrast, two more recent works by James W. Earl and by Gillian R. Overing propose radically different perspectives. Earl's "*Beowulf* and the Origins of Civilization" demonstrates how psychoanalytic criticism can offer a strong model of readerly identification with the poem, one that appears to carry with it the promise that patriarchy—like masculinism—will remain hegemonic.[5] Overing's *Language, Sign, and Gender in "Beowulf"*, on the other hand, suggestively exposes masculine desire in the poem from the perspective of a feminist reader, and invites, for me at least, a reexamination of how patriarchy and masculinity operate in the internal thematics of the poem itself. Both arguments help me to suggest how the concepts of masculinity and patriarchy inform our understanding of *Beowulf* in the second part of this essay.

These issues of masculinity and patriarchy differ from those addressed by other recent feminist criticism, either on the poem or on Old English literature in general. Work by, for example, Jane Chance or Helen Damico primarily addresses text-internal issues, and is prompted by a desire to reclaim and map out roles for the female in the poem in view of the antifeminist tradition of much of its critical reception.[6] One limiting feature of this kind of feminist approach is that emphasis on the female figures—vital though it is as an intervention in critical writing on *Beowulf*—has left unexplored and, in some cases, reified the male figures. The trap, of course, is essentialism—one of the targets of the feminist agenda. While building on such feminist work, my own differs in two respects. First, I see the critical reception of the poem as part of the continuing history of its meaning; second, I argue that gender—as one mediating element in this history—implies a reexamination of the interplay between masculine *and* feminine issues, both internal and external to the poem.[7] The poem's readers, after all, are men and women, however much they present themselves as disinterested, objective, or ungendered.

Tolkien's New Critical Reader

But in the centre we have an heroic figure of enlarged proportions.
J. R. R. Tolkien, "*Beowulf:* The Monsters and the Critics"

In a brilliant riposte to an earlier generation of critics such as W. P. Ker, who viewed *Beowulf* as fundamentally flawed, Tolkien's "*Beowulf*: The Monsters and the Critics" defends the poem's integrity on three fronts: aesthetically, structurally, and thematically. The essay is grounded on, and framed by, an assertion of the poem's right to be read as poetry rather than as poetic historical document: this is, in other words, an early and important example of New Criticism in Anglo-Saxon studies.[8] Tolkien was fully aware of his intervention in mainstream *Beowulfiana*, and prefaces his analysis with a brief apologia, the real force of which is to demonstrate that the poem still awaits its critic: "*Beowulf* has been used as a quarry of fact and fancy far more assiduously than it has been studied as a work of art" (Tolkien, 5).

It is clear both from the title of Tolkien's article, with its delightful ambiguity, and from these prefatory remarks that Tolkien offers himself as the poem's (New) literary critic. Appropriately enough, then, his own account of the poem's reception is cast not simply in terms of a brief historical survey (6-14), but also metaphorically or, as Tolkien puts it, "allegorically":

> As it set out upon its adventures among the modern scholars, *Beowulf* was christened by Wanley Poesis—*Poeseos Anglo-Saxonicæ egregium exemplum*. But the fairy godmother later invited to superintend its fortunes was Historia. And she brought with her Philologia, Mythologia, Archaeologia, and Laographia. Excellent ladies. But where was the child's name-sake? Poesis was usually forgotten; occasionally admitted by a side-door; sometimes dismissed upon the door-step. "*The Beowulf*," they said, "is hardly an affair of yours, and not in any case a protégé that you could be proud of. It is a historical document. Only as such does it interest the superior culture of today." (6)

This extended metaphor is followed by a second that reinterprets the first and prefaces Tolkien's own reading of the poem:

> A man inherited a field in which was an accumulation of old stone, part of an older hall. Of the old stone some had already been used in building the house in which he actually lived, not far from the old house of his fathers. Of the rest he took some and built a tower. But his friends coming perceived at once (without troubling to climb the steps) that these stones had formerly belonged to a more ancient building. So they pushed the tower over, with no little labour, in order to look for hidden carvings and inscriptions, or to discover whence the man's distant forefathers had obtained their building

> material. Some suspecting a deposit of coal under the soil began to dig for it, and forgot even the stones. They all said: "This tower is most interesting." But they also said (after pushing it over): "What a muddle it is in!" And even the man's own descendants, who might have been expected to consider what he had been about, were heard to murmur: "He is such an odd fellow! Imagine his using these old stones just to build a nonsensical tower! Why did he not restore the old house? He had no sense of proportion." But from the top of that tower the man had been able to look out upon the sea. (7-8)

The difference between these two narratives registers Tolkien's distance from prevailing critical approaches as well as his desire to forge an alternative reading. Unlike earlier critics, who read *Beowulf* as history, and respond to it with historical analysis, Tolkien reads the poem as art and prefaces his response to this artistry with his own narratives. Both merit careful attention for the ways in which gender is deployed by this "new" critic.

In the first, Tolkien recasts the earlier critical tradition (what we might now call the philological school of Anglo-Saxon studies) as symbolically feminine by treading the well-worn path of personification allegory. The kernel of the allegory is self-evident: the poem has been ill served by its historical critics. But look again. Humfrey Wanley, eminent early Anglo-Saxonist, with the full weight of paternal authority as godfather to *Beowulf* and cataloger of the manuscript, recognizes the document as poetry (*Poesis*). On the other hand, the fairy godmother (or is it wicked stepmother?) *Historia*, supported by her grammatically feminine relatives (philology, myth, archaeology, and folklore), forgets, dismisses, and even abandons her adopted child, poetry. Godfather and godmother play asymmetric, nurturing roles to the orphaned and authorless poem, and it is clear where Tolkien's sympathies lie: the godfather (Wanley) empowers *Beowulf* as poetry, the godmother (*Historia*) disables it.

Tolkien rewrites the first allegory in his second and modifies this binarism by rejecting—rather than simply devaluing—the symbolically feminine and the maternal. There are no godmothers here, only men, fathers, forefathers, descendants, and friends interwoven through time in a genealogy of conflict and misunderstanding. This second narrative restores to the poem its filial critic and its fatherly author—both of whom, though criticized for their lack of proportion, are able to look out upon the sea, unified in one perspective. In fact, critic and author come perilously close to being the same figure: the "man" in the allegory can be read as both poet and critic; the tower as both poem and critical interpretation, capable of construction, destruction, and reconstruction. Poet and critic use the tower to empower their transcendental gaze: they look out *upon* the sea, not *at* the object of their construction, the tower/poem/interpretation. No longer the abandoned child of the first allegory, the poem is now a collection of old stones, perhaps ultimately a barrow, certainly a house or hall (which mirrors Heorot), and, above all, a tower. Like the poet, critics are builders, excavators, and miners. In short, Tolkien's condemnatory view of *Beowulf* as a "quarry of fact and fancy" is redeployed to symbolize the poem as a man-made artifact in which lived experience is generated (the house/hall/tower). This view of the poem as artifact or object is, of course, one of the founding premises of New Criticism and resurfaces time and again in Tolkien's subsequent interpretation.

Only in relation to the first allegory can the second be interpreted as symbolically masculine. Tolkien works through the feminine – the older school of philology – in order to erect his own interpretation. That interpretation, which is allied with the poet's own vision by the figure of the tower (the poem, the masculine, the Phallus), looks out upon the sea (the Other, the feminine, the past). Historical criticism, in Tolkien's eyes, fails at least in part for reasons associated with gender: both the "feminine" and the "masculine" allegory have the potential to destroy, or rather deconstruct, the poem. At the same time, and in both allegories, Tolkien casts the poem's "true" defenders as male (Wanley, the poet, and the critic). The second allegory offers Tolkien a means of reconstructing the poem's aesthetics, replacing philological criticism with the New Critical universality of the transcendental gaze. The masculinism of this second allegory, in other words, offers a beginning for literary criticism.

The structures of gender are more complex, therefore, than the binarism female/male suggests, for it is only the second allegory that carries with it the promise of masculinism – creating both an artifact and a criticism to transcend gender. Small wonder that Tolkien's own reading of *Beowulf* expels the female even more dramatically than does the poem. As is well known, Tolkien's monsters are Grendel (the monstrous son) and the dragon; Grendel's mother and other female characters are not mentioned.

"Man" in Tolkien's essay emerges as the liberal humanist construct of the universal male; "we," the unifying perspective of masculinism. Read in the light of these two allegories, Tolkien's comment on the hero Beowulf, "He is a man, and that for him and many is sufficient tragedy" (18), takes on quite a different light. Gender, or more precisely the unifying discourse of masculinism, mediates between the critic's metacritical commentary (the two allegories) and his practice of criticism, his reading of the text. In the remainder of "The Monsters and the Critics," Tolkien sets out to rebuild the poem and finally, poem, poet, and reader are united in a climactic defense of aesthetics. *Beowulf*, built from the "masonry" of its lines (30), transcends its historical moment as "we" look on: "At the beginning, and during its process, and most of all at the end, we look down as if from a visionary height upon the house of man in the valley of the world" (33). In such a reading, the poem, the poet, and the critic transcend time, conquering it as does the hero, Beowulf, at the moment of his death.

Part of Tolkien's critical project is to reconceptualize the significance of Beowulf to demonstrate that he is indeed a hero worthy of a place in the pantheon of the heroes of classical epic, even if (especially if) he fights monsters. There is no gainsaying that, at least in conventional literary critical terms and certainly in Tolkien's time, epic heroes are men, and his analysis demonstrates how masculinity, maleness, becomes an index of humanity. In fact, Tolkien concentrates on the hero's humanity—as man—and the universality of his experience as a shared and representative focus for all readers—or men.[9] Beowulf, for Tolkien, is a man faced with the inevitable consequences of his knowledge "that man, each man and all men, and all their works shall die" (23). In such a reading, the monsters are a very real presence that signifies the limits of the male world: Beowulf's encounters with Grendel and the dragon thematize the hero's will to death, or his struggle against "Time" (18). The poem's power to generate affect is thus inextricably linked to the temporal humanity of the hero or, in gender terms, his masculinity: "that for him and many is sufficient tragedy" (18).

Beowulf's humanity, moreover, becomes a trope for the vexed question of structure: the two halves of the poem are read metonymically as the rise and fall of one man's life. In the process, Beowulf the man (fighting Grendel) becomes Beowulf the hero (fighting the dragon). Enter the dragon, enter the hero: or, as Tolkien puts it "that first moment, which often comes in great lives, when men look up in surprise and see that a hero has *unawares* leaped forth" (32; emphasis added). This is the classic matrix from which many subsequent interpretations of *Beowulf*—the *great* poem—and Beowulf—the man and hero—emerge. But this transformation of Beowulf from man to hero simultaneously provokes a response in Tolkien the reader, who moves from identification to admiration. There is little the critic can do once this stage has been reached: Tolkien's admiration for "an heroic figure of enlarged proportions" (31), which echoes the laudatory final lines of the poem, signifies distance and closure, and "The Monsters and the Critics" ends shortly after.[10] But, judging from the lengthy appendices attached to the essay, Tolkien's resolution was far from satisfactory; yet the article itself heralded a new generation of critics, all anxious to assign a role to Beowulf (the heroic warrior, the young man, the wise/old/proud king), to enlarge, as it were, Tolkien's preliminary analysis.

What does it mean to call Beowulf a man? Tolkien does not explicitly pose this question (nor should we expect him to—this essay is very much a product of its time), but nevertheless the answer is inextricably linked to the project of New Criticism: Beowulf is a representative of all men and is every man's hero. In the process of analysis, masculinity is pressed into the service of masculinism, and the feminine is expelled from the unified gaze, the shared perspectives of poet, hero, and reader. To put it another way, Tolkien's Beowulf is not simply a man. I do not wish to be too critical of the fact that Tolkien does not address questions of gender; my reinterpretation of Tolkien's essay from just such a perspective, however, reveals the extent to which his argument rests on the untheorized assumption that all his readers will read, as he does, as "men."[11]

Gender and Interpretation

By contrast, James W. Earl's "*Beowulf* and the Origins of Civilization" offers a more self-conscious model for reading that examines the poem's patriarchy in psychoanalytic terms. Patriarchy here becomes the key to understanding the poem's, and the hero's, unique power to generate ambivalence in the poem and in the reader. As a result, Earl addresses the very issues that remain implicit and unfocused in Tolkien's essay. To examine the relationship between the hero and the reader in terms of identification, Earl reads Tacitus's well-known comment on the two heroic codes of warrior society ("The lord fights for victory, the companions for the lord"; cited by Earl, 81) from the stance of a creative Freudian psychoanalysis. Earl adapts Freud's theory of the group to explicate how the poem enforces a radically authoritarian patriarchy in its readers by splitting identification between Beowulf as heroic ideal or superego and Wiglaf (the loyal retainer) as brother of the group or *comitatus*. The fact that Tolkien admires or idealizes the hero and thereby defends him from criticism is thus precisely the point: "The heroic ideal, then, is not simply a model of excellence or virtue to be imitated but is also a forbidden and unattainable desire, highly defended against, sharply distinguished from the ego itself and highly critical of it" (Earl, 83). As ideal, the hero is defended from the reader's criticism in much the same way as Tolkien's hero "unawares leaped forth" (Tolkien, 32).

The ambivalence felt by readers is a direct result of their admiration of the hero, "the idealization of the hero, which frees him from criticism, is accompanied by self-criticism among his followers—and the audience"

(Earl, 83). The catch, of course, is that the poem's ability to continue to produce these ambivalent effects demands that the reader uncritically occupy a subject position *within patriarchy*. As a symbol of the superego, Beowulf is, of course, the Father. Earl's theory is thus defended more sharply than Tolkien's against the perspective of an Other reader (female or feminist, e.g.), who may have a different investment in patriarchy. As with Tolkien, the process by which Earl arrives at this conclusion has considerable implications for our understanding of the interrelationship of gender and interpretation. In place of Tolkien's two allegories, Earl offers two dreams, both of which use female figures. The (female) sphinx in the first dream symbolizes the riddle of *Beowulf* (read as the riddle of Oedipus), which occupies the position of the superego (like Beowulf in the latter part of the poem) and silently analyzes its readers as they seek to analyze it.[12] In the second dream, the poem itself is a fabulous doll:

> I dreamed about a little girl who had a fascinating, unusual doll, every part of which—arms, legs, head, torso—seemed to be made from other dolls, all of different colors and proportions. I knew where it had come from: the little girl's brother had collected all the old, broken dolls he could find around the neighborhood, and he had loaded them into his red wagon, and pulled them home behind his bicycle; then he had made a single doll out of all their parts and had given it to his sister. Far from thinking it was junk, she thought it was beautiful, and loved it—first of all because it was unlike any other doll, and yet like them all; also because it was so interesting, and also because her brother had made it for her, and because he had made it so well. (Earl, 73-74)

This dream is brilliantly analyzed by Earl himself, who, however, never identifies the doll—or poem—as female, yet there are some suggestive hints: in the splitting identifications of the dream, Earl as reader is female as well as male ("Insofar as I am a reader of *Beowulf* I identify with the girl"; 74), and the reader to whom the gift of the doll is made is also identified as female ("You are the sister I am trying to please"; 74). I freely admit that this is a somewhat partial view of Earl's own analysis of his overdetermined dream (which also concentrates on his identification with the poet), but it heuristically foregrounds the problem of gender in his two dreams. In both, the poem is read as symbolically female. Earl explains the second dream as follows:

> The dream also brings rather delicate problems of gender to consciousness. *Beowulf* is a markedly antifeminist poem, and making it a gift to the little girl is my attempt at compensation, though nec-

> essarily condescending: she is still being strongly marginalized, after all. I do not see any way around that, since the poem so strongly marginalizes the female reader already. My simultaneous identification with her, however, indicates my deep ambivalence about the *patriarchal* project of the poem and the *patriarchal* project of its criticism (not to mention the *patriarchal* structures of professional life, teaching, and marriage). Beyond that, moreover, the bond of love between her and her brother, both of whom I identify with strongly, though in different ways, indicates how far from such ideological criticism my psychoanalytic responses to the poem really are. (74-75; emphasis added)

Who is marginalizing the female here: Earl the dreamer or Earl the analyst? The dream itself focuses on the female—the little girl and the beautiful doll—as much as it does on her brother, whereas the analysis admits to, and attempts to compensate for, a desire to marginalize her. The deep divide between Earl's psychoanalytic response to the patriarchal structures of the poem and his resistance to the ideology of patriarchy as an institution of gender relations (note the number of times "patriarchal" is repeated in the above quotation) leads me to suggest that what is still being avoided is gender. Indeed, his essay skirts the "delicate problems of gender" posed by the poem while simultaneously promoting the Law of the Father. The result is that for Earl, reading as one man, patriarchy and its psychic structures are presented as hegemonic, and gender highly defended against: "I do not see any way around that," Earl says (74).

At the heart of Earl's analysis lies a vital contribution to *Beowulf* criticism, namely, the role of identification and transference in eliciting and constructing interpretation. Whether or not the poem marginalizes the female reader (as opposed to the evident marginalization of women *in* the poem), many women do read it, and Earl's analysis of his own dreams points to an understanding of identification that can include us. It is obvious enough to suggest that women readers may identify differently with the poem and its hero—Freud's insistence on primary bisexuality, for example, allows for a broad range of oedipal conflicts, resolutions, and, hence, identifications across the sexes. The poem, in other words, may attempt to enforce an authoritarian patriarchy upon its readers, male or female, but there is no guarantee it will succeed as Earl suggests. In spite of this, patriarchy here assumes the same conceptual status that liberal humanism (as New Criticism) does in Tolkien's essay: it is, as Earl implies, a transhistorical and universal theory of the relationship of the individual to the group, of the rule of the Father. The way around this problem may be to consider a second (nonpsychoanalytic) interpretation of patriarchy as a social system of *dominance of men over women.*[13] This definition of patriarchy enlightens Earl's anxieties, as his resistance is not to the female (as is clear in his second dream) but to his own interpretation of her, which produces an analysis of how men maintain dominance, not simply in the poem, but in the project of its criticism. As Earl himself says, he is deeply ambivalent about the patriarchy of the poem and of its criticism: his dreams attempt to compensate for the marginalization not simply of the woman, but also the man, whose identification with the poem might usher in a male oedipal failure and an identification with an authoritarian patriarchy.[14]

We can demystify Earl's project of patriarchy in ways similar to my reading of Tolkien's project of New Criticism. The parallels between the two essays, though clearly not intentional, are nevertheless notable. Like Tolkien, Earl uses gender (his gendered dreams) as a beginning—this time for a psychoanalytic reading. Again, the symbolically female is replaced by the symbolically male, this time to provide a sophisticated account of the structures of patriarchy in *Beowulf* with considerable power to explain the psychological processes whereby obedience is enforced and maintained within a necessarily male warrior class (Earl, 84). In the process, Earl targets the ambivalence that the poem itself expresses toward this patriarchal project—a point to which I shall return later. If Tolkien reads the poem from the perspective of the universal "man," however, Earl reads more self-consciously as just one "man."

It is precisely in opposition to reading as a "man" that the first wave of feminist criticism on *Beowulf* is produced. Part of a widespread feminist project that seeks to reclaim the female, its critical insights are frequently purchased at the price of remaining firmly tied to gendered binary assumptions. The ideological underpinning of criticism in general remains unquestioned by these moves: to Beowulf the hero is added Chance's *Woman as Hero*; to the male warrior figure is added Helen Damico's valkyrie; to the male roles of hero and king are added the female roles of peace-weaver and queen; and so forth. These analyses are conducted with varying degrees of sophistication, but they are based on a conception of binarisms as equal and opposite rather than asymmetric, and offer little explanatory power with which to analyze the patriarchy of the poem or the patriarchal assumptions of much of its criticism, including their own. The feminist gaze on the poem remains firmly on the female, which has the curiously unfeminist effect of leaving the question of the male protected and hidden. We could say that such readings stem from the same masculinist assumptions as Tolkien's allegories: the critical gaze looks beyond the artifact of its own creation.

By contrast, Earl's analysis of the reader urges the importance of examining our critical constructs (and their unconscious motivations), and a similar position is adopted in Gillian R. Overing's *Language, Sign, and Gender in "Beowulf,"* which examines the patriarchy of *Beowulf* from an Other, feminist perspective to demonstrate how its perceived hegemony is neither consistent nor without consequences. Overing starts with a premise similar to Earl's—that the text may be said to invent its readers (Overing, xiii)—but she theorizes *Beowulf*'s patriarchy using a feminist semiotic and psychoanalytic understanding of desire: "Who wants what in *Beowulf* and who gets it?" (69) thus usefully contrasts with Earl's questions of identification. Casting desire as the centerpiece of the symbolic economy of the poem (read as masculine), Overing suggests that the male characters of the poem cast their objects of desire as Other and, through subjugation and appropriation, maintain their own Sameness (xxiii, 69-70). Women, the feminine, thus have no position from which to signify—nameless, silent, or even resistant, as use-objects within this economy they can have little investment in it. Though marginalized, women may usurp their position of Other by hysteria. They disrupt, displace, and deflect what Overing calls the dominant masculine desire of the poem—revealing it and, at the same time, intersecting with the process of its drive toward death. The problem of the marginal female is fully addressed as a critical issue, and what is presented as a source of anxiety in Earl is given centrality by Overing, who, by acknowledging the asymmetry of the binarisms—man/woman; active/passive; silent/speech—resists recuperation of the female by making her the Same as him.

As we have seen, Earl's analysis clears the ground for an understanding of readerly identification that is ostensibly male but need not exclude the female while pointing to the poem's manipulation of patriarchal structures. Equally important, Earl concentrates on the poem's, and the reader's, idealization of the hero. Overing suggests a similar idealization but approaches it from the Other's direction—Beowulf, in his speech community of one, is potentially the male hysteric of the poem (84):

> Beowulf forms a speech community of one, however, he is judge and jury. His heroism demands a degree of self-absorption that closes the social circuit of language; he creates his separate relation to reality. (93)

From the position of Other (which can be occupied by both female and male subjects), Overing deliberately unsettles the reader with her comments on Beowulf as hysteric: to her, Beowulf is not the universalized hero but man-as-scapegoat, as Other. The power of the masculine hero as analytic construct, which is used to unify the critical perspectives on the poem by Tolkien and Earl, is therefore severely tested. Following Hélène Cixous and Catherine Clément, Overing suggests that the appropriation of the role of Other can be used to unsettle and challenge the hold of patriarchy.[15] From this position as Other, it is possible to return our gaze onto the masculine economy of the poem and use Overing's emphasis on the female to rethink Earl's emphasis on the male. We can ask what it means to be a signifying subject in *Beowulf*, what it means to be a man, bearing in mind the problems of essentializing the categories of either man or woman.

Patriarchy, Masculinity, "Beowulf"

Beowulf creates an almost exclusively male world, as I said at the beginning of this essay, but, in spite of Tolkien's assertions, it does not claim to be a poem about men or masculinity in general. Rather, as both Earl and Overing imply but do not develop, it is a poem about a particular group of men, associated by their aristocratic rank, their kin, and their lords. It is also a poem that directs much of its attention to one man, Beowulf, of the same class, similar family structure, and lords. What unifies these two groups – Danes and Geats – is the ethic of warrior behavior: only warriors from this rank act to become heroes, leaders, kings. As is often remarked, this world is further circumscribed: women are markedly marginal, as are the family and domestic relations between the sexes – institutions that might be expected to parallel the world of the warrior. There are, in other words, deliberate constraints on this masculine poetic world that can be understood in terms of their relationship with the ideological institutions of rank, family, and ethical (or cultural) norms. By examining the social matrix of such constraints in the poem, we can modify and complement Earl's insights into their psychological components.

Contemporary social theorists have observed similar matrices that underpin masculinity and patriarchy, which can be usefully tested against a reading of the poem, despite radical differences in time and subject. Sylvia Walby, for example, argues that the principal sites for the contestation of patriarchy, understood as a social system of gender inequalities that enforces male dominance over women, are waged work, culture, housework, sexuality, violence, and the state.[16] Each of these sites will necessarily vary from culture to culture and period to period as patriarchy is reconstructed and remodified, but they have some usefulness as the beginnings of analysis. As Arthur Brittan reminds us, ideologies of power such as masculinism (male domination of other men) and patriarchy (male domination of women) are never simply givens imposed on any particular society, but are contested by individuals within particular institutions.[17]

Beowulf is a poem in part about history, but it is not a work of historiography: if we wish to understand more fully the patriarchal structure of Anglo-Saxon society, this poem will give us only notoriously limited answers. The subject of the poem is not Anglo-Saxon England and, as is well known, critics cannot even agree on its date and place of production.[18] *Beowulf* as a poem is, nevertheless, part of this culture's social formation and, given its careful construction of a particular kind of masculine world, it is reasonable to consider just what kind of perspective on men in what kinds of institutions *Beowulf* offers. We can extend the insights of Earl and Overing into the relationship between gender and interpretation by reexamining the poem's re-presentation of patriarchy and of masculine values.

The patrilineal family is a useful place to start and broadens Earl's focus on the *comitatus* while complementing Overing's concentration on the marginalized position of the female figures within the family. The poem opens with the patrilineal family of the Scyldings – the ruling family of motherless Danes – and the ruling dynasties, whether Danish or Geatish, form one of its fundamental preoccupations. What is immediately striking is the severe pressure under which these motherless families operate. Scyld's glorious founding family is in radical stasis within three generations (and many fewer lines), with the twelve-year persecution of Hrothgar's hall by Grendel. Intimations of future discord between his nephew, Hrothulf, and his sons Hrethric and Hrothmund haunt Beowulf's successful slaughter of Grendel's mother (1180b-91). Similarly, Beowulf's own father, Ecgtheow, was indebted to the Danish family because of feuding (459-72) and plays an extremely curtailed role in his son's life, who is far more closely identified with his uncle Hygelac and his grandfather Hrethel, of the Geatish ruling family. The Geats too are beset with problems of kingly succession, partly as a result of feuding with the Swedish ruling family. By the end of the poem, the Geats are lordless, without an obvious successor because Beowulf leaves no direct heir, as he himself acknowledges (2729-32a). While praising these dynasties, the poem leaves us in no doubt of their tenuous hold on life in the hall. The maintenance of patrilineal genealogy is no easy thing.

In fact, *Beowulf* concentrates on what we might call the crucial sites in genealogical or patrilineal succession. The poem opens with a fatherless father whose past is unknown, Scyld, and closes with the death of a childless son, Beowulf. Patrilineal relationships cement strong bonds between a father and a son – the family of Scyld is a matter for praise and memory – and yet they are also fragile ones. The memory of Ecgtheow is similarly conflicted – the father of Beowulf found himself in need of Danish assistance. Succession within the same family leads as often to conflict, as in the case of Hrothgar, as it does to relative stability, as in the case of his grandfather, Beowulf Scyldinga (12-19). Relationships between uncle and nephew, brother and brother, are equally tense: Beowulf is the loyal nephew of Hygelac, who ends up the most famed king of the Geats, but it was the accidental slaying of Hygelac's own brother, Herebeald, by his other brother, Hæthcyn, that brought Hygelac to the throne (2435-40). Indeed, the most potent bonds between man and man are not necessarily those of father and son but those of lord and noble retainer. The poet uses such bonds to underscore the symbolic conflict between kinship ties and rank affiliations that can always erupt into literal violence. Significantly, the poet reserves his most emotional language to express these displaced bonds. Hrothgar becomes a metaphoric father in his speeches to Beowulf and weeps at his parting (1872b), Hrethel before him (2426-34) and Hygelac after him both treat Beowulf as a son. By contrast, the most stigmatized though equally poignant relationship in the poem is that of the father living on alone after the unavenged death of his son, as Beowulf laments in one of the most sustained metaphors in the entire poem (2444-61a).

The focus on patrilineal genealogy therefore provides the poem with a particularly conflicted set of male relationships. The attitude of the poem toward these relationships is deliberately ambivalent: the institution cannot guarantee the continuity of kingly life, but it is the only institution available. The poem's focus is therefore on individual men who sustain, interact with, and reinterpret this institution. It is perhaps no accident that Beowulf dies in battle with the only major figure in the poem without a genealogy: the dragon. Genealogy offers the ambiguous promise of male succession; how this power is managed by men forms one aspect of the broader patriarchal dynamics of the poem. The focus on genealogy, however, is a narrowly circumscribed one, defined by the interests of the ruling families as measured in kinship bonds or loyalty ties. Accordingly, social power is always concentrated in a few male hands.

Patriarchy is most commonly defined as a system of gender inequalities by which men preserve their dominion over women, and, as Overing indicates, this is certainly the case in *Beowulf*. The poem, however, is arguably as much preoccupied with the ways in which aristocratic warriors dominate other men as they do monstrous Others. This is expressed in terms of the language of masculinism: *Beowulf* ritualizes aggression both physically *and* verbally[19] to enforce obedience of the dominated to the dominant. Aggression is central to the maintenance of power in the ruling families and is formulated throughout the poem in terms of a heroic ideology, or code. Most of the events enacted or recited in the poem are attempts to control or resolve violent situations. Violence may be implicit in the structure of warrior society and therefore man-made—as represented in the complex clashes of kinship and revenge in the Finnsburh episode (1068-1159a)—or represented by the challenges of the alien or the Other—clashes of man and monster, man and woman (the example of Modthryth springs to mind).

Beowulf is a bloody poem. It dwells on death and lingers on the tearing of vertebrae, the severed arm, the burnt body. Grendel relishes blood:

> Ne þæt se aglæca yldan þohte,
> ac he gefeng hraðe forman siðe
> slæpendne rinc, slat unwearnum,
> bat banlocan, blod edrum dranc. (739-42)

[Nor did the monster think to delay but on the first occasion he quickly seized a sleeping warrior, tore without hindrance, bit bone-links, drank blood from veins.]

So too does the poem, as the description of Grendel's mortal wound makes plain:

> Licsar gebad
> atol æglæca: him on axle wearð
> syndolh sweotol; seonowe onsprungon,
> burston banlocan. (815b-18a)

[The terrible monster experienced body-pain: a huge wound gaped on his shoulder; sinews sprung apart, bone-links burst.]

But Grendel is not alone in desiring blood, the ethos of the heroic world demands it. There is, however, a crucial difference between Grendel's desire for aggression and that of the heroic world he attacks. Grendel's desire is channeled into the production of death; warriors too produce death, but their desires are channeled into a social ethos that ritualizes desire as heroic choice, thus ensuring the preservation of that ethos.[20] The institution of the warrior caste encodes the desires of its members, and warriors choose death as a means of its reproduction—the warriors fight on even after the death of their lord, as Earl reminds us. At the same time, however, the poem tells us that this institution does not guarantee success, and its reproduction is fragile.

Deeds of aggression are therefore necessarily as praiseworthy as the patriarchal family—they too are the matter of memory and of song. Good deeds and bad are preserved in the communal songs of *Beowulf*. As a good king and one who demands loyalty and tribute, Scyld Scefing acts forcefully, rules through territorial expansion and subjugation, and leaves a son: "þæt wæs god cyning!" (11b). To be a good king is also to be a dead one. The parameters of the poem's masculine heroic world are inscribed in the opening lines (4-11), and are subject to redefinition and reinterpretation throughout. The leader comes from elsewhere, from the unknown, reinstates order though aggression, rules successfully (as measured by the assent of his subjects and poets), and dies, returning to the unknown. Continuity is ensured in two ways—through the memory of his actions and through his sons—but neither is reliable. The heroic actions of the past are not predictable guides to those of the present or future: "þæt wæs god cyning!" is statement, not advice. Scyld Scefing's line will be threatened by Grendel and destroyed by feuding.

The actions of dead kings and dead heroes, however, provide the only guides for interpreting action in *Beowulf*. After Beowulf's battle against Grendel, his actions are celebrated with a song about two other heroic men: Sigemund and Heremod (874b-906). The successful slaying of one monster prompts the recall of another famous monster-slayer, Sigemund, and it would appear that Beowulf's present actions are to be analogically interpreted via this song. But Beowulf is not Sigemund. Beowulf has killed Grendel and will later kill a dragon, but he will die in the encounter, unlike Sigemund, who survived. In the song, Sigemund is contrasted with the ignoble Heremod, who does not fulfill his early promise as a good king. Later Hrothgar too urges Beowulf to contemplate the lesson of Heremod (1709b-22). But Beowulf, unlike Heremod, lives out the promise of the heroic ethos and the institution of kingship. Although the poem invites us to measure man against man, the coordinates of the past offer only superficial parallels. As with genealogy, patriarchal power within the institution of the warrior class is managed and tested by its individual male members.

Beowulf, as a result, is as much about the limits of aggression in this male aristocratic heroic world as it is about its successes. By resting its gaze on Beowulf, the poem gives us a man who exposes the workings of these institutions—that is to say, an example of how one man (the hero) manages its obligations to maintain power in the male hands of ruling dynasties. It is with the representation of this one man that the poem images the ambiguous functions of the masculine world, which can produce an Unferth and a Beowulf: hence, Beowulf's power to unsettle and disturb critical thought as hero, which all the best commentators on the poem have understood. Beowulf is the only warrior in the poem not fully sanctioned by a legendary or mythical lineage. His own line has ambiguous overtones because of his father's earlier feuds, and his earlier life is subject to challenge and redefinition. Beowulf is therefore only partially assimilable to the heroic world of either Danes or Geats. Associated with the Danes via his father's debt to Hrothgar as well as his heroic actions, he is seen as a threat to the ruling family by at least one member (Wealhtheow), whereas Hrothgar views him as a promising candidate for the throne of the Geats (1844-53a), and perhaps too for the Danes. In his own country, however, Beowulf comes to power only as a result of the interminable Swedish-Geatish wars. Beowulf, moreover, refutes the promise of genealogical succession by dying without a son, even while making alternative arrangements for Wiglaf to succeed him (2800a-2801b).

In terms of the management of aggression, Beowulf occupies a privileged position as the only successful warrior in Denmark. But, as Tolkien, Earl, and Overing all note, Beowulf is the outsider as hero, like Scyld before him. Unlike Scyld, however, Beowulf demonstrates that the successful management of events is not a matter simply of actions but of words. As Overing says, Beowulf is "a speech community of one" (93). In the series of highly ritualized encounters that mark Beowulf's advance from the seashore to Heorot, Beowulf progressively reveals in speech his own past until that past is climactically appropriated by Hrothgar (372-76). In fact, he is always the privileged speaker in the poem and the poem becomes in part *his* narrative. We hear his rhetorical mastery of personal memory in combat with communal memory represented by Unferth's challenge, when hc cxposes the illusions of the Danes, whose best riposte is discord, and whose best account of Breca is Unferth's (506-28). Beowulf triumphs in words before he defeats Grendel, and succeeds not because his version of the contest is "true" (that truth is unverifiable by those in the present), but because his words carry the authority of one who has rhetorically restructured the past to best suit the present. This restructuring continues throughout the poem. Beowulf retells of his struggles against Grendel and Grendel's mother time and again, on each occasion reformulating the account to mold it to present circumstances (958-79, 1652-76, 2069b-2143). He relates to Hygelac his interpretation of the political situation in Denmark (2020-69a), foregrounding the internal dynastic feuds that were simply allusions earlier in the poem. And he shares with the narrator the stories of the Swedish-Geatish wars that precipitate his rise to power (2426-2509). Beowulf speaks as both warrior and king from the privilege of both personal and communal experience. The successful manipulation of patriarchal power, therefore, rests on one discourse, as well as on one body.

As the poem repeatedly emphasizes, power is played across the bodies of individual men: desire, chaneled through the institutions of heroism and family, comes to rest in the dead body of Beowulf, as he himself reminds us in his penultimate speech (2729-51). Here, Beowulf laments the absence of an heir to his body ("lice gelenge"; line 2732a) to whom he could present his war-gear. Beowulf is a great king but even he cannot resist the dragon. He comes into the poem from across the seas (like Scyld), from the unknown, and is buried looking out upon the sea. Finally, he is only one more dead but praiseworthy man—warrior and king: the only good hero, after all, is a dead one.

Conclusion

Concepts such as gender mediate in our interpretations of *Beowulf*, and my own position has been to illustrate how the patriarchal project of *Beowulf* criticism (to paraphrase Earl) can create a reading of the poem that naturalizes gender and thereby promotes masculinism. We need only turn to Earl and Overing to see how crucial the concepts of patriarchy and gender are to reading. As both suggest, the masculinity of *Beowulf* may be self-evident, but its construction—how masculinity works in the poem—is by no means transparent. The construction of this masculine world is bought at a huge price: women, men, and monsters are all sacrificed to an artistic vision that focuses on the desires of a very narrowly defined warrior class. The ideologies of patriarchy and masculinism help define the matrix of this circumscribed world by attending to the relationship between the patrilineal aristocratic family and the institutionalized aggression of its warrior class, by whom it maintains power. The poem does not condemn these warriors, but its patriarchal gaze is simultaneously appreciative *and* critical. The challenge readers face is how to explore the difference, or alterity, of this poetic world without falling into glib and easy statements about its apparent celebration of male violence. Although *Beowulf* is a poem that is frequently cast in a sentimental light, there is nothing sentimental about its ambiguous and ambivalent gaze on men.[21]

Notes

1. J. R. R. Tolkien, "*Beowulf*: The Monsters and the Critics," *Proceedings of the British Academy* 22 (1936): 245-95, reprinted in *The Monsters and the Critics and Other Essays*, ed. Christopher Tolkien (London: Allen & Unwin, 1983), 5-48 (at 18); Gillian R. Overing, *Language, Sign, and Gender in "Beowulf"* (Carbondale: Southern Illinois University Press, 1990), xxiii. All subsequent references to these works are by page number and author, when relevant; page numbers for Tolkien's essay are from the 1990 reprint.

2. The theoretical distinction between beginnings and origins is applied to the discipline of Anglo-Saxon studies in general by Allen J. Frantzen, *Desire for Origins: New Lan-*

guage, Old English, and Teaching the Tradition (New Brunswick, N.J.: Rutgers University Press, 1990), 1-26, especially 23-24.

3. An interesting and broadly materialist study of masculinity is that by Arthur Brittan, *Masculinity and Power* (Oxford: Basil Blackwell, 1989); see also Toril Moi's pertinent comments in "Men against Patriarchy," in *Gender and Theory: Dialogues on Feminist Criticism*, ed. Linda Kaufman (Oxford: Basil Blackwell, 1989), 181-88. One of the best introductions to materialist criticism generally is Raymond Williams, *Marxism and Literature* (Oxford: Oxford University Press, 1977).

4. Brittan uses the term *masculinism* to distinguish the ideology of masculine power from the concept of masculinity, that is to say, those aspects of male behavior that are subject to change over time and that suggest that (male) identity is fragile; see *Masculinity and Power*, 3-4.

5. James W. Earl, "*Beowulf* and the Origins of Civilization," in *Speaking Two Languages: Traditional Disciplines and Contemporary Theory in Medieval Studies*, ed. Allen J. Frantzen (Albany: State University of New York Press, 1991), 65-89. All subsequent references are by author and page number.

6. Jane Chance, *Woman as Hero in Old English Poetry* (Syracuse, N.Y.: Syracuse University Press, 1986); Helen Damico, *Beowulf's Wealhtheow and the Valkyrie Tradition* (Madison: University of Wisconsin Press, 1984). See also Helen Damico and Alexandra Hennessey Olsen, eds., *New Readings on Women in Old English Literature* (Bloomington: Indiana University Press, 1990). For a survey of feminist approaches to Old English literature, see Helen T. Bennett, "From Peace Weaver to Text Weaver: Feminist Approaches to Old English Studies," in *Twenty Years of the "Year's Work in Old English Studies,"* ed. Katherine O'Brien O'Keeffe, *Old English Newsletter*, Subsidia 15 (1989): 23-42; and, more briefly, Helen T. Bennett, Clare A. Lees, and Gillian R. Overing, "Gender and Power: Feminism and Old English Studies," *Medieval Feminist Newsletter* 10 (Fall 1990): 15-23.

7. Gender is, of course, only one such mediation; others would be race and gender, for example, Williams, *Marxism and Literature*, 95-100, offers a useful discussion of the concept of mediation. For another discussion of mediation, directly related to Old English, see Frantzen, *Desire for Origins*, 103-5.

8. As Frantzen notes; *Desire for Origins*, 79.

9. Whereas, according to Allen J. Frantzen, the poem itself distinguishes *only* Beowulf's behavior as an index of human behavior, superior to other men (and women); see his "When Women Aren't Enough," in "Studying Medieval Women: Sex, Gender, Feminism" (special issue), ed. Nancy F. Partner, *Speculum* 68 (1993): 445-71. I am grateful to Professor Frantzen for letting me read and refer to this essay prior to its publication.

10. Fr. Klaeber, ed., *Beowulf and the Fight at Finnsburg*, 3d. ed. (Lexington, Mass.: D. C. Heath, 1950), lines 3180-82. All subsequent references to *Beowulf* are to this edition, by line number.

11. For an introductory discussion of the concept of gendered reading, see Patrocinio P. Schweikart, "Reading Ourselves: Toward a Feminist Theory of Reading," in *Gender and Reading: Essays on Readers, Texts, and Contexts*, ed. Elizabeth A. Flynn and Patrocinio P. Schweikart (Baltimore: Johns Hopkins University Press, 1986), 31-62. Gillian R. Overing applies the concept to Old English literature in "On Reading Eve: *Genesis B* and the Readers' Desire," in Frantzen, *Speaking Two Languages*, 35-64.

12. "Falling asleep recently while thinking about *Beowulf*, I dreamed of a sphinx, not quite buried in the desert sand; in fact, no matter how hard I tried to bury it, one eye always remained uncovered. The sphinx is *Beowulf*, of course; but it is also my superego" (Earl, 73).

13. As Juliet Mitchell says, "Psychoanalysis is not a recommendation *for* a patriarchal society, but an analysis *of* one." Juliet Mitchell, *Psychoanalysis and Feminism* (Harmondsworth: Penguin, 1975), xv. A useful discussion of feminist approaches to psychoanalytic theory remains Michèle Barrett's, *Women's Oppression Today: The Marxist/Feminist Encounter* (London: Verso, 1980, rev. 1988), 42-83.

14. This passage into patriarchy is assessed by Earl, who offers this strongly marked compensation cast in terms of his own gaze on the poem: "I must admit that my pleasure with this understanding of *Beowulf* and its effects on the audience sits rather uneasily with my own individuality, and my own resentful attitudes toward authority. The oedipal failure the poem tries to enforce is intended to socialize us into a radically authoritarian world. It is balanced, thank goodness, by the spectacle of the hero's awesome, if unobtainable, freedom" (87).

15. Hélène Cixous and Catherine Clément, *The Newly Born Woman*, trans. Betsy Wing (Minneapolis: University of Minnesota Press, 1986).

16. Sylvia Walby, *Theorizing Patriarchy* (Oxford: Basil Blackwell, 1990), 21. Anthropological studies of men also indicate some transcultural similarities in the construction of male identities; see, for example, Stanley Brandes, *Metaphors of Masculinity: Sex and Status in Andalusian Folklore* (Philadelphia: University of Pennsylvania Press, 1980); and David D. Gilmore, *Manhood in the Making: Cultural Concepts of Masculinity* (New Haven, Conn.: Yale University Press, 1990).

17. Brittan, *Masculinity and Power*, 19-45.

18. See, for example, Kevin S. Kiernan, *"Beowulf" and the Beowulf Manuscript* (New Brunswick, N.J.: Rutgers University Press, 1981); David M. Dumville, "Beowulf Come Lately: Some Notes on the Palaeography of the Nowell Codex," *Archiv für das Studium der neueren Sprachen und Literaturen* 225 (1988): 49-63; and the essays in Colin Chase, ed., *The Dating of "Beowulf"* (Toronto: Toronto University Press, 1981).

19. As Ward Parks reminds us in *Verbal Dueling in Heroic Narrative: The Homeric and Old English Traditions* (Princeton, N.J.: Princeton University Press, 1990).

20. These brief comments on desire as a psychoanalytic mechanism for production have been stimulated by Klaus Theweleit's analysis of fascism, *Male Fantasies*, vol. 1, trans. Stephen Conway in collaboration with Erica Carter and Chris Turner (Minneapolis: University of Minnesota Press, 1987), 215-28. Theweleit also draws some suggestive parallels between the fascist male and men in general: "I don't want to make any categorial distinction between the types of men who are the subject of this book and all other men. Our subjects are equivalent to the tip of the patriarchal iceberg, but it's what lies beneath the surface that really makes the water cold" (171).

21. See, for example, Fred C. Robinson, *"Beowulf" and the Appositive Style* (Knoxville: University of Tennessee Press, 1985). To James W. Earl and Gillian R. Overing, I owe a special debt for the patience and generosity with which they responded to my questions about their work and read my own. In addition, I thank Thelma Fenster and Julian Weiss for their insightful comments and productive criticism.

CHAPTER 9

Men in the *Roman d'Eneas*
The Construction of Empire

Christopher Baswell

The *Roman d'Eneas* forms part of an important group of Old French texts, the so-called Romances of Antiquity, through which the narratives of Thebes, Rome, and Troy were progressively made available to a new audience of aristocratic readers who had little or no access to the Latin works in which the stories had first been transmitted to the Middle Ages. Renewed access to antiquity was all the more important because this readership saw itself as genealogically connected to the survivors of Troy and founders of Rome. The *romans d'antiquité* in turn were part of the fuller legendary history of the Normans and Angevins, including the *Brut*, with which these romances were sometimes grouped in manuscript. While only Benoît de Ste. Maure, author of the *Roman de Troie*, is definitely connected with the literary patronage of the court of Henry II, all the antique romances (otherwise anonymous) fall within the period and dialectal realm of his Angevin empire.[1]

The *Roman d'Eneas*, however, did not offer just a racial background and historical precedent for Angevin imperialism. More ambitiously, the *Eneas* created a space in which its aristocratic readership could examine manhood and heroism for its own time, and imagine the old dangers and new pressures under which its concept of manhood labored, and the new forms into which it was struggling to emerge. Most particularly in the pages below, I am interested in showing how the figure of Eneas proposes a model of male heroism peculiarly apt to the kingship of Henry II, a strong ruler whose strength was expressed less in the martial violence of the feudal past than in the forms of patriarchal genealogy, centralized kingship, and judicial deliberation toward which the rule of his ancestors had been slowly moving.

Of all the subjects in the Romances of Antiquity, an accessible version of the *Aeneid* would have had an especially strong appeal for the Angevin court, by providing that court with a justificatory and triumphant prehistory—what might even be called a secular typology—for its own more recent past. Like many European aristocrats, Henry II claimed Trojan ancestry;[2] as an Angevin monarch, he was the heir of westward-moving conquerors who had overwhelmed a weaker, even slightly senescent Anglo-Saxon kingdom; and he gained his largest territory through a wife (Eleanor of Aquitaine) who had been attached to another ambitious prince (Louis VII). The Trojan hero of the *Aeneid* was tellingly similar: he was a westward-moving conqueror whose territorial control could be certain only once he had taken a wife (Lavinia) and her lands from the local prince Turnus. Through these narrative similarities as well as much subtler means, the social and political modes of male-dominated, aristocratic Angevin society are encoded in the *Eneas*'s version of an antique—and therefore authoritative—Latin epic.[3]

Unlike the predominant critical response to the romance, then, I will argue that this carefully worked and highly self-conscious poem, whatever its ultimate literary influence, explores patriarchal power and imperial foundation at its structural and thematic center, far more than it explores the feminine eroticism at its margins. The great bulk of criticism and scholarship on the *Roman d'Eneas* has centered on the role of women in the poem, and in turn the poem's decisive impact on later erotic courtly romances, particularly through its adaptation of Ovidian psychology and rhetoric of love.[4] But in fact, the great and central bulk of the poem, roughly six thousand lines intervening between the two erotic episodes of Dido and Lavine, is about war and aristocratic social order.[5] From this narrative of empire there emerges, I will show, a model of male power and social action relevant to the Angevin court under whose intellectual influence the poem was produced.

The formal structure of the narrative reflects its central reexamination of the modes of masculine power. The poem is carefully constructed, with mirrored or analogous episodes (Dido at the beginning and Lavine at the end, for instance) concentrically bracketing its center. The arena for a revisionary model of heroic manhood lies solidly at the middle of the *Roman d'Eneas*, in the narrative of the Trojan conquest of Latium, whereas the poem's beginning and end feature challenging versions of the feminine—Dido, Camille, Lavine—that must be (variously) shunned, killed off, enclosed, or ultimately negotiated with. I will return to these specifically feminine challenges and the ways they help provoke and articulate the new manhood of the *Eneas*. This exploration of male values in the poem begins, however, at the numerical center of the *Eneas*, and a story of two heroes who derive closely from the *Aeneid*, and yet provide the high point in the French poem's elaborate restructuring of its Virgilian source.

At the center of Virgil's twelve books are Aeneas's descent to the underworld and arrival in Latium (*Aeneid* 6-7), in which the guidance of the Sibyl plays so key a role. The *Roman d'Eneas* radically dislocates this Virgilian center, and circles instead around the matter of Virgil's later books: feudal war and disagreement over the legal possession of land and woman. The exact middle ground between Dido and Lavine, in the French poem, is held by the heroic sacrifice of Nisus and Eurialus (4906-5278), a tale of militant male bonding from which women (even women present in Virgil's version) are wholly excluded.[6]

This is a decentered – even digressive – and less positive episode in Virgil (9.176-502). In the *Aeneid,* the episode of Nisus and Euryalus stands apart from the action, a self-contained epyllion, distinct in its straightforward speeches and almost Homeric tone from the surrounding book.[7] At this point in the action, the Trojan camp is besieged by Turnus's forces, but Aeneas has departed up the Tiber to seek military allies. Nisus and Euryalus – inseparable fighters and perhaps lovers in the mold of Achilles and Patroclus – reconfirm their service to Aeneas's son Ascanius, volunteering to sneak out among the drunken Latins and take word to Aeneas of his people's jeopardy. But they pause on their way through the enemy camp, slay their sleeping opponents in a burst of carnage, and Euryalus disastrously takes booty from his victims. A passing Latin troop sees moonlight reflected from Euryalus's pillaged helmet. Euryalus is captured, and Nisus sacrifices his own life trying to rescue his companion. *"Fortunati ambo,"* Virgil calls the pair; their end is noble if also exceedingly violent, and they typify for Virgil both the glorious commitment of fellow warriors and tragic service to Aeneas and the Trojan cause.

Where Virgil's *Aeneid* centers on the transformation of the hero and his historical and Pythagorean education under a woman's guidance in the underworld, the revised center of the *Eneas* is this entirely male, military, and amatory though not explicitly erotic union of Nisus and Eurialus. The episode is among the *Eneas*'s most extended close redactions of the Latin epic, although the French version seems not to share Virgil's moral ambivalence about the blood of sleeping enemies or Euryalus's eagerness for booty. The only considerable element from the *Aeneid* left out by the French redactor is, significantly, the Virgilian reference to Euryalus's mother and her mourning (*Aen.* 9.216-18, 283-302, 473-502). The female, even the maternal, is thus wholly suppressed at this point in the French version, leaving all the more prominent its focus on male militarism and fidelity. At the midpoint of the French poem, Nisus and Eurialus provide a model of exclusively, even exclusionary, male values, issuing in a glorious and sacrificial death in arms.

Even as this story articulates and centralizes one mode of male heroism for its Angevin readers, however, it also adumbrates without comment two dangers that lurk within that mode of heroism. First, there resides in the bonding of Nisus and Eurialus an unspoken theme of homoeroticism, which challenges the emergent principle of the patrilinear transmission of kingship in the Angevin world. Insofar as this fear extends to Eneas, there is the danger that he may be heterosexually unmanned. Second, the diversion that Nisus and Eurialus allow themselves while they slaughter and pillage the sleeping Latins enacts the potential for disaster when private vendetta displaces service to a dynastic ruler – a persistent problem throughout twelfth-century Europe. When vendetta extends to Eneas, there is the danger that he will be feudally unmanned. It is the work of much of the rest of the *Eneas* to give fuller voice to those dangers, then conquer and replace them. The dangers are brought into the open by two companies of opponents: women and Turnus. And it is in the person of Eneas that an alternate, even an evolved, version of manhood emerges, as he ultimately conquers Turnus and marries Lavine.

Along with establishing Eneas as the primary example of a new manhood, moreover, the poem also reflects several aspects of the social order toward which Angevin society was hesitantly striving. This broader model of empire, pervading the center of the poem, is to be seen in (1) a continuing theme of patrilinear genealogy, (2) an integration of legal, deliberative rhetoric into the Italian conflict and its resolution, and (3) a move from feud (even vendetta conflict) to the judicial duel (*judicium Dei*). These themes, of course, are not original to the redactor of the *Eneas*; some can be found in concurrent Latin traditions surrounding the *Aeneid* and the Troy story. I turn now to this ambient reception of the *Aeneid* in the intellectual world of northwestern Europe and its fuller development in the *Eneas* itself. Only then will I return to the structural margins and narrative suspensions where the *Eneas* nervously records its sense of an opposing system of power and a version of the feminine with which it must finally reconcile itself.

The suppression of a feminine role that we have seen at the *Eneas*'s central point, and that poem's broader emphasis on imperial conquest, recall the preoccupations of a Latin Troy poem, "Viribus, arte, minis . . . ," written by a tutor of Henry II.[8] This Latin poem deals with the story's most dangerous woman, Dido, in an analogous manner: it leaves her out altogether, and concentrates instead on the story's historical setting, on male militarism, and on the establishment of genealogy. These themes, and related modes of imperial power such as law and rhetoric, occupy the center and the real bulk of the *Eneas*.[9] The most persistent of these is a continuing theme of genealogy and the establishment of a male line. Howard Bloch has pointed to the increasing transmission of land through blood kin, ever more narrowly conceived in terms of patrilineal descent, during the twelfth century.[10] The theme of lineage, of course, is fully present in the *Aeneid* itself, where Latinus (for instance) outlines the ancestry of the Trojans and Dardanus's travel eastward from Italy and through Crete to Troy (*Aen.* 7.207ff.). But lineage is further emphasized in marginal commentary surrounding the *Aeneid* in its twelfth-century manuscripts, and it becomes even more persistent in the *Eneas.*

Interest in lineage, and the particular attention to a theme of lineal return through Dardanus, is very widespread indeed in the commentaries. The late-antique commentator Servius outlines the ancestry of the Trojans in several places, and simplified versions occur in many English and Norman manuscripts of the *Aeneid.*[11] An entry in a twelfth-century English or Norman Virgil (MS London, B.L. Addit. 27304) is especially intriguing: "Teucer and Dardanus were Aeneas's original fathers, and thus Aeneas heard in the oracles 'Seek your first father.' "[12] The oracle "quoted" in the final words of the gloss is not Virgilian and seems, on the contrary, to usurp Virgil's oracular counsel to seek the *antiquam . . . matrem* (*Aen.* 3.96). This oracle pointing to a mother and the confusion to which it gives rise in the *Aeneid* (because of Troy's double genealogy from the Cretan Teucer and the Italian Dardanus) are both effaced in the *Eneas*, where the Trojans consistently seek only a fatherland, descending from Dardanus. Eneas is simply instructed "that I should depart and go to the land from which Dardanus, our ancestor, came."[13]

An *accessus* added at the end of another twelfth-century *Aeneid* manuscript (London, B.L. Addit. 32319A) gives an even more telling summary of the Latin epic's events:

> For he shows that Eneas, after the destruction of Troy, was counselled by Apollo that he should seek his mother's breast—words interpreted by Eneas's father Anchises—and came with a number of ships (namely twenty) via Thrace to Crete, whence Anchises, since he was not ignorant of former times, said Teucer had come. But when a great pestilence arose there they were forced to depart. They entered their ships a third time and, passing through Sicily where Anchises died, and Carthage where they finally lingered a long while, they came to Italy, whence Dardanus had come. At the time when Eneas came to Italy, Latinus reigned there. Hearing of Eneas's arrival, Latinus immediately promised him the hand of his daughter, whom her mother had earlier promised to Turnus. For this reason a war arose between Turnus and Eneas; finally Turnus was defeated. But his mother, not daring to remain, fled to Flanders and founded

> there a city called Tournai from the name of her son. These brief points are made about the book's content.[14]

Several points emerge from this passage. First, the *accessus* lays primary emphasis on lineage and social foundation. The prominent details about Teucer and Dardanus derive more from preoccupations in the commentary tradition than from Virgil. Second, and linked to the issue of lineage, is an interest in the naming of places. Significantly, the *Eneas* too closes with a reference to Romulus's foundation and naming of Rome. Third, this is a summary about knowledge and empire passing from father to son, rather than about historical or erotic loss. Troy is quickly dismissed; Lavinia does not possess a name here and no reference whatsoever is made to Dido.[15] Finally, the passage shows a fascination with the continuing westward movement of those touched by the Trojan war. This of course is exactly the context in which the *Eneas* was produced, a context further marked by its manuscript association with the *Brut*.[16]

The *Eneas* equally makes the attachment of land to a new race through an ancient male lineage a central theme, carefully looking forward to the link of Latin and Trojan blood through Eneas's offspring. Indeed, in the much-reduced underworld episode in the *Eneas*, the redactor nonetheless retains most of the information about Eneas's line, repeatedly using the term *ligniee*, although he trims much of Virgil's historical and mythological elaboration, understandably enough.[17] Beginning with the Trojan arrival in Latium, the *Eneas* employs, with increasing prominence, Virgilian themes of paternal genealogy and divine destiny to justify the Trojans' imperial claims. Latinus repeatedly stresses Eneas's divine genealogy, and the gods' wish that he marry Lavine ("il est prochains de lor ligniee," 3349; see also 6553-58). And Eneas insistently recounts his genealogical claim to Latium through Dardanus. Just before his single combat with Turnus, for instance, Eneas tells the assembled Latins:

> "Seignor, mon droit mostrer vos voil
> que nel m'atornoiz a orgoil
> que par force voille conquerre
> autrui enor ne autrui terre.
> De ci fu mis ancestres nez,
> qui Dardanus fu apelez;
> de ceste terre s'an ala,
> en la nostre s'edefia.
> Molt fu forz hom et molt vesqui.
> De son linage Tros issi,
> qui fonda Troie et le donjon,
> et qui li anposa son nom;

mes peres fu de son linage.
. . .
Li damedeu d'iluec me pristrent,
ça m'envoierent el pais
dunt mes ancestres fu naïs;
otroiee m'ont tote Itaire,
qui fu mon aire et mon besaire." (9347-66)

["My lords," he said, "I wish to explain my right to you, so that you do not accuse me of wishing to conquer, out of pride, another domain or another land by force. My ancestor, who was called Dardanus, was born here. He left this land and established himself in ours, where he was a very strong man, and conquered much. From his lineage issued Tros, who founded Troy and its fortress, and who gave it his name; my father was of his lineage. . . . The gods took me from there and sent me here to this country where my ancestor was born. They have granted me all Italy, which is as it were my grandparent and great-grandparent."]

These themes of course would ring loud in the ears of an audience accustomed to hearing Angevin propaganda justify the Norman conquest of England. Moreover, as Bloch reminds us, the twelfth century generally, and the Anglo-Norman world particularly, saw the older control of land through feudal relation being replaced by control through the relation of blood.[18] An audience sensitive to such a change would see Turnus arguing from the declining system of armed service, personal oath, and expandable family, and would see Eneas buttressed by legal language (*mon droit*) issuing from paternal genealogy and narrowing notions of family relation. Eneas's claim to Latium thus is simultaneously contemporary with his Angevin readership and, in its appeal to divinity, beyond historical challenge. In a final genealogical gesture, the *Eneas* closes by extending the Virgilian narrative into later history, looking forward to the nation and imperial lineage that will arise from the marriage of Eneas and Lavine (10131-56).

Just as important in the *Roman d'Eneas*'s construction of a simultaneously ancient and contemporary version of male power is the integration of legal rhetoric into the Italian conflict and its resolution. The role of law and debate is constant in the *Eneas*. The poem gives repeated emphasis to baronial councils in which leaders take the advice of their nobles. Between them there is a shared thread of judicial rhetoric that has much in common with the rhetorical emphasis observed in marginalia of some high medieval manuscripts of the *Aeneid*. These councils gain prominence as Eneas approaches Latium (for example, the council he holds in Sicily; 2228-41), and thereafter become part of the narrative rhythm of battle and truce. Legal terminology already strongly colors Eneas's final encounter with Dido, in the underworld, as he is prepared for his genealogical destiny. Whereas Virgil's Aeneas merely weeps and blames the gods for his unwilling departure from Carthage (6.455-66), the French Eneas engages in legalistic self-defense. He insists that while he may have been the immediate occasion (*acheison*) for her death, he is legally blameless: "Ge n'i oi colpes ne tort" (2634; "I have no guilt or wrong in it").[19]

Once Eneas is in Italy, his claims to the land through lineage are also formulated in the language of legal right (again, see his reference to *mon droit* at 9347, quoted above). At the same time, Eneas, Turnus, and Latinus all call councils in which rhetorical strategy is as important as military strategy. Turnus in particular articulates his sense of his barons' rights in giving or witholding military aid.[20] After he gathers his army, he adresses his barons, again using the diction of law (*droit, tort*) and feudal obligation:

"Seignor," fait il, "escotez moi;
mon afaire mostrer vos doi,
por que vos ai ci asanblez,
et se mon droit i antandez,
sel m'aidiez a maintenir,
de droit ne me devez faillir;
se vos oëz que ge tort aie,
pri vos ne m'en portez menaie,
mais dites moi que me repos,
et ge crerrai bien vostre los;
no voil a tort rien comancier,
no vos ne m'en devez aidier." (4115-26)

["My lords," he said, "hear me; I must explain my affairs to you, because of which I assembled you here, so that you may understand my right and help me to sustain it; in justice you should not fail me. If you see that I am wrong, I pray you that you bring me no assistance, but tell me that I should desist, and I will indeed accept your advice. I do not wish to begin anything wrongly, nor that you should aid me in such a venture."]

And Eneas argues his rights by arguing from the law of lineage, to which I will return.

Third, and most important for the *Eneas*'s embedding of contemporary social and political structures, is the poem's move from uncontrolled feud to the judicial duel (*judicium Dei*). It is through Turnus, and by contrast to him, that the poem articulates this social model of the newly translated empire, for Turnus proposes to carry out his resistance to the Trojan empire in Latium through the armed medium of feud.[21] Feud was exactly the archaic but still widespread mode of resolving political or legal differences that the Norman and Angevin kings, especially Henry II, were at pains to suppress.[22] Turnus thus offers the danger of a history that could easily run backward toward the private conflicts of the earlier feudal era—a form of conflict we glimpsed even in the admirable figures of Nisus and Eurialus. Turnus poses an old danger, the danger of decentralized, early feudal rule and the chaos of private war.

It is a messenger from Amata who first brings word to Turnus that his engagement with Lavine, and indeed all of Latinus's prior "convenance" (3424), have been abrogated. In the face of these broken oaths, the messenger further urges Turnus to undertake what emerges more and more clearly as a private war against Eneas:

> Prent soldoiers, asanble gent,
> ne te tarder mes de noiant,
> lo Troïen coite de guerre,
> tant qu'il te guerpisse la terre,
> ou que l'aies vencu ou pris
> ou qu'il s'an alt par mer fuitis. (3431-36)

[Take soldiers, gather an army without delay, and press the Trojan with war, until he abandons the land to you, or you have conquered or captured him, or he departs a fugitive by sea.]

Private war, skipping over any legal recourse that might be available (however weak), was the aristocratic course to justice in the earlier feudal period, and of course remained a temptation for any sufficiently powerful baron. It was, according to Bloch, "a persistent fact of life in the Middle Ages, vengeance carried out independently by private individuals did not necessarily involve either public or semipublic legal process."[23]

Turnus's response here and after hinges on the power of prior oath and the rights thereby guaranteed him, to Lavine and to her lands:

> Li mes s'en vet, Turnus remaint,
> a ses amis privez se plaint
> del roi, qui ne li tient convent
> ne fiance ne seremant. (3491-94)

[The messenger departs and Turnus remains, complaining to his close friends about the king, who has not kept covenant with him, or faith, or oath.][24]

Turnus's objection thus is to the breaking of specific, public feudal covenants; Latinus and Eneas, as we have already seen, respond with the superior (though, in the twelfth century, still contested) claims of male lineage, royal will, and the desires of the gods as revealed to Latinus in that most private forum, the dream.[25] The poem thus displays the restructuring of male power under the Angevins, from elective feudal oath and public covenant to patriarchal lineage and the monarch's private will.[26]

Ascanius's slaughter of Silvia's stag gives Turnus the "occasion" (*acheison*, 3497, 3507; again, a legal term that recalls Eneas's final encounter with Dido in the underworld) he has been seeking to initiate his war; he calls together his barons to hear his complaint and render counsel.[27] From this point on, however, simultaneous with the armed struggle on all sides, efforts are made in council to move Turnus's war into a legal setting, or at least to limit it to a judicial duel between himself and Eneas. Along with the rise of patrilinear inheritance, the period of Angevin consolidation was also an era of judicial duel (*judicium Dei*), and of early efforts to suppress even that mode of justice in favor of legal procedure.[28] When Turnus first appeals to Latinus, he refuses to involve himself, preferring to let the forces of Turnus and Eneas settle the matter in open battle. But even in Turnus's initial meeting with his barons, one of them, Mesencius, counsels "measure" and an appeal to steps of legal procedure (4201-10). This is rejected by the violent Mesapus, who prefers the swifter, old-fashioned recourse to feud (4211-36). The latter advice prevails, but it is significant that the better counselor, Mesencius, goes on to an explicitly noble death in battle on Turnus's behalf.

Once the war between Latins and Trojans is under way, its movement, however often postponed and frustrated, is from the earlier model of feud or private war, to the high medieval model of judicial duel, with Turnus or his allies repeatedly dragging it back toward the more archaic form. It is Drances, as unattractive in the *Eneas* as in Virgil, who again proposes a *judicium Dei* in Latinus's council (6699-706). And this time the call for judicial duel succeeds:

> Se cors a cors la puet conquerre,
> si ait la feme o tot la terre. (6801-2)

> [If he can win her, man against man, then let him have the girl with all the land.]

The duel is interrupted as in Virgil, but not through another intervention by Juno. Rather, one of Turnus's own knights articulates for a final time the old aristocratic resistance to individual *judicium Dei*, and then reignites general battle:

Franc chevalier, nel dretés ja,
combatons nos o çals dela,
ne nos metons an tel mesure
sor un sol home an aventure. (9421-24)

[Noble lords, do not allow it; let us do battle against our enemies, and let us not place ourselves on the action of one man alone.]

Finally, Turnus sees his fortune in decline and calls for a renewal of the single combat. At this point, as in Virgil, his historical fate crosses with the suspended memory of Pallas through the relic Turnus had been reserving to himself, in this case a ring that had belonged to the slain boy. Virgil's emphasis on the violence of this moment is replaced in the *Eneas* with a focus on the closure and peacemaking Turnus's death allows. Eneas is depicted as pacific and friendly toward the Latins, eager to cement his presence in the country by a royal marriage with Lavine (9825-38).

The poem's movement from the archaic disorder of feud to a more ordered and judicial mode of political action—and thus its restructured vision of manhood—can also be sited within contemporary discussions of the just war.[29] These discussions allow us to see Turnus's war as perhaps initially just, but moving ever more surely away from accepted standards of appropriate martial action. Simultaneously, Eneas wages what looks like a holy war, supported by the will of the pantheon, and behaves more and more clearly according to approved norms.[30]

Even as early as the Romans, war was considered acceptable as a just response, even "an extraordinary legal process," upon the abrogation of contractual agreements.[31] And, as shown above, it is exactly such a contractual breach that is first reported to Turnus and drives him to war. Yet at the same time, according to Gratian, who wrote in the decades just before the *Eneas*, the just warrior must always have peace in view. Turnus's bellicose speeches move swiftly away from any such attitude; and Gratian explicitly condemns "implacable and unsatisifed vehemence."[32]

By contrast, Eneas seems to embody the inner charity and wish to reestablish peace that Gratian demands of the just warrior. He is consistently calm in the face of his enemies, and repeats several times his desire to avoid war altogether. Writing around 1157, even closer to the date of the French poem, the commentator Rufinus accepts the necessity of violent self-defense in the face of violence—which would again justify Eneas—but insists that one should not recommence battle after peace without judicial authority. This of course is just what Turnus and his forces do during the first effort at judicial duel.

It is not surprising that these moves from private warrior to peacemaker, from fighter to talker, from open and group battle to something very like judicial duel, should all come in a text of Angevin origin.[33] As Bloch and others before him point out, the Normans and Angevins were among the first to codify the legal processes that slowly replaced private war with judicial combat, and ultimately judicial combat with legal inquest: William the Conqueror had tried to restrict private campaigns, and Henry II was the most effective ruler in his time to work against judicial duel and toward legal procedure.[34] If the Anglo-Norman empire was at a delicate point of transition from feudal assignment to patrilinear inheritance, and from open warfare to *judicium Dei*, then Eneas's language of lineage, law, and divine right points readers forward, while Turnus's and his cohort's preference for swift and wholesale war looks back.

The French poem's insertion of feudal obligation and law into an ancient epic context, far from being a naive "modernization" by a redactor unable to understand his source, is a canny prehistory and legitimation of his culture's recent war over imperial inheritance, and that culture's wish to move past feudal war and into judicial order. As the redactor moves into the imperial half of the Latin source, his themes and narrative converge with Virgil's, at the same time altering Virgil's focus by rendering that imperial half his own center. And his use of Turnus shows a brilliant sensitivity to the archaism of Virgil's Latin prince, genuinely translating him into the embattled protector of values newly archaic in the middle of the twelfth century. The *Eneas* centers on ancient imperial history, but a history that simultaneously validates a changing concept of heroism and patriarchal order occurring in the redaction's own time. The poem's central narrative thus inscribes the emergent manhood of Angevin imperial order within the ancient, authoritative Latin epic.

By all the procedures surveyed above, the *Eneas* redactor creates a structural and narrative center in which female characters (Lavine especially) are only the audience – or only brief if important interruptions – of their men's story. This internal audience, acknowledged but marginalized, has analogies among the multiple audiences that would have used a vernacular poem such as the *Eneas*. The *Eneas* is not just a popular version of Virgil's epic for the non-Latinate; rather, it is a highly learned text serving several audiences simultaneously: male aristocrats (many with some considerable Latinity), learned clerics with their own preoccupations and bases of verbal power, and a growing and powerful audience of women who, even as readers, tended to be limited to the romance vernaculars.[35]

This is not to say that the *Eneas* does not make place for female characters greatly expanded from Virgil. It does so, famously. These women, however, further articulate specters or dangers – some already latent, we have seen, in the central episode of Nisus and Eurialus – that the Trojans must suppress or co-opt as they enact the poem's examination of new manhood.[36] Dido's erotic delay of Eneas threatens Trojan destiny in Italy, and Camille's proud rejection of sexuality threatens lineage itself. But these episodes of women, and the dangers they pose, are carefully delimited, even bracketed off from the imperial narrative, which is the first sign of their containment. What power these women do have centers on their eroticism (as against their political and military leadership) to a far greater extent than in Virgil: Dido's pursuit and Camille's refusal of desire both provoke more comment in the French poem than in the Latin.[37] Moreover, after their deaths Dido and Camille are ritually entombed at points of emphatic closure. Thus, although they are not denied a role or impact in the story—indeed Camille's corpse is carefully preserved, an ongoing physical presence—they are ultimately placed beyond action, beyond history, even (as the tombs are ever more marvelously elaborated) beyond reality.

Dido occupies the initial margin of the poem. Her power is real, her erotic danger considerable. But even she, along with her city of Carthage, is described in terms that tend to privilege economic force and the challenge that a rising mercantilism posed to traditional land-based aristocracy in the twelfth century. And of course Dido dies at her own hand and is enclosed safely in a magnificent tomb (2135-44). When the imagery of her dress and her city's mercantile wealth reappear in the poem, they do so transformed into the stuff of male ritual lament and mobile imperial militancy: the bier of Pallas (see below) and Eneas's fortress tent.[38] Camille, closer to the center of the poem, poses an opposite danger to Angevin concepts of manhood. Camille is the woman warrior, much expanded from Virgil, who would refuse the woman's role in genealogy. She too is swiftly if regretfully consigned to a tomb elaborately reminiscent of Dido's (7531-7637). Women and the modes of their power are thereby rendered, thus far in the poem, figures of delay for the most part—loops (as with Lavine, see below) and suspensions (as with the tombs of Dido and Camille)—in marginal contest with a more central, linear, and male narrative of imperial conquest.

Despite this tension between a central and dominant (if interrupted) imperial discourse and feminine challenges to its assumptions, there is also an ongoing negotiation between them, which must ultimately be resolved if the imperial theme of patriarchal lineage is to be validated and extended by the marriage of Eneas and Lavine. Toward the close of the poem, the redactor creates virtually from whole cloth a large role for Lavine and a distant love between her and Eneas that culminates in their marriage. Yet with the advent of Lavine, the poem also articulates the central specter in its embedding of Angevin manhood and patriarchal genealogy in antique history. This is the threat of homoeroticism.

It has already been suggested above that the devotion of Nisus and Eurialus, and the exclusively masculine world they inhabit, allows the themes of militant brotherhood and homoeroticism to approach convergence at the poem's center.[39] There is no overt implication of homosexuality in this pair, and, indeed, Norman readers would not have known the Homeric models (like the lovers Achilles and Patroclus) that Virgil recalls to his readers' attention. But between the French Nisus and Eurialus there is what could reasonably be called a homosocial bond, based on established sentimental attachment, the link of youth and age, and militant virtues.[40]

The sense of danger posed by Trojan homosexuality arises again, more forcefully and threateningly, in the analogous attachment of Eneas and Pallas. Their relationship is little specified in the poem, until Pallas's death at the hand of Turnus, whereupon Eneas begins his mourning in restrained but tellingly ambiguous lines:

> "Amis," fait il, "ce est domage,
> que vos estes por moi ocis.
> Amenai vos d'autre païs,
> nostre amor a petit duré,
> malvés garanz vos ai esté." (5850-54)
>
> ["Friend," he said, "it is pitiful that you have been killed for me. I led you here from another country, but our love has been short-lived. I have been a poor protector to you."]

Whatever hints of an erotic history attach to this speech must be reinforced when Pallas lies on his bier, clothed in the rich robe that Dido had given Eneas "quant elle l'anama [when she loved him]" (6124). This robe on Pallas's corpse creates a provocative image, triangulating militant, male aristocracy with the twin threats posed to it by Carthaginian mercantilism and gay sexuality.[41]

Militant brotherhood and connections to erotic desire remain merely convergent, not explicit, however, until Lavine reveals to her mother her own love for Eneas, whereupon Amata explodes in a frankly obscene attack upon the sexual practices of the Trojans:

> Cil cuiverz est de tel anture
> qu'il n'a gaires de femmes cure;
> il prise plus lo ploin mestier;
> il ne velt pas biset mangier,

molt par aimme char de maslon;
il priseroit mialz un garcon
que toi ne altre acoler. . . .
. . .
De cest sigle seroit tost fin,
se tuit li home qui i sont
erent autel par tot lo mont;
ja mes feme ne concevroit,
grant sofraite de gent seroit. (8567-73, 8596-8600)

[This wretch is of the sort who have hardly any interest in women. He prefers the opposite trade: he will not eat hens, but he loves very much the flesh of a cock. He would prefer to embrace a boy rather than you or any other woman. . . . It would quickly be the end of this life if all men were thus throughout the world. Never would a woman conceive; there would be a great dearth of people.]

Amata not only brings this challenge to Angevin manhood to the poem's surface, but also articulates its specific danger to genealogical transmission.[42] By this moment, however, in a gesture that repeats the poem's treatment of other erotic challenges, the only object of Eneas's overt male affection has already been killed. Pallas is then placed in a tomb whose details also link it to Dido's before and Camille's later (lines 6409-48). The echoes between Pallas's and Dido's tombs repeat the triangulation of dangerous hetero- and homoeroticism noted above in the use of Dido's robe on his bier. Lavine herself once again accuses Eneas of homosexuality, when she fears he is unresponsive to her overtures (9130-70). Lavine's complaint, however, like Amata's, has been forestalled, denied before it is even spoken, by what the reader already knows: first that Pallas is dead, and then that Eneas is deeply in love with Lavine.

Like other such challenges to Angevin manhood in the poem, then, the danger of homosexuality, if articulated, is always already contained by some form of narrative bracketing. Even once this theme is left behind, as Eneas begins to respond to Lavine's overtures, the very fact that she initiates those overtures must itself be recuperated, I think, by two means. First, Lavine's love for Eneas is itself bracketed and preempted by the male negotiations for the *judicium Dei* between Eneas and Turnus, which precede and follow her discovery of love. And second, as Eneas becomes sensible to Lavine and his desire for her, he begins to adopt (we may even say co-opt) her habit of internal deliberative discourse. Indeed, in the passage immediately before Lavine's accusation of homosexuality, Eneas uses for the first time a form of divided internal dialogue that up to now has been limited exclusively to Dido and Lavine. It is in this divided discourse, especially, that we see Eneas, the model for the Angevin new man, adopt from women the mental and verbal habit so critical for the forms of judicial deliberation toward which (as I have shown above) Angevin society was slowly striving.

Lavine, like Dido before her, learns to love Eneas through her own eyes and her own will, and even opposes her mother's preference for Turnus. Yet this gesture of feminine wilfullness only serves to align Lavine with the wishes of her father, and replicates a decision he has already taken on her behalf. She erupts at this point into a series of extended internal dialogues between voices of desire and logical self-interest, and begins to dominate the text even more than did Dido (see 8047-8775, especially 8127-8334, 8343-8444, 8679-8775). But we must remember that this episode occurs during an eight-day truce between the decision to settle Lavine's fate by single combat and the (ultimately delayed) combat that Eneas does win (7829-56, 9275-9424). Her interior discovery of Amors is bracketed, textually contained, by the military and judicial discussions among men that will actually decide her future; and her "independent" desire for Eneas only replicates her father's preference. The story of Lavine's power thus occupies a loop, really just a delay, in an episodic progression already determined among men. This narrative containment of Lavine climaxes the whole series of strategies by which the poem controls challenges to the order of patriarchal will or divine power.

Yet Lavine, because of her genealogical role, is the one female character whose will, once acknowledged, must finally be integrated by the epic. And in fact, both before and after his military triumph over Turnus, Eneas himself continues to engage in internalized erotic debates very like Lavine's (8940-9099, 9929-10078).[43] This adoption of a language heretofore wholly limited to women represents, I think, not a male appropriation of feminine values, but rather a genuine and significant (because final) admission of a specifically feminine discourse into the work of empire, even as Lavine moves into empire's genealogical work. At the same time, the carefully balanced argument of these dialogues, both in Lavine and in Eneas, also points toward the deliberative rhetoric necessary to the legal forms of social order that were struggling to emerge in the Angevin world. It is particularly emblematic that when Lavine's love letter, shot toward Eneas wrapped around an arrow, threatens to disrupt a truce, Eneas responds not with immediate battle but with verbal protest and the promise of legal evidence – the arrow itself (8845-60). This arrow (soon to be transformed metaphorically into Cupid's dart) carries Lavine's letter (and with it a particular form of erotic discourse) into the realm of battle and appeals to law. It is immediately after this episode that we witness Eneas in his tent learning the language of love and, simultaneously, of logical debate.

If the tone and structure of the *Eneas* are made up of several plates shifting between epic and romance, if the poem looks in both directions, it equally addresses several overlapping readerships, but it does not address them equally. The *Roman d'Eneas* is not an early courtly romance pulling eagerly and inevitably away from its source in Latin imperial epic, as it is still too generally thought to be. Rather, it is a carefully controlled social and political work that articulates and then limits new feminine powers, and leaves them, moreover, at the margins of a far more central construction of emergent Angevin manhood and patriarchal imperialism. Though it does address a marginal audience, vernacular and in good part female, it also much more centrally describes arenas of male power to which that audience has little access *except* as audience. Structurally, too, the feminine audience is marginalized by having its major internal models placed far more at the edges than they are in Virgil; and Virgil's own middle is equally shifted, from the feminine guidance of the descent to hell in the *Aeneid*, to the archetypal scene of militant male bonding and sacrifice, the *Eneas*'s version of Nisus and Eurialus. Whatever the thematic and gender negotiations that go on at the beginning and end of the poem, its center is devoted to the investigation of a new patriarchy as represented by Eneas's divinely fated empire, the wars by which men claim it, and the modes by which they order it.

Notes

I am grateful to Professor Thelma Fenster, to W. Duncan Stalker, and to the press's anonymous readers, whose comments led to substantial improvements in this essay.

1. A useful survey of the materials, and current bibliography, can be found in the *Dictionary of the Middle Ages* (New York: Scribner's, 1985, 1987), 5:243-45, 5:253-54, 8:225-27. Angevin patronage is explored in Walter F. Schirmer and Ulrich Broich, *Studien zum literarischen Patronat im England des 12. Jahrhunderts* (Cologne: Westdeutscher Verlag, 1962). The fullest discussion of date and provenance of the *Eneas* itself, with full references to earlier arguments, is by Giovanna Angeli, *L' "Eneas" e i primi romanzi volgari* (Milan: Riccardo Ricciardi, 1971). Angeli argues for a *terminus a quo* of about 1155, and for an author working in the immediate context of the Angevin court; see viii, 100, 141.

2. Hugh A. MacDougall, *Racial Myth in English History: Trojans, Teutons, and Anglo-Saxons* (Montreal: Harvest House, 1982), 8.

3. In an important essay, Lee Patterson speaks of the *Eneas* as suppressing most of the darker complexities of Trojan history it found in Virgil, in order to make it a more palatable model for the imperial project of the Angevins. Yet he also acknowledges that "the *Eneas* is not immune to a counterawareness . . . of the human cost of the historical life," seen especially in the marvelous. See Lee Patterson, "Virgil and the Historical Consciousness of the Twelfth Century: The *Roman d'Eneas* and *Erec et Enide*," in *Negotiating the Past: The Historical Understanding of Medieval Literature* (Madison: University of Wisconsin Press, 1987), 170-83, especially 181. In what follows I will focus more on the careful insertion of contemporary modes of social action in the poem.

4. For an eloquent study of courtly love themes in the poem, see Helen C. R. Laurie, " 'Eneas' and the Doctrine of Courtly Love," *MLR* 64 (1969): 283-94. Angeli, *L' "Eneas,"* 107-14, however, argues that the eroticism of the poem is rather more Ovidian than courtly.

5. Raymond J. Cormier, *One Heart One Mind: The Rebirth of Virgil's Hero in Medieval French Romance* (University, Miss.: Romance Monographs, 1973), proposes a tripartite division of the poem that also centers on the struggle with Turnus and emphasizes the expanded role of *Aeneid* 7-12 in the French redaction (see especially 108-10). Cormier's study has provided a fundamental impetus for serious critical treatment of the poem in the past two decades.

6. *Eneas: Roman du XIIe siècle*, ed. J.-J. Salverda de Grave, 2 vols. (Paris: CFMA, 1925-29; reprinted 1973); trans. John A. Yunck, *Eneas: A Twelfth-Century French Romance*, Records of Civilization 93 (New York: Columbia University Press, 1974). All line citations are from this edition and from Yunck's translation, with occasional minor alterations.

7. See the excellent comments by R. D. Williams in his edition, *The Aeneid of Virgil, Books 7-12* (London: St. Martin's, 1977), 290-91.

8. Walter (Hans Walther, *Initia carminum ac versuum medii aevi posterioris latinorum. Alphabetisches Verzeichnis der Versanfänge mittellateinischer Dichtungen*, 2d ed. [Göttingen: Van den hoeck und u Ruprecht, 1969]), no. 20582. P. Leyser, *Historia poetarum et poematum medii aevi* (Halle, 1721), 404-8, and following him PL 171, col. 1451-53, print the poem as an uninterrupted continuation of a Troy poem of Simon Aurea Capra. Edélestand du Méril, *Poésies populaires latines antérieures au XIIe siècle* (Paris, 1843), 400-5, prints it as an independent work.

9. Christiane Marchello-Nizia explores the *Eneas* as a poem of dynastic foundation in "De l'*Énéide* à l'*Eneas*: les attributs du fondateur," in *Lectures médiévales de Virgile*, Collection de l'école française de Rome 80 (Rome: École française de Rome, 1985), 251-66.

10. R. Howard Bloch, *Etymologies and Genealogies: A Literary Anthropology of the French Middle Ages* (Chicago: University of Chicago Press, 1983), 66-79.

11. See Servius at *Aeneid* 1.380 and 3.104; *Servii Grammatici qui feruntur in Vergilii carmina commentarii*, ed. Georg Thilo and Hermann Hagen, 3 vols. (Leipzig: Teubner, 1881-84; reprinted Hildesheim: Georg Olms, 1961). A typical simplification is found in the earliest layer of marginalia surrounding the *Aeneid* in MS London, B.L. Additional 27304 (probably a generation or so later than the *Eneas*), at 3.102: "teucer venit a creta, dardanus ab italia. anchises putans febum dixisse de teucro fecit eos ire ad cretam. et ita decepti fuerunt." A widespread late eleventh- or early twelfth-century commentary, attributed to Anselm of Laon, gives a fuller version at 1.235: "*reuocato sanguine*. non enim ad teucrum, sed ad dardanum reuocabantur. dardanus enim de ithalia profectus est. et uenit ad loca illa ubi troia fuit. et fecit quasdam paruas domos. Teucer autem de creta et post ad eadem loca uenit et augmentauit" (MS London, B.L. Additional 33,220). Often the marginal material also supplies the generations between Dardanus and Aeneas, as in MS London, B.L. Additional 32319A, at 1.245: "iupiter dardanum dardanus erictonium erictonius troeam troes asaracum asaracus capin capis anchisen."

12. At 1.235: "teucer et dardanus fuerunt primi pater [*sic*] enee. Unde eneas in responsis accepit petite primum patrem."

13. "que m'en tornasse, / et an la terre m'en alasse, / dont Dardanus vint nostre ancestre" (1187-89). See also 38-41: "et ce li comandent li dé / que il aut la contree querre / dunt Dardanus vint an la terre, / qui fonda de Troie les murs [The gods commanded him thus: that he should go in quest of the country from which Dardanus, who founded the walls of Troy, came to this land]."

14. "Ostendit enim quod ipse eneas post destructionem troie, cum aliquot nauibus scilicet uiginti, monitus ab apolline ut materna peteret ubera, anchisse [*sic*] patre eiusdem enee verba interpretante, per traciam cretam uenit, dicens tamquam uetustatis non inscius teucrum inde uenisse. Sed orta ibidem maxima pestilencia coacti sunt recedere, et tercium ingressi naues suas, per siciliam ubi anchises mortuus est, et cartaginem ubi aliquando diu commorati sunt, in italiam uenerunt unde dardanus uenerat. Eoque tempore quo eneas ital-

iam uenit, latinus ibidem regnauit. Audito autem aduentu enee, statim latinus ei natam suam despondit, quam mater sua prius turno spoponderat uxorem. Unde ortum bellum inter turnum et eneam. Tandem turnus uictus est. Mater uero ipsius non ausa remanere, aufugit in flandriam ibidemque ciuitatem unam a nomine filii sui dictam tornacum condidit. Hec de materia breuiter dicenda sunt (B.L. Additional 32319A, fo. 149v).

15. Just as interesting, however, a woman is allowed power at the edge of the story, just where the *Eneas* as a whole similarly allows feminine power to remain. Women, in this summary, are excluded from the narrative of Roman refoundation; but the mother of the defeated local prince flees to found a northern town.

16. Both the *Eneas* and the *Brut* are found in MSS Paris, B.N. fr. 1416, fr. 1450, and fr. 12603; and Montpellier, École de médecine 251. See the edition of Salverda de Grave, iv-v.

17. See, for instance, 2819-20, which closely translate *Aen.* 6.681-82; the redactor follows Virgil where he emphasizes lineage and number. Again at 2879-82 lineage is emphasized by explicit terms (cf. *Aen.* 6.716-18). And finally at 2933-68 Anchises sketches the Roman imperial line. Patterson, "Virgil and the Historical Consciousness," 174-76, makes a telling argument for the suppression of a dangerous past in so neatly linear a genealogy. Marchello-Nizia also emphasizes genealogical themes in the poem, especially in the context of its elaborate tombs; see "De l'Énéide," 254-56.

18. Bloch, *Etymologies*, 69.

19. In old as in modern French, *tort* carries a specific legal sense of wrongdoing. See A. J. Greimas, *Dictionnaire de l'ancien français* (Paris: Larousse, 1968). In this setting, the somewhat looser *colpes* would take on a legal tone that is clear in its medieval Latin analogues. See J. F. Niermeyer, *Mediae latinitatis lexicon minus* (Leiden: Brill, 1984), s.v. *culpabilis*; the term has a legal context at least as early as the *Lex Salica*.

20. As I will suggest below, this is part of Turnus's attachment to earlier modes of feudal obligation, whereas Eneas's genealogical claims look forward to the model of royal power toward which the Angevins were striving.

21. Even in the twelfth century, feud remained a crucial part of the negotiations by which aristocratic disputes were settled in the continuing absence of a sufficiently powerful royal judiciary and administration. For an excellent recent treatment of feud and disputes, see Stephen D. White, "Feuding and Peace-Making in the Touraine around the Year 1100," *Traditio* 42 (1986): 195-263.

22. See ibid., 200, n. 24. Alfred Adler discusses Turnus's commitment to an aging feudal system in "Eneas and Lavine: *Puer et Puella Senes*," *Romanische Forschungen* 71 (1959): 82-83. See also comments on the archaism of Turnus's social assumptions by Cormier, *One Heart One Mind*, 187-95.

23. R. Howard Bloch, *Medieval French Literature and Law* (Berkeley: University of California Press, 1977), 64; see also 66.

24. Turnus's later speech to Latinus will be even more replete with terminology of feudal possession and obligation; see especially lines 3847-68.

25. Indeed, Latinus's willingness to break so important an oath simply by recourse to his will and that of the gods, and without the consultation of his barons, might reflect the gestures of near-sovereign power by the Norman and Angevin kings through "mere will"—*per voluntatem*. See J. E. A. Jolliffe, *Angevin Kingship* (London: Adam and Charles Black, 1963), 5, 14-39.

26. The Norman and Angevin kings, "where equity or policy or profit dictated, . . . wielded their supreme force of distriction by mere will. . . . This power—*vis et voluntas*—the sovereigns assumed for themselves openly, as it were unconsciously, yet without hesitation, and it was near a full sovereignty." Ibid., 5-6.

27. See lines 3881-96. White discusses the ease with which a new and much larger feud could grow out of an earlier, only tangentially related conflict; "Feuding and Peace-Making," 216-17, 237.

28. Bloch, *Law and Literature*, 16-21, 64-66, 108-20.

29. In what follows, I am constantly indebted to Frederick H. Russell, *The Just War in the Middle Ages* (Cambridge: Cambridge University Press, 1975).

30. On the uncertain distinctions between just and holy war, see ibid., 2.

31. See ibid., 4-5.

32. Ibid., 60-61.

33. In many ways the Latinus of the *Eneas* is the same ineffectual king of the *Aeneid*. But his willingness to detach territory from Turnus and give it to Eneas may well echo habits of distraint and disseizin by which the Angevin kings established their administrative power, often without prior recourse to law or baronial council. See Jolliffe, *Angevin Kingship*, 57-76.

34. Bloch, *Law and Literature*, 9, 112, 120.

35. The "bookishness" of the *roman antique* and the self-conscious readerliness (*clergie*) of its redactor are discussed by Renate Blumenfeld-Kosinski, "Old French Narrative Genres: Towards the Definition of the *Roman Antique*," *Romance Philology* 34 (1980): 143-59. For the patronage of vernacular literature, see Diana B. Tyson, "Patronage of French Vernacular History Writers in the Twelfth and Thirteenth Centuries," *Romania* 100 (1975): 185-86, 190-95, 219-20. Tyson notes the dominance of the Anglo-Norman court in the encouragement of vernacular history.

36. I examine a sequence of specific objects, closely associated with Dido and Camille, which are then recuperated for the ends of Trojan hegemony, in my article "Eneas's Tent and the Fabric of Empire in the *Roman d'Eneas*," *Romance Languages Annual* 2 (1990): 43-48.

37. When the rumor of Dido's affair with Eneas spreads among the local barons, they complain that she has chosen a man less worthy then they. They articulate the stereotypes of women's unreliability ("Fous est qui an fame se fie"; 1600), and are particularly angered that she has broken her vow of fidelity to Sicheüs (1598-99). More important, the narrative voice makes a rare and emphatic entry into the story to approve the barons' complaints – "et si ont droit" (1589). This is the sort of scene that Virgil's Dido feared (*Aen.* 4.320-25), but Virgil does not actually describe. Camille is the object of an analogous and extended reproach. Virgil's Tarcon seems to sneer at Camilla and her women warriors, but never speaks to them directly (*Aen.* 11.732-40); the Tarcon of the *Eneas*, by contrast, addresses a long and offensive speech to Camille, discoursing on women's sexual insatiability and offering to buy her sexual services (7073-7106). Camille swiftly kills him (7107-16), and the narrator does nothing explicitly to approve Tarchon's attack; but the male fear of Camille's militancy, and the wish to render her an object of sexual purchase, is nonetheless registered (if in nearly parodic form) by his speech.

38. See Baswell, "Eneas's Tent."

39. For a survey of the revival of homosexual practices and homoerotic literature during the twelfth century, see John E. Boswell, *Christianity, Social Tolerance, and Homosexuality: Gay People in Western Europe from the Beginning of the Christian Era to the Fourteenth Century* (Chicago: University of Chicago Press, 1980), 207-66.

40. For a brief discussion of "homosocial desire" that has rightly become classic, see Eve Kosofsky Sedgwick, *Between Men: English Literature and Male Homosocial Desire* (New York: Columbia University Press, 1985), 1-5.

41. The connection seems to have historical roots. Boswell argues that the resurgence of a gay subculture in the twelfth century was connected to the growth of mercantile cities; see *Christianity*, 207-9.

42. Along with the growth of gay culture in the twelfth century, Boswell points out, there also arose an angry hostility (largely clerical and generally ineffectual) to homosexual practices; see ibid., 210-16. By contrast, there also developed a literature of passionate male friendship intriguingly reminiscent of Eneas's speech over the body of Pallas; for discussion and samples, see ibid., 218-26.

43. For discussion of this dialogue, see Cormier, *One Heart One Mind*, 241-46.

CHAPTER 10

Representing "Other" Men
Muslims, Jews, and Masculine Ideals in Medieval Castilian Epic and Ballad

Louise Mirrer

Kien kisiere tener plazer,
déla de palos a su muxer.

Dámelo judío, y dártelo he quemado.
medieval Castilian proverbs[1]

Masculine Ideals

The literary texts of medieval Castile provide a clear picture of the traits and attitudes considered ideal for men in the society. Aggressive behavior, sexual assertiveness, and menacing speech all figure prominently in these works as characteristic of "real" men. In popular as well as in learned texts, masculinity is proved not through biology, but through force, intimidation, and the use of threatening language.[2]

The notion that manliness involves – much more than anatomy – acts of aggression is in fact at the heart of a well-known story by Juan Manuel (1282-1348), the medieval Castilian Christian writer and statesman. Juan Manuel relays the puzzling advice given to the count of Provence by the Muslim sultan, Saladin, to "marry [his] daughter to a man," explaining, in the course of the tale, that what Saladin meant by "man" was a male willing, able, and ready to use the sword.[3] In another story, Juan Manuel makes even clearer the concept that manhood must be proved through aggressive behavior. He tells of a Muslim bridegroom who demonstrates his masculinity by "taming" his new bride. This bridegroom commands, threatens, and insults his dog, cat, and horse, then hacks them to pieces for their disobedience, all to show his wife the mastery of the man who uses verbal and physical force when his orders are disobeyed. Indeed, a significant consequence of the bridegroom's violent behavior in this story is the silencing of the bride. Prior to her husband's aggression, this woman had been portrayed as "fierce and truculent" (*fuerte y brava*). By the close of the tale, she wordlessly obeys her husband's every order, including, apparently, the one to sleep with him.[4]

The stories told by Juan Manuel, as well as by many other medieval Castilian male Christian writers of the thirteenth through fifteenth centuries, drew on Arabic sources and Islamic customs known and admired throughout medieval Spain. Their characterizations reflect masculine ideals shared by Christians and Muslims alike, for Christian writers appropriated Muslim culture only to the extent that it affirmed precisely those qualities prized by Christian men like themselves.[5] It is, for this reason, not surprising that Juan Manuel, a Christian, used Muslim men to purvey the masculine ideal of aggression.[6]

In the depictions of Muslim men found in oral-traditional Castilian texts specifically treating Muslim-Christian military conflict (i.e., the Reconquest), however, this trait is almost entirely absent.[7] Although the texts do sometimes point to a common store of prized qualities—Christians, for instance, may admire the beauty of Muslim architecture[8]—the male Christian-composed epic (e.g., *Cantar de Mío Cid* [*CMC*], c. 1207) and frontier ballads (fourteenth through fifteenth centuries) almost never look to Muslims or to Islamic culture for examples of culturally exalted masculine practices and attitudes. Indeed, in these texts, Muslim men—like the women in Juan Manuel's stories—have only the most limited access to such behaviors.

The standard manner of analyzing this type of representation of Muslim men is to say that it reflects the friendly and mutually respectful relations that obtained between Muslims and Christians, even in the midst of heated battle, when many of these texts were composed—a kind of cross-religious sympathy (unlike the cross-sexual antipathy of Juan Manuel's stories).[9] Yet it is almost always Muslim, not Christian, men who are "friendly" in the texts.[10] Muslim men console their Christian captives by offering them their sisters as concubines;[11] they speak with great courtesy to Christians who seek to divest them of their holdings;[12] they address their Christian opponents as *amigo*;[13] and they weep sorrowfully when their Christian captors set them free.[14] Christian men, on the other hand, threaten, insult, intimidate, and act violently toward Muslim men freely. They enslave them,[15] they starve them,[16] and they rape their women.[17] Whereas a Muslim king such as Almozorre of the mid-thirteenth-century *Poema de Fernán González* may be described as wielding great amounts of power over other Muslims, this description only underscores the much greater power of the conquering Christians whose authority extends well beyond their own membership.

Why did the epic and frontier ballads so often deny Muslim men the "manly" traits and attitudes that Muslim, as well as Christian, culture so valued? And why, indeed, did the texts rely so heavily on masculine ideals to distinguish Muslim from Christian men? It was, after all, *religious*, not sexual, difference that fueled the Reconquest.[18]

An answer to these questions seems to lie, at least partially, in the nature of the war against the Muslims. As it emerged in the late Middle Ages, the fight against the Muslims involved not only reconquest, but, ultimately, the attainment of the Christian goal of orthodoxy in the region. Muslims were eventually expelled from Spain (as were Jews), and the cultural pluralism that had characterized medieval Castile for some seven centuries came to an end.

To affirm and legitimate this militant Christian ideal, the epic and frontier ballads reproduced a system of social arrangements that had already generated (particularly in literary representation)[19] the dominion of one group over another—that is, gender relations, a system whose structure guaranteed positions of power to men alone.[20] Thus, the texts, which largely denied Muslim men masculine sexual and status identity—repeatedly linking them to their mothers[21] and portraying them as rather predictably defeated, incapable of "making good" on threats of rape against Christian women,[22] and polite—patently disqualified them from holding or attaining positions of power in Castile. (It is interesting to note that a similar tactic was used in the ballad to disqualify a legitimate fourteenth-century Castilian king from rule.)[23]

Other related motivations for the emphasis on sexual, rather than religious, difference in the epic and frontier ballads may be found in the proverbial associations—perpetuated in the folklore and speech of Spain and other countries to the present day—of masculine with military values, of military with sexual conquest, and of powerlessness with women.

The connection between military prowess and "manliness" is discussed often in modern studies of "manhood." Gilmore, for example, points out that many societies test "manliness" by placing men at risk on the battlefield or in confrontation with their fellows.[24] Pleck notes that male sex-role identity is frequently seen to be demonstrated when men are militaristic—apparently manifesting the sex-appropriate traits that validate or affirm their biological sex.[25]

In the epic and frontier ballads that focus specifically on the war between Muslims and Christians, "manliness" is repeatedly linked to the military superiority of the Christians. It is, moreover, proffered as a quality that increases in proportion to the number of Muslims defeated: the Cid's beard flourishes with every successful campaign against the infidel; Minaya Alvar Fañez speaks *a guisa de varon* (in the fashion of a man) in the *CMC* when, laden with booty taken from the Muslims, he approaches King Alfonso; young Christian men "prove" themselves in anti-Muslim raids;[26] and a truly "great" man is one with whom the Muslims fear doing battle.[27]

This concept of "real" or "great" men as warriors is also commonly evinced in folklore and folk speech, as Brandes's study of contempory Andalusia demonstrates. Brandes notes that popular jokes frequently link military and sexual conquest.[28] He gives two striking examples – both uttered by male informants: "Spain conquered America not by the sword, but by the prick," and "America was conquered by Spaniards who were carrying the cross in one hand and the prick in the other."

In the epic and frontier ballads, the language of militarism is also often couched in a sexual idiom.[29] Muslim men are presented to Christian warriors' girlfriends as tokens of love,[30] Muslim-controlled cities are cast as women and addressed with flirtatious language or "seduced,"[31] and Muslim leaders are shamed through Christian appropriation of their daughters.[32]

In Brandes's study, the connection between masculinity and militarism is made, too, through what Brandes terms the enforced "feminization" of enemies. Brandes speaks of men who prove dominance over rivals by forcing them to adopt a "feminine" role, citing, as one example, the harvest ritual, *hacer las facas del rey*, in which male genitals are obscured.[33]

An examination of the language and imagery of the epic and frontier ballads suggests a similar phenomenon. Male Christian poets at times perform a kind of symbolic conversion of Muslim men and their holdings into women in order to demonstrate, as in Brandes's study, supremacy. The texts, for instance, speak of soon-to-be-taken Muslim strongholds in terms of female marital conditions (e.g., brides, matrons, widows) and call cities held by Muslim rulers potential "brides" of Christian kings;[34] they focus on feminine aspects of the clothing worn by Muslim men, such as the finely embroidered caps with veils that cover the men's faces;[35] they associate Muslim cities lost in battle with (female) loss of honor;[36] they diminish Muslim men in size;[37] and they tell of Muslim towns, transformed into women through personification, that powerful Christian men surround and penetrate with artillary fire.[38] In this manner, the texts identify Muslim men with the powerless in medieval Castile – a group tied intimately, in the act of literary representation, to female sexual and status identity.

One further explanation for the texts' emphasis on sexual symbolism lies in the works' implication of Christianity in the culturally exalted masculine ideal of aggression. Through its association with brave and usually victorious soldiers – not to mention such fighting clerics as the *Cantar de Mío Cid*'s Bishop Jerome and the ballads' Bishop of Jaén – Christianity dramatically surfaces in the texts as the more "muscular," "manly," or potent faith (a familiar enough characterization in works of a more recent vintage).[39] Indeed, in the epic and frontier ballads, Muslim submission appears as a metaphor for the dominion of Christianity, as well as for the mastery of those who fought for its supremacy.

In fact, the Muslims were, at the time of frontier ballad composition, at or near the nadir of their power. Vassals of Christian rulers, they could no longer depend on help from their coreligionists in North Africa. Yet, while the frontier texts bore witness to the waning of Muslim military might and the final stages of Christian reconquest in Spain, they, as well as historical documents of the period, show that Muslims could still be a formidable enemy, capable of winning battles, if not the war, with Christians.

At the time of epic composition (e.g., the *Cantar de Mío Cid*, thought to have been composed during the first decade of the thirteenth century), Muslims still did pose a threat to Christian hegemony in Spain. As Duggan points out in his recent study of the text:

> The poet no doubt entertained the possibility that a very real alternative to his own Christian, Castilian civilization could come to dominate Spain, namely the civilization of the Almohads which had recently asserted its presence so forcefully that some Castilians must have been led to doubt that their own cause would prevail.[40]

Thus the representation of Muslim men as predictably defeated, docile,[41] and often "unmanly" witnesses to the strength and military superiority of the conquering Christians did not draw on historical reality alone (the legendary story of Boabdil, the last Muslim king in Spain, epitomizes this: Boabdil's mother is said to have mocked her son, as he cast a glance backward toward his lost kingdom, with the words, "Do not weep now like a woman for what you could not defend like a man"). Indeed, such representation can be said to have heralded a new reality—one that would refuse Muslim men equality—and, ultimately, coexistence—with Christians in Spain.[42]

Muslim men were not the only groups so depicted in the epic and frontier ballads. Jewish men, too, were frequently accorded the sexual and status identity of the powerless. Indeed, representing "other" men in the epic and frontier ballads was always a matter of limiting access to traits and behaviors considered ideal for *men* in medieval Castile[43]—a phenomenon generated, it would seem, by the processes of exclusion of, and discrimination against, all "others" in the society that produced and transmitted the texts.

The following pages of this study will draw on three specific texts—the frontier ballads *Jugando estaba el rey moro* (The Moorish king was playing [chess]) and *Junto al vado de Xenil* (Near the Ford of the River Xenil), and the epic *Cantar de Mío Cid*—in order to discuss the specific mechanisms through which this representation was carried out. The main focus of the analysis will be the direct discourse and the "physical phrases"[44] found in the works, for the texts make frequent recourse to dialogue[45] and to "directions" to performers in reinforcing their point of view.[46]

Muslim Men in the Ballad

Jugando estaba el rey moro

In a frontier ballad dating from the Reconquest period of Spain,[47] a Muslim king of Granada wins at cards against his opponent, the Christian *adelantado* (frontier governor), Pedro Fajardo. The king's prize is supposed to be the Christian city of Lorca, but when he claims it, the *adelantado* refuses to give in. Instead, he tells the king to "shut up" (*calles, calles*) and vows military action against the Muslims should their leader persist in his demand for the city. Surprisingly, the Muslim king makes no complaint against his opponent's failure to honor the terms of the game. Indeed, he reacts with good grace, respectfully assuring the *adelantado* of his intention to drop the matter entirely and complimenting him on his chivalry:

> Allí hablara el rey moro,
> bien oiréis lo que decía:
> "No juguemos más, Fajardo,
> ni tengamos más porfía,
> que sois tan buen caballero
> que todo el mundo os temía."[48]

The conciliatory image of the Muslim projected onto the resolution of this ballad is striking for its placement in a work that suggests, through the metaphor of the game, that Muslims still "play"—and indeed, win—in the war with the Christians. The point appears to be that Muslims know Christians will not tolerate their gains. Once stepping "out of line," they quickly make amends, reverting to the submissive behavior appropriate to the weak and vulnerable, and employing politeness strategies aimed to disarm real physical threats posed to them. In fact, the text represents the Muslim king as using the very same politeness strategies that women frequently use in cultures where unsubmissive female behavior is not tolerated by men (e.g., women are beaten for threatening men's reputations). The king, like such women, uses language to convince his addressee that he appreciates his strength and respects his "face," taking special care not to offend the *adelantado*, for he knows he is vulnerable to the Christian's reprisals.[49] The Muslim king's speech also echoes medieval courtesy books' exhortations to women to speak temperately

Table 10.1 **Strengtheners (powerful language) in *Jugando estaba el rey moro,* by religion of principal speaker**

	Principal speaker	
Strengtheners[a]	Rey moro	Fajardo
Threats[b]	–	2
Imperatives[c]	–	2
Pejorative expressions/Insults[d]	–	–
Total	0	4

[a]The subcategories of strengtheners are not mutually exclusive. I have therefore assigned instances into the categories into which they most clearly fall, and have specified in the notes to each category which instances have been placed in the category.

[b]"Que aunque me la ganases / no se te daría que defenderían."

[c]Calles, calles."

[d]The above instance (*calles*) also falls into this category.

Table 10.2 **Weakeners (powerless language) in *Jugando estaba el rey moro,* by religion of principal speaker**

	Principal speaker	
Weakeners[a]	Rey (Muslim)	Fajardo (Christian)
Polite expressions/flattery[b]	2	–
Meek/self-effacing utterances[c]	2	–
Naive utterances[d]	1	–
Total	5	0

[a]The subcategories of weakeners are not all mutually exclusive. I have therefore assigned instances into the categories into which they most clearly fall, and have specified in the notes to each category which instances have been placed in the category.

[b]"Que sois tan buen caballero / que todo el mundo os temía."

[c]"No juguemos más, Fajardo / ni tengamos más porfía."

[d]"La villa de Lorca es mía."

and in a conciliatory manner, as opposed to the aggressive linguistic behavior prescribed for men in many medieval documents.[50] Indeed, the Muslim king's speech is characterized by the very linguistic markers generally seen to constitute powerless language—the language that women, even today, are supposed to speak. He uses polite expressions, flattery, and meek, self-effacing, and naive utterances. In striking contrast, the speech of the Christian *adelantado* is characterized by threats and commands—the kind of powerful language that is most often linked to men.[51] Tables 10.1 and 10.2 indicate the type of language used by each protagonist.

To some critics, the powerless speech of the Muslim is proof of the friendly and respectful relations that obtained between the text's protagonists. Wright, for example, comments, "The two sides respect each other, but feel they have to hold on to what is theirs. . . . Peaceful relations are maintained."[52] Wright takes the fourth line of the text, which, in indirect speech, notes the Muslim king's "love" for the Christian *adelantado* (*"con amor que le tenía"*) as further evidence of a great friendship between the pair.

Yet, as in many other, similar texts, it is only the Muslim who appears respectful and friendly in the work, and only the Muslim who attempts to maintain peace. As the tables show, powerful features dominate the speech of the Christian, who uses commands and threats to intimidate his Muslim opponent. Thus, whereas the Muslim king is depicted as respectful, the Christian *adelantado* is portrayed as aggressive and militant; nowhere does he express a friendly, respectful, or loving attitude toward his adversary. Far from suggesting relations of friendship and solidarity in the text, the powerless features used by the Muslim king reflect a perceived lack of power vis-à-vis the Christian *adelantado*. His polite language serves only to emphasize his own position of vulnerability and inferiority.

It may be surprising at first glance that the text should choose to portray a king, of all Muslims, as weak and inferior. The king, after all, represents the pinnacle of his faction's power structure—a point the text in fact develops through its report of the protagonists' nonreciprocal use of titles: the Muslim is addressed by the *adelantado* as *"Señor rey,"* whereas the *adelantado* is addressed by the Muslim simply as "Fajardo." But the text represents the Muslim king's access to the powerful ranges of speech as limited by physical, not social, factors. The emphasis on his social status indeed underscores this, for if a Muslim king is powerless to withstand a Christian's threats, so too must be his people.

In effect, by representing the Muslim king as submissive, vulnerable, and powerless, the text demonstrates his—and all Muslim men's—difference. It makes clear that, in a society that valued men for their aggressive and militant behavior, the conciliatory or docile Muslim man had no "proper" place.[53] Moreover, the Muslim man's difference, grounded as it is in spoken language, could not have been made plainer than in an oral genre such as the *romancero*, where a performer could easily have exploited the distinctiveness of protagonists' speech styles. One can only imagine the modulations of voice (falsetto, exaggerated rhythmicity, and so on) fifteenth-century *juglares* might have used to underscore their representation of the *rey moro* not as a true king—that is, a manly warrior worthy of respect—but instead as a wimp, culturally relegated to a secondary status relative to Christian men.

Junto al vado de Xenil

King Boabdil of Granada, called by Christians, the *Rey Chico* (Little King), was the last Muslim king in Spain. When Boabdil sought to exploit his demoralized Christian enemy after this group's resounding and humiliating defeat in Ajarquía (1483), he was captured. A strategic decision was made by the Christians to ransom Boabdil back to his people; the Muslims were in the midst of a civil war and the king's absence mitigated factional strife, thus strengthening Muslim forces. Much was made in the Castilian court of Boabdil's humiliation at the hands of the Christians—indeed, one of the salient issues was whether the Muslim king should be made to kiss the hands of King Ferdinand upon leaving the Christians.[54]

In the ballad, Boabdil's capture and its aftermath are described in a large segment of direct discourse spoken by an unidentified Muslim soldier. The segment reads as follows:

"Que se perdió el rey chiquito
y los que con él han ydo,
y que no escapó ninguno,
preso, muerto o mal herido,
que de quantos allí fueron
yo sólo me he guarescido
a traher nueva tan triste
del gran mal que ha succedido.
Los que a nuestro rey vencieron,
sabed, si no havéys sabido,
que fue aquel Diego Hernández,
De Córdova es su apellido,
alcayde de los donzeles,
hombre sabio y atrevido,
y aquel gran Conde de Cabra
que en su ayuda avía venido.
Éste venció la batalla
y aquel trance tan reñido,
y otro Lope de Medoça,
que de Cabra havía salido
que andava entre los peones
como león bravo metido.
Y sabed que el rey no es muerto
mas está en prisión rendido,
yo le vide yr en trahilla

en acto muy abatido.
Llevan lo drecho a Lucena,
junto a donde fue vencido."[55]

In the solider's discourse, evaluative devices are heavily relied on to reinforce the point of view of his story.[56] Like the features of powerlessness that characterized the Muslim king's language in *Jugando estaba el rey moro*, the evaluative devices employed here ensure a representation of Muslims as powerless – unable either to stand up to Christians or to measure up to the masculine/military ideals valued by both cultures.

Consider, for example, the soldier's initial announcement of his king's defeat. This announcement is evaluated in a long string of clauses that emphasize the resounding humiliation of the Muslims' loss. A double negative and quantifiers stress that *not one* of the king's men, except for the soldier, himself, escaped imprisonment, death, or grave injury ("y que no escapó ninguno, / preso, muerto, o mal herido, / que de quantos allí fueron / yo sólo me he guarescido"; 13-16). Positive evaluation, on the other hand, characterizes the soldier's description of the Christian victors. Such titles marked for high social status and power as *alcayde*, (mayor, 23) and *conde* (count, 25) stress the victors' membership in Christian nobility; the citing and repeating of their names and surnames (Diego Hernández, Conde de Cabra, Lope de Mendoça; De Córdoba) reinforce their prestigious identity. Moreover, attributives and comparators that positively evaluate the fighting of the noble Christians, such as the description of one as a skilled and daring man (24) and the comparison of another's behavior to that of a fierce lion (32), highlight the aggression and military superiority of those who won the battle.

In stark contrast to the victorious, brave, and noble Christians is the defeated Muslim king. The soldier, in his evaluation, focuses particular attention on the abject state of the Muslim ruler. He reports, for example, that the king lies subdued in prison (line 34), and he stresses, through the repetition of words relating to the king's humiliation, the lowliness of the ruler's appearance and conditions – reinforcing his description by insisting that his words are no exaggeration: he claims he has firsthand knowledge of the king's circumstances, declaring that he saw the king being led on a leash, in a very humiliating state (35-36).

To some critics, the evaluative devices employed in the soldier's discourse serve to engage audience sympathy for the Muslims, for they draw attention to their plight and that of their leader.[57] But the text, which goes on, in indirect speech, to describe the Christians' ransoming of the king to the Muslims, who bankrupt themselves buying their humiliated leader back, in fact makes the Muslims look ridiculous without in the least diminishing the valor of their Christian victors. The king whom the Muslims are so keen to have back is, after all, not much of a king. The text shows that though the Muslims mourn his captivity, his presence is rather sorry and diminutive. Indeed, the text repeatedly assigns him an epithet designed to exaggerate his small size, thereby diminishing him even further: he is called in the work not simply the "little" king, as he was commonly known by Christians (*Rey Chico*), but the *tiny* king (*rey chiquito*) (11, 56-57). Moreover, that the text makes the Muslim soldier call the king by this name firmly establishes the fiction of its "Moorish point of view." Only to Christians was Boabdil known as the "Little King"; his Muslim supporters would never have diminished him this way. Indeed, the very fact that the text makes a Muslim man articulate the discriminatory attitudes of Christians appears to be part of its strategy for reassuring its audience that the threat of "other" men has been reduced. Muslims, once tamed, also sing the praises of Christians.[58]

Once again, one can only imagine the intervention in the text during performance of contemporary *juglares*, who could easily have used gestures, along with modulations of voice, to make clear the contrast between the "manly" noble Christians, who won the battle, and the defeated little Muslim king, led around by the neck on a leash. This text, like *Jugando estaba el rey moro*, imaginarily asserts male Christian Castilian privilege and power.

Jewish Men in the Epic *Cantar de Mío Cid*

The *CMC* is one of Castile's earliest and most treasured texts. The work narrates some two decades of events relating to the life of a noble Christian Castilian military leader, Rodrigo Díaz de Vivar, or the Cid. When the epic begins, the Cid has been denounced by enemies and exiled by his king. In the course of the text, he manages to win his way back into the king's good graces by defeating vast numbers of Muslims and plundering their wealth.

Among the most salient and memorable characters in the text are two Jewish men—moneylenders called Rachel and Vidas. A great deal has been written about this pair from whom the Cid borrows, but never repays, six hundred marks. It is, nevertheless, interesting to look at the two in the context of medieval masculinist ideologies.

Like the male Muslims in the ballads, Rachel and Vidas are powerless men—a point evinced in the classically "powerless" language they are made to speak in the work. Their language style is, for example, characterized by speech in unison. The pair is initially described as "together as one" (*"en uno estavan amos"*; 100) and only once does one speak alone.

The two also make pointed use of ritual utterances (for example, the proverbial expressions "Non duerme sin sospecha / qui aver trae monedado, [He who has money with him sleeps uneasily]," 126; and "Non se faze assi el mercado, / si non primero prendiendo / e despues dando, [Business is done first by taking, then by giving]," 139-40), expressions and gestures of respect and appreciation for Christians' "face" (for example, Rachel exclaims, "Ya Campeador / en buen ora çinxiestes espada! [Ah, Great Warrior / in a good hour you girded your sword]," 175), empty threats (for example, when the Cid fails to repay the loan, the pair threaten to come after him, 1438, even though the text has made clear that their locus of activity is the home), and flattering epithets—aptly characterized by Walsh as "the flattery of the desperate."[59]

Rachel and Vidas are also represented as powerless through the text's descriptions of their physical behavior. In the space of a short interview (thirty-one lines, 152-82) with the Cid, for example, the Jews kiss the hand of the newly exiled Christian warrior no fewer than four times. (The first three instances are described as actual gestures; the fourth is a verbal "kiss," given the Cid by Rachel at the end of the interview: "Cid, beso vuestro mano [Cid, I kiss your hand]," 179.) Although kissing the hand of a superior is not an unusual activity in the text, it is, in the case of the Jews, greatly exaggerated. Elsewhere in the work, one kiss per interview usually suffices.[60]

While the text appears to revel in the pair's act of submission, using the repeated gesture of the kiss to demonstrate Rachel and Vidas's subordination to the Christian warrior, it also makes clear that the Jews' behavior must be distinguished from that of other subordinates in the work. Their gesture does not stem, as does that of other characters, from their position as vassals. Not only are they not vassals of the Cid, but the text makes it clear that the Cid's vassals kiss his hand as an entrée to productive, income-earning labor on the battlefield, whereas the Jews pursue only unearned profit, remaining at home and collecting interest on their wealth.[61] Nor does the Jews' gesture result from their subordination as women. They are, of course, both men—in spite of Rachel's female-coded name and the fact that he asks the Christian warrior to bring him a gift so "feminine" seeming (an ornate and exotic crimson-colored skin) that at least one critic has found in it enough evidence (now discredited) to claim that Rachel is in fact a woman, Vidas's wife, not his business partner.[62] Finally, the Jews' gesture of submission cannot be a consequence of the honor they feel the Cid deserves as ruler, for he is not a king and, in fact, is in disgrace at this point in the work.

That it is *masculine*, not simply Christian, beliefs and attitudes the Jews are excluded from in the text is made clear in the work's express affirmation that the attitudes and ideals of the Cid and his vassals belong specifically to men. The Cid, for example, has to instruct his wife and daughters in these attitudes, for as women, they are ignorant of them. The women must, for instance, learn from the men to view war as a window of opportunity; the Muslim invasion of Valencia will, the Cid argues, ultimately advantage them materially ("ca todo es vuestra pro"; 1664). The Cid also teaches the women not to fear Muslims, but to dominate them, reassuring his wife and daughters that the Muslim's drums, which make them fearful, will soon hang in the church as trophies of Christian victory and dominion.[63] The women must also learn to dehumanize "other" men, for these are not truly men, but alien objects to be appropriated as their own; the Muslims, he tells his wife, are no more than wealth to be taken as dowries for her daughters.[64]

In this context of exalted male aggression and extroversion, the otherness of the Jewish men could not be plainer. Over and again the text makes the point that the Jews' locus of activity is the home, whereas that of "men" is the battlefield. It dwells on the image of the Jews returning to the enclosed spaces of their residence after agreeing to make a loan to the Cid, laying a carpet on the floor, then placing a fine white sheet on top of it—all to make a comfortable "bed" for the silver coins they throw out (182-84). It is no wonder Martín Antolínez, the brave Christian warrior, itches to leave the Jews' house for the Cid's tent in the countryside ("Grado exir de la posada"; 200). The text also stresses Rachel and Vidas's sedentary behaviors and eagerness to profit from, but not engage in, war. One can only picture the contortions of singers as they described how the Jewish men strained themselves, not in glorious battle as "real" men ought, but in lifting sand-filled chests they stupidly believed held great treasure (171-72). One can picture also the ironic representation of Rachel and Vidas as repeatedly rejoicing over the expectation of profit—profit they would never receive because, unlike "real" men who battled Muslims for their money, they did nothing to earn it.

By the end of the *CMC*, the Jewish men, like the Muslim kings in the frontier ballads and Juan Manuel's "tamed" bride, are silenced. Their final plea for the Cid to repay them—even without interest—is ignored, and they speak no more in the work, although it is only less than half over at this point.

Conclusion

In stripping male Muslims and Jews of their markers of sexual identity, the epic and frontier ballad texts displace, rather than signify, these groups' reality, for Muslims and Jews in fact shared the masculinist ideologies of Christians. Thus, the texts must have sought to establish difference by presenting two distinct and contrasting images of men during the Reconquest – "manly" Christians and docile and defeated Muslims and Jews – shoring up Christians' masculine identity while imaginarily formulating Muslims' and Jews' future exclusion from Spain.

In this context, it is interesting to see how Christians' experience of "other" cultures in Spain, particularly as recorded and popularized in epic and frontier ballad, later provided them with a template for describing their cultural encounters in the New World. *Romances*, sung with fervor by Spaniards as they fought for dominion in America, lent a semblance of continuity from Reconquest to conquest in their equation of Christianity with manliness and muscle. Above all, the description of Christian victories against Muslim aristocrats in the medieval texts provided a ready-made formula for evoking Christian privilege and power in New World images, from the defeated Indians of *La Araucana* to *La Malinche*, the aristocratic young Aztec woman given as a gift to Cortés.

Notes

1. "Whosoever wishes to have pleasure should beat his wife"; "Give me a Jew, and I'll have him back for you burned." Translations here, as well as elsewhere in this essay, are mine.

2. For an interesting discussion of manhood as different from simple anatomical maleness, see David D. Gilmore, *Manhood in the Making: Cultural Concepts of Masculinity* (New Haven, Conn.: Yale University Press, 1990).

3. I refer here to "What Happened to the Count of Provence, and How He Was Freed from Prison," in Juan Manuel, *El Conde Lucanor*, ed. John England (Warminster, England: Aris & Phillips, 1987), 157-67. I have used England's edition here to facilitiate references for nonspecialists.

4. For an interesting discussion of this story, see Alberto Sandoval, "De-Centering Misogyny in Spanish Medieval Texts: The Case of Don Juan Manuel's XXXV Exemplum," *Ideologies and Literature* 4 (Spring 1989): 65-94.

5. This much is clear from the remarks Juan Manuel, for example, makes at the end of each of his tales. The stories end with the comment that the author found "good" or "truth" in them and that is why he included them in his book.

6. The sexual aggression of Muslim men is, in fact, proverbial in Spanish culture, even in the modern period. See David Gilmore, *Aggression and Community: Paradoxes of Andalusian Culture* (New Haven, Conn.: Yale University Press, 1987), 129. Gilmore quotes an informant as saying, "Everyone knows . . . that they [Moors] have sexual organs twice the size of Europeans. They are all satyrs (129)." See also David J. Viera, "The Treatment of the Jew and the Moor in the Catalan Works of Francesc Eiximenis," *RCEH* 9, (Winter 1985): 203-13. Viera discusses the medieval Catalan tradition of the Muslim's inordinate desire for sexual satisfaction.

7. The Castilian epic and frontier ballad belong to an oral tradition. The best-known epic text, the *Cantar de Mío Cid*, was composed c. 1207. Frontier ballads were composed during the last two centuries of the Reconquest – that is, the fourteenth and fifteenth centuries. Although not a great deal is known about the reception of these texts, it is widely theorized that the *CMC* encouraged men to take active part in the Reconquest by emphasizing the possibilities for financial gain in warfare. For a recent study of this aspect of the

work, see Joseph J. Duggan, *The "Cantar de mio Cid": Poetic Creation in Its Economic and Social Contexts* (Cambridge: Cambridge University Press, 1989). Regarding the frontier ballads, or *romances fronterizos,* as they are known in Spanish, the large number of texts cited in works from the fifteenth century onward suggests that the tradition was well known and popular among all social groups—despite the remarks of some fifteenth-century learned poets that they were a form of diversion for "people of low and servile condition." See Ramón Menéndez Pidal, *Romancero hispánico (hispano-portugués, americano y sefardí): teoría e historia,* 2d ed., vol. 2 (Madrid: Espasa-Calpe, 1968), 21.

8. In, for example, the *Romance de Abenámar,* King Juan II of Castile asks, in reference to the beautiful buildings of Granada, "¿Qué castillos son aquellos? / ¡Altos son y relucían! [What castles are these? / They are tall and are shining!]." For complete text, see Roger Wright, *Spanish Ballads* (Warminster, England: Aris & Phillips, 1987), 106; and Colin Smith, *Spanish Ballads* (Oxford: Pergamon, 1971), 125. I have used Wright's and Smith's editions of Spanish ballads to facilitate references for nonspecialists. Wright provides translations of the texts (although translations in this study are mine and differ somewhat from his) and Smith's notes and comments are in English.

9. Wright, *Spanish Ballads,* 236, calls this cross-religious sympathy "normal" in frontier ballads. For a different view, see Israel Burshatin, "The Docile Image: The Moor as a Figure of Force, Subservience, and Nobility in the *Poema de mio Cid,*" *KRQ* 31, no. 3 (1984): 269-80; and idem, "The Moor in the Text: Metaphor, Emblem, and Silence," *Critical Inquiry* 12 (1985): 98-118.

10. Only rarely are Muslim men portrayed as equally, or more, aggressive than their Christian opponents. One example is *Alora la bien cercada,* in which a Muslim outsmarts and kills the Christian *adelantado,* Diego de Ribera. See Smith, *Spanish Ballads,* 127; Wright *Spanish Ballads,* 107.

11. In *Pártese el moro,* for example, the Moorish king, Almanzor, is said to feel such pity for his captive, Gonzalo Gustos, who has lost all of his sons, that he sends his beautiful sister to sleep with him. Another son is born to the Christian as a result of this union. See Smith, *Spanish Ballads,* 82-85.

12. The Muslim, Abenámar, in the *Romance de Abenámar,* is expressly courteous when the Christian King Juan seeks to take the city of Granada from the Muslims. See Smith, *Spanish Ballads,* 125-27; Wright, *Spanish Ballads,* 106-7.

13. For example, *En los campos de Alventosa*; see Smith, *Spanish Ballads,* 147-49.

14. In the *CMC,* the Moors of Alcoçer weep as the Cid leaves the city he has taken by force. These Muslims had been made to serve their Christian captors. See Colin Smith, *Poema de mío Cid* (Oxford: Clarendon, 1972), 851-56. I have used Smith's edition, with notes in English, to facilitate references for nonspecialists. All subsequent line citations appear in text.

15. See ibid., 617-22, for one example.

16. For example, *De Antequera partió el moro*; see Smith, *Spanish Ballads,* 118-21; Wright, *Spanish Ballads,* 101-3.

17. For example, *Romance de la Morilla Burlada*; see Smith, *Spanish Ballads,* 191-92; Wright, *Spanish Ballads,* 111.

18. Indeed, there are traditional Spanish texts that directly address the religious aspect of hostilities in Reconquest Spain. The Judeo-Spanish ballad *El idólotra de María,* for instance, speaks of the superior power of the Jewish faith in its story of a Christian ship captain who prayed to the Virgin Mary for relief from turbulent seas and drowned, while his Jewish sailors prayed to God on High and were saved.

19. When women are represented as powerful in the literature of the period, they are almost always criticized. Juan Manuel's fierce and truculent bride is but one of many examples.

20. This is notwithstanding such powerful female political figures of the Castilian Middle Ages as María de Molina and Catalina de Lancaster. A discussion of the "problem" male writers and statesmen encountered when faced with these powerful women goes beyond the

scope of this essay. It is sufficient to note here that the presence of such figures in medieval Castile did not significantly alter the subordination of women either within or outside of literature.

21. King Boabdil of Granada is a prominent example of the identification of Muslim men with their mothers (e.g., *Reduán, bien se te acuerda*; Smith, *Spanish Ballads*, 116-18). Christian men, on the other hand, are generally associated with their fathers (e.g., *Por aquel postigo viejo*; Wright, *Spanish Ballads*, 76) and the ballads concerning the Cid (e.g., *En Santa Gadea de Burgos*; Smith, *Spanish Ballads*, 96-98).

22. For example, see *Moricos, los mis moricos*; Smith, *Spanish Ballads*, 116.

23. This was the ballad cycle relating to King Pedro I of Castile (*el Cruel*). Pedro is forced into the "feminine" sphere in a number of the texts, in which he is said to be under the influence of his mistress, María de Padilla, who makes decisions for him.

24. Gilmore, *Manhood in the Making*, 12-14.

25. Joseph H. Pleck, "The Theory of Male Sex-Role Identity: Its Rise and Fall, 1936-Present," in *The Making of Masculinities: The New Men's Studies*, ed. Harry Brod (Boston: Allen & Unwin, 1987), 21-38.

26. For example, *Día era de San Antón*; Smith, *Spanish Ballads*, 129-31.

27. For example, *Dadme nuevas, caballeros*; ibid., 131-33.

28. Stanley Brandes, *Metaphors of Masculinity: Sex and Status in Andalusian Folklore* (Philadelphia: University of Pennsylvania Press, 1980), 92.

29. Gilmore's studies of contemporary southern Spain show a related phenomenon – the language of sex is couched in a military idiom: "A man makes conquests; a woman is prey; she capitulates; battles are won or lost; a rejected suitor is defeated, and so on. Andalusian notions of sexuality, then, are deeply steeped in the mentality and language of forceful assertion, competition, and conflict, of waging campaigns, that is, aggression." *Aggression and Community*, 126.

30. For example, *Día era de San Antón*; Smith, *Spanish Ballads*, 129.

31. For example, *Alora la bien cercada*; ibid., 127-28.

32. For example, *Moro alcayde, moro alcayde*; Wright, *Spanish Ballads*, 112-14.

33. In this ritual described by Brandes, *Metaphors of Masculinity*, 154-55, one obliterates the genitals of one's masculine opponent by covering them with mud. Brandes comments: "To eliminate a man's genitals symbolically is to emasculate him and thereby to emphasize one's own comparative potency" (155). Throughout his study, Brandes stresses that dominance is proved through the emasculation or feminization of enemies.

34. In *Abenámar*, for example, King Juan II proposes to the city of Granada.

35. For example, *De Antequera*; Smith, *Spanish Ballads*, 118-21; Wright, *Spanish Ballads*, 101-3.

36. In *Reduán*, the Muslim king's mother speaks of the "honor" of Granada, a Muslim city about to be lost to the Christians. See Smith, *Spanish Ballads*, 116-18; Wright, *Spanish Ballads*, 100-101.

37. The *rey chico* becomes the *rey chiquito*. See Wright, *Spanish Ballads*, 116-18.

38. For example, *Alora*; see ibid., 107-8.

39. Gilmore, *Manhood in the Making*, 18, discusses the suggestion of the nineteenth-century English publicist Thomas Hughes and his colleagues, who argued also for the "manliness" of Christ and Christianity.

40. See Duggan, *The "Cantar"*, 146.

41. This is Burshatin's term; see "The Docile Image."

42. The epic and ballads' emphatic distinction of Muslim from Christian men resonated in late medieval ordinances that legislated special signs of "difference" to be worn by Muslims, such as the yellow "capuche" and turquoise "moon." See Fernando Díaz-Plaja, *Historia de España en sus documentos*, Siglo XV (Madrid: Cátreda, 1984), 23.

43. This applies to the representation of non-*Castilians* in the literature as well. Two salient examples are found in the depiction of Ramón Berenguer and the Infantes de Carrión in the *CMC*.

44. See Colin Smith and J. Morris, "On 'Physical' Phrases in Old Spanish Epic and Other Texts," *Leeds Philosophical and Literary Society Proceedings* 12, no. 5 (1967): 129-90.

45. I am speaking here of "constructed" dialogue, or direct discourse created by singers in order to impart a sense of the speech they present as "reported" or "natural." See, for discussion, Deborah Tannen, "Introducing Constructed Dialogue in Greek and American Conversational and Literary Narrative," in *Direct and Indirect Speech*, ed. Florian Coulmas (Berlin: Mouton de Gruyter, 1986), 311-32.

46. For discussion, see John Walsh, "Performance in the *Poema de Mío Cid*," *RPh* 44 (August 1990): 1-25.

47. Frontier ballads characteristically deal with events of the war against Granada in the final century of the Reconquest. The texts, which were composed by Christians, may have served to stimulate enthusiasm for the completion of the Reconquest of Spain and the expulsion of non-Christian groups. For discussion, see Angus MacKay, "The Ballad and the Frontier in Late Medieval Spain," *BHS* 53 (1976): 15-33. This text is from Smith, *Spanish Ballads*, 133-34.

48. Thus spoke the Moorish king,
well will you hear what he said:
"Let's not play anymore, Fajardo,
nor have any more arguments,
for you are such a good knight
that the whole world lives in fear of you."

49. For discussion of these phenomena, see Penelope Brown, "How and Why Are Women More Polite: Some Evidence from a Mayan Community," in *Women and Language in Literature and Society*, ed. Sally McConnell-Ginet, Ruth Borker, and Nelly Furman (New York: Praeger, 1980), 111-36.

50. For further discussion of medieval courtesy manuals, see Diane Bornstein, *The Lady in the Tower: Medieval Courtesy Literature for Women* (Hamden, Conn.: Archon, 1983).

51. My categories are adapted from the work of, among others, Robin Lakoff, *Language and Women's Place* (New York: Harper & Row, 1975), on women's speech; William M. O'Barr and Bowman K. Atkins, " 'Women's Language' or 'Powerless Language'?" in McConnell-Ginet, Barker, and Furman, *Women and Language in Literature and Society*, 93-110, on powerless language; and William Labov, *Language in the Inner City* (Philadelphia: University of Pennsylvania Press, 1972), on oral narrative. These categories by no means constitute an exhaustive catalog of features, but they are the features relevant to the study text.

52. Wright, *Spanish Ballads*, 235.

53. See Luce Irigaray, "Sexual Difference," in *French Feminist Thought*, ed. Toril Moi (Oxford: Basil Blackwell, 1987), 118-30. Irigaray discusses an analogous issue: women's "proper" place (121).

54. See L. P. Harvey, *Islamic Spain, 1250-1500* (Chicago: University of Chicago Press 1990), 278-83.

55. "The Tiny King is lost
and those who went with him as well,
no one escaped at all,
imprisonment, death, or grave injury,
of those who went over there
I alone have survived
to bring this so sad news
about the great misfortune that has befallen us.
Those who vanquished our king,
you should know, if you didn't already,
included that Diego Hernández,
De Córdova is his surname,

a member of the royal household,
a skilled and daring man,
another was that great Count of Cabra
who came along to help.
These ones won the battle
and the perilous struggle and fight,
another of them was Lope de Mendoça,
who came from Cabra,
and plunged in among the infantrymen
to fight like a fierce lion.
And know that our king is not dead
but lies subdued in prison instead
I saw him led round by the neck
in a very humiliating state.
They took him straight to Lucena,
near to where he was vanquished."

56. Evaluative devices include repetitions, ritual utterances, negatives, futures, modals, comparators, attributives, appositives, conjunctions, and causals that enter into the narrative for the purpose of explicating or evaluating a particular action. See Labov, *Language in the Inner City*, for discussion of evaluative language.

57. Wright, *Spanish Ballads*, 241, comments, "We might expect a Spanish poem to gloat over the Muslim distress . . . but there is no hint of such an attitude in the text."

58. See Wlad Godzich, "The Further Possibility of Knowledge," in Michel de Certeau, *Heterologies: Discourse on the Other* (Minneapolis: University of Minnesota Press, 1986), xiii.

59. For example, they call Minaya Fañez *cabellero de prestar* (worthy knight), 1432. See Walsh, "Performance in the *Poema*," 2.

60. The Cid's followers, for example, each kiss his hand a single time, as they join his company (298). The Cid's wife, Doña Jimena, also kisses his hand – once as the couple prepares to part (265), a second time some seventy lines later, when they actually do part (369), and then in a few scattered reunions throughout the text, with one kiss per occasion. When the Cid's vassal, Alvar Minaya Fañez, brings gifts to King Alfonso on behalf of the Cid, he makes a verbal representation of the action. He tells the king that the warrior kisses both his hands and his feet (e.g., 879, 1322-23) and his hands alone (1338). Yet, in these sections of the text, the actual *physical* act of kissing the king's hands is accomplished in a single gesture alone, by Minaya (894, 1320). The only segment of the *CMC* in which the text is comparably saturated with hand kissing is the interview between the Cid and King Alfonso, as the latter pardons the former. But here, as the text makes clear, there are specific reasons for such behavior relating to the special, overdetermined nature of the occasion. The Cid kisses the King as anyone would kiss a ruler; he kisses the King to assure him that he, once suspected of treason, is respectful and loyal; he kisses the King because he is relieved upon the news of his pardon; and he kisses the King because he is grateful to the ruler who, having once banished him, now honors him (2025 and passim).

61. Walsh "Performance in the *Poema*," 10, notes that they are described counting their wealth ("en cuenta de sus averes"; 101) as if that were their perpetual exercise.

62. See J. M. Solá-Solé, "De nuevo sobre las arcas del Cid," *KRQ* 23 (1976): 3-15.

63. "Aquelos atamores a vos los pondran delant / . . . colgar los han en Santa Maria"; 1666-68.

64. "Riqueza es que nos acreçe / maravillosa e grand; / ¡a poco que viniestes / presend vos quieren dar; / por casar son vuestras fijas: / aduzen vos axuvar!"; 1648-50.

Contributors

Christopher Baswell is associate professor of English at Barnard College, where he is also chair of the program in medieval and Renaissance studies. He publishes on classical tradition in the Middle Ages and on the concept of marginality in medieval culture. In 1993-94, he will be a fellow at the National Humanities Center.

Vern L. Bullough is SUNY distinguished emeritus professor of history and social studies at SUNY College, Buffalo. He is the author of numerous studies on various aspects of human sexuality. One of his most recent books is *Cross Dressing, Sex and Gender*, coauthored with Bonnie Bullough.

Stanley Chojnacki is professor of history at Michigan State University. The author of numerous articles on the politics and society of late medieval and Renaissance Venice, he is currently writing a history of the Venetian patriciate from 1300 to 1530. His essay in this volume addresses issues dealt with more fully in that study.

John Coakley is professor of church history at New Brunswick Theological Seminary. He has published essays in *Images of Sainthood in Medieval Europe*, edited by Renate Blumenfeld-Kosinski and Timea Szell (1991), and *Church History*. He has also coedited, with E. Ann Matter, *Creative Women in Medieval and Early Modern Italy* (forthcoming).

Thelma Fenster teaches French medieval literature at Fordham University. She has published on Christine de Pizan and has been coeditor of the *Medieval Feminist Newsletter*.

Clare R. Kinney is associate professor of English at the University of Virginia, where she teaches both medieval and Renaissance literature. Her publications include *Strategies of Poetic Narrative: Chaucer, Spenser, Milton, Eliot* (1992) as well as articles on *Beowulf, Sir Gawain and the Green Knight*, Chaucer, Shakespeare, and Sidney. She is currently working on a study of gendered representation and the metamorphoses of Petrarchism in Renaissance romance.

Clare A. Lees was an assistant professor in Old and Middle English in the English department of Fordham University before joining the English department at the University of Pennsylvania. In addition to her feminist studies on medieval literature in both Old and Middle English, she has published a number of articles on Old English religious prose and is currently working on a study of Anglo-Saxon belief.

Jo Ann McNamara is professor of history at Hunter College. Among her works on women in the Middle Ages are *A New Song: Celibate Women in the First Three Christian Centuries* (1983), and *Sainted Women of the Dark Ages* (1992). She is at present completing *Sisters in Arms: Two Millennia of Women Religious in the Catholic Church.*

Louise Mirrer is professor of Spanish and comparative literature at Fordham University. She is the author of *The Language of Evaluation: A Sociolinguistic Approach to the Story of Pedro el Cruel in Ballad and Chronicle* (1986) and the forthcoming *Women and Others (Jew and Muslims) in the Texts of Reconquest Castile.* She also edited *Upon My Husband's Death: Widows in the Literature and Histories of Medieval Europe* (1992).

Harriet Spiegel is associate professor of English literature at California State University, Chico. She has published an edition of the Anglo-Norman *Fables* of Marie de France and an accompanying verse translation (1987) and several articles on the fables and other medieval beast literature. She is on the editorial board of *Bestia*, the yearbook of the Beast Fable Society.

Susan Mosher Stuard is professor of history at Haverford College. She has an interest in economic and social history and writes on women's history. Her most recent book is *A State of Deference: Rogusa/Dubrovnik in the Medieval Centuries* (1992).

Index